Harbin to Hanoi

 Global Connections

School of Modern Languages and Cultures
The University of Hong Kong

Series General Editor: H. W. Wong

The Global Connections series explores the movement of ideas, people, technologies, capital, and goods across national and regional borders. Books in the series reveal how these interconnections have the power to produce new global forms of cultures, politics, identities, and economies. Seeking to explore the dynamics of change, the series includes both historical and contemporary topics. It focuses on interactions between the world's diverse cultures through the production of new interdisciplinary knowledge.

Also in the Global Connections series:

Narratives of Free Trade: The Commercial Cultures of Early US-China Relations
    Edited by Kendall Johnson
Europe and China: Strategic Partners or Rivals?
    Edited by Roland Vogt

Harbin to Hanoi

The Colonial Built Environment in Asia, 1840 to 1940

Edited by Laura Victoir and Victor Zatsepine

香港大學出版社
HONG KONG UNIVERSITY PRESS

Hong Kong University Press
The University of Hong Kong
Pokfulam Road
Hong Kong
www.hkupress.org

ISBN 978-988-8139-41-5 *(Hardback)*
ISBN 978-988-8139-42-2 *(Paperback)*

British Library Cataloguing-in-Publication Data
A catalogue record for this book is available from the British Library.

10 9 8 7 6 5 4 3 2 1

Printed and bound by Paramount Printing Co., Ltd. in Hong Kong, China

To the Main Building of HKU, which inspired us.

To the Main Building of HKU which inspired us

Contents

Contributors

G. A. Bremner, School of Arts, Culture and Environment, University of Edinburgh

Peter Cunich, Department of History, University of Hong Kong

Quang-Vinh Dao, Architect, Geneva

Lisa Drummond, Department of Social Sciences, Urban Studies Program, York University

Caroline Herbelin, Department of Art History, University Paris IV, Sorbonne

Danielle Labbé, Institut d'Urbanisme, Université de Montréal

Liu Yue, Curator, Tianjin Museum of Modern History

Klaus Mühlhahn, Institute of Chinese Studies, Freie Universität, Berlin

Cole Roskam, Department of Architecture, University of Hong Kong

Bill Sewell, Department of History, Saint Mary's University, Halifax

David Tucker, Department of History, University of Central Florida

Laura Victoir, Department of History, Hunter College, City University of New York

Victor Zatsepine, Department of History, University of Hong Kong

Zhang Chang, Center for Science, Technology, and Society, Tianjin University

Illustrations

Table

Figures

Plates

Plates

Acknowledgements

The efforts behind this book were generously funded by the University of Hong Kong's School of Modern Languages and Cultures, with support from the History Department. We thank them both for intellectual, financial, and logistical support. We would like to thank Hong Kong University Press for helping us to publish this edited volume. We thank Michael Duckworth, Clara Ho, Jessica Wang, Christy Leung, and Serina Poon. We appreciate your advice, professionalism, patience, and attention to detail.

1
Introduction

Victor Zatsepine and Laura Victoir

This volume is the result of a discussion between its editors, both historians of empires, about the possibility of comparing the experiences of imperial European powers and Japan in the Pacific region during the period of time between the First Opium War (1839–42) and the Second World War (1939–45). This foreign intrusion and presence generated a large amount of material evidence on the eastern coast of the Asian continent. As a result, several Asian cities had entire districts designed and built by imperial powers. Several generations of Europeans, Russians, and Japanese moved to the colonies, treaty ports, and leased territories of Asia in search of economic gain, adventure, or government positions. The histories of individual imperial powers and colonial cities in different regions of Asia have been studied in great detail.[1] However, the relationship between the built environment and history of colonialism and imperialism in Asia still deserves much needed cross-disciplinary attention. We came to realize how little dialogue exists between historians in different areas of study, not to mention the lack of scholarship comparing British, French, Russian, German, and Japanese imperialism, colonial practice, and built forms in Asia.

The purpose of this book is to use the built environment to analyze the multiple experiences of colonial powers in China and northern Indochina. The colonial built environment can be viewed on several levels: as an expression of imperial aspirations, a manifestation of colonial power, a tool in the mission to civilize, a re-creation of a home away from home, or simply as a place to live and work for the colonizers and the colonized. The built environment is also a tangible artifact, one that had real impact on the daily life of those who resided and toiled there.[2] Yet, the colonial space and structures, as they are presented to us in their physical forms today, tell only a very limited story of the people and powers behind them. The buildings themselves do not explain the process of designing, financing, and choosing the location, or legal arrangements involving land purchase, lease, and taxation. We learn little or nothing about the lives of construction workers, about the controversies and conflicts resulting from disruption of traditional life, for example the damage caused by European railways to rural trade, local *fengshui,* or ancestral temples. While diplomatic historians have analyzed different forms of European imperial expansion in Asia, such as gunboat diplomacy, military invasion, and opium trade, much remains unknown about everyday life in the colonies and treaty ports in Asia, and especially about interactions between Europeans and local populations.

This volume brings together scholars working in city planning, architecture, and Asian and imperial history, to provide a more detailed picture of how colonization worked both at the top and at the bottom levels of society, and how it was expressed in stone, iron, and concrete. We show that the process of creating the colonial built environment was multilayered, complicated, and unpredictable. Our volume demonstrates that the relationship between the colonizers and colonized and the built environment transformed over time: the structures changed tenants, functions, surroundings, and even ownership. Some buildings were expanded, while others were destroyed or replaced with new ones, reflecting the emergence of new forces, historical circumstances, and preferences. Colonial built environments in Asia have outlived the empires that founded them to create lives of their own.

This book explores three main themes: the first one is the interaction between colonial powers. We reject the idea that each empire or state had a purely unique colonial agenda, policy, or practice. Royal family ties and common interests of European powers in Asia created the need to negotiate and co-operate on issues ranging from diplomacy and military affairs to sharing space and services in the colonial setting. European empires and Japan went through common experiences in establishing and defending their spheres of influence. Their relations were further strengthened by the logic of international trade. They interchanged ideas, technology, resources, and housing arrangements. As European communities in Asia grew, the partnership between them became more complex, both on official and non-official levels. Expanding global trade and economies linked colonial enclaves with each other and the rest of the world. This book strives to underline how, in the colonial world, global and local forces coexisted, as well as the necessity for colonizers to both compete and co-operate with one another. At the same time, the colonial enterprise was diverse and heterogeneous. This volume stresses the regional diversity of the colonial built form found from Harbin to Hanoi. The chapters in the volume attest to the variety inherent in colonial projects.

The second theme of this book is the adaptations and accommodations made between different sides in the process of colonization. This volume examines the elite as well as other actors of colonization, such as entrepreneurs and minor colonial officials, whose geographic distance from the European metropolis allowed them flexibility in dealing with local society in both formal and informal ways. We aim to dispel traditional assumptions about indigenous societies as only victims of colonization by demonstrating abilities to learn from, work within, and challenge their assigned roles in the colonization process. Despite the unequal treaties, extraterritorial rights, as well as endemic racism and segregation, there also existed dialogue and interaction between the colonizers and the colonized.

The colonial built environment is most misleading in its visual expression of self-confidence and grandeur, as it attempts to conceal the risks and anxieties associated with living in colonial settings. Our third theme is the uncertainties of colonial and semi-colonial regimes. We recognize that colonialism should be viewed on different scales. Micro-studies demonstrate that the colonial enterprise was a messy, unpredictable, and often dangerous affair.[3] While imposing colonial buildings epitomized metropolitan power, confidence, and prestige, the reality on the ground was often lawless, unpleasant, and dangerous. During times of peace, the colonizers were concerned about disease and natural disasters. Their reliance on local labor was accompanied by the possibility of insubordination, desertion, or revolt. Local authorities were another source of conflict. Moreover, the case studies in this volume illustrate that during the high tide of imperialism, starting from the late-nineteenth century, the fear of rebellion and war was constant and real. We illustrate that the official versions of empire building gloss over the precariousness of colonial life.

This collection brings together case studies about the regions where the concentration of Western and, later, Japanese influence, money, and people were at its maximum. We examine urban colonial places and the urban aspects of colonization, such as city planning, infrastructure, and spatial arrangements. We do not discuss the countryside, where the majority of local populations in East Asia lived, as their encounters with the urban centers were limited. This volume does not discuss the Portuguese in Macau, for by the mid-nineteenth century their influence both in Europe and in this region was limited. We do not include discussion of the United States' activities in China. Even though the United States was involved in colonial practices in the Caribbean and the Pacific during this period, it did not have formal colonies or spheres of influence in China or Vietnam although American missionaries, traders, and entrepreneurs did participate in colonial life in these places, and American-designed buildings testified to this.[4] Japanese imperial expansion in coastal China can be considered part of this story because of its ability to adopt and adapt earlier European colonial models and integrate them into its own expansionist policies in Asia, as Bill Sewell demonstrates in his chapter.

We go beyond one geographic region and the fixed notions of Northeast, East, and Southeast Asia to examine the coast bordering the South and East China Seas. Here, full-scale colonization started later than in other parts of the world; the intensity of colonial projects reached its peak in the late nineteenth century and endured much longer, as in the case of Hong Kong. It is difficult to draw borders between East and Southeast Asia on the coast of the South China Sea: both geographic regions have similar natural conditions, their indigenous populations and cultures are mixed, and they were affected by Confucian culture. In addition, it is there that French, Portuguese, and British colonial projects and influence overlapped. Instead, we examine a long geographic belt, a north-to-south axis extending from Northeast China to Northern Vietnam, which best represents the diversity of Imperial Russian, German, Japanese, British, and French colonization projects. Along this belt, regional variations were most pronounced in topography and climate, posing different challenges to the colonizers. Proximity to the ocean, in Hong Kong for example, meant exposure to typhoons. Living near mighty rivers, like in Harbin, Shanghai and

Hanoi, meant dealing with seasonal floods. Building on mountainous Hong Kong Island was complicated by hazards of landslides, lack of water, and poisonous snakes. Cold places like Manchuria required solid building materials and heating during long winters. Unbearable summer heat and humidity, paired with cool winters, were part of life in the subtropical climate of South China and Tonkin.

Encounters between the colonizers and local populations also depended on the choice of geographic location. Some places had well-established local populations. For example, recent scholarship emphasizes that Shanghai was a trading center on the Yangtze River since the thirteenth century, becoming a major cotton and silk production center during the Ming dynasty (1368–1644).[5] Hanoi's history goes back to 1010 when it became a capital of the Ly dynasty (1009–1225).[6] Other colonial cities were built from scratch. Harbin was nothing more than a small village when Imperial Russia started to build the Chinese Eastern Railway in Manchuria in 1896. When the British established Hong Kong as their colony in 1842, they found a handful of fishing settlements with a population of some 5,600 people.[7] As the British discovered in Hong Kong's New Territories or the Russians and Japanese in what is now Northeast China, building on a sparsely populated location often proved to be an advantage to the colonizers as they did not have to deal with strong resentment from settled local communities with established traditions. New settlements and cities also made it easy to attract cheap labor from neighboring areas.

The places discussed in this volume had access to the sea: either direct, via rivers or, eventually, by railway. European and Japanese colonizing powers all came from the sea (with the exception of the Russians) with the purpose of establishing permanent outposts, first on the coast and later with their sights inland. Proximity to the sea allowed them to exploit local economies and resources for the purpose of colonial and international trade. These cities became colonial seaports and trading hubs and were connected by networks of merchant and military ships, government offices, industries, railways, banks, hotels, and churches. Once the colonizers settled in, they built houses, schools, hospitals, factories, sports facilities, parks, and cemeteries. The natural outcome of their presence was small enclaves of Europe and Japan in Asian urban centers, where they invested money and technology and practiced different forms of government and authority.

The events covered in this volume span a period of one hundred years and begin with the First Opium War, starting with the arrival of the British Navy, which signaled the end of the Canton trade system (1760–1842) and the opening of China's treaty ports. It concludes with the advent of China's Resistance War (1937–45), which crippled European aspirations of semi-colonial control in China. The century saw an unprecedented growth of treaty ports and spheres of influence on China's coast, the expansion of Imperial Britain's colonial influence in Hong Kong, and of Imperial France in Vietnam, Laos, and Cambodia. The length of colonial and semi-colonial presence in Asia varied among the different imperial powers. British colonial rule in Hong Kong lasted from 1842 to 1997. French colonial rule in Tonkin lasted from the 1880s until 1954, with the last decade marked by the bloody French-Indochina War, which resulted in Vietnam's independence and division between the north and the south. Imperial Russia's colonial claims in China span from 1860, when it annexed Qing territory north of the Amur River and east of the Ussuri River, until the end of the Romanov dynasty in 1917. From 1860 to 1895, Imperial Russia did not expand further into China. After this lacuna, Russia claimed Manchuria as its exclusive sphere of influence until 1905, when it lost South Manchuria to Japanese influence after its defeat in the Russo-Japanese War. The extensive railway network was the most important legacy of Imperial Russian and Japanese presence in Manchuria. In addition, the Soviet Union kept a naval presence in Dalian from 1945 until the early 1950s.

The Imperial German presence in China was the shortest of all the colonial powers, with Germany staking claim to parts of Shandong province from 1897 to 1914. Yet it was this imperialist presence that triggered one of the most forceful anti-foreign movements, the Boxer Rebellion, which briefly threatened all external imperial powers in China in 1900, and which was brutally suppressed by the Eight Allied Forces of Great Britain, France, Austria-Hungary, Italy, Germany, the United States, Russia, and Japan. During World War I (1914–18), Germany lost its possessions in Shandong to Japan, which controlled these areas until 1922. Even as a latecomer to China, in less than seventeen years, Imperial Germany had built a strong colonial enclave centered in the city of Qingdao. But it was Imperial Japan that posed the greatest threat to China's sovereignty and to the European powers in Asia. Imperial Japan's colonial rule in China lasted from 1895, when it colonized Taiwan (Formosa), to 1945. From 1905 Japan occupied South Manchuria, and in 1931, the rest of Manchuria, establishing the puppet state of Manchukuo. As a result of Japan's war with China from 1937 to 1945, most of China's coast was occupied by Japanese troops and several puppet regimes were set up. Japan's quest for empire in East Asia became the ultimate challenge to the imperial claims of European powers, weakening their influence in China and uniting different forces within Chinese society. These forces of resistance and nationalism became crucial in terminating Japanese and European colonial rule. Most damage to the colonial built environment (in the period covered by this study) was done in the early years of China's Resistance War against Japan (1937–45), when Japan systematically bombed China's coastal cities.

The built environments in the locations discussed in this volume were the products of different forms of colonial and semi-colonial rule. British Hong Kong and French Cochinchina had status of full colonies, whereas France considered the remaining parts of the Indochinese Union (Annam, Tonkin, Cambodia, and Laos) as protectorates.[8] European powers established a semi-colonial presence in China through unequal treaties following the First Opium War by granting themselves treaty ports, leased territories, legation quarters, foreign settlements,[9] as well as railway and natural resource concessions. The combination of these arrangements allowed European powers to create their own competing spheres of influence in different parts of China. These powers were rarely bound by early treaties and agreements, and took advantage of opportunities to claim more territory and rights. For example, in Tianjin, the original British Concession covering 76 acres in 1860 increased to 588 acres in 1903. Ultimately, its total area was nearly half of all the territory of foreign concessions in town.[10]

We use the term "colonial" to describe European presence on the China coast, most of which was never formally colonized, because the European presence was based on unequal treaties and power dynamics. Edifices, railways, and roads were built by local coolie labor, without regard to the needs or desires of the local authority. They were often built in defiance of local laws, indigenous forms, spatial arrangements, and traditions.

While the European presence in Vietnam and China was not guaranteed to exist in perpetuity, the colonial built environment became a permanent claim over space. European powers, and later Japan, designed new urban districts and cities on a grand scale, with the amenities of modern European civilization. In doing so, they did not shy away from destroying or relocating existing local settlements, temples, and cemeteries and displacing indigenous populations. Once the railways, cities and buildings were complete, it was very difficult to physically remove them, even though some attempts by the native population to destroy them were an inevitable part of the colonial experience. For example, the Chinese Eastern Railway was completed by Imperial Russia in 1903 as planned, despite the destruction of its lines by Chinese Boxers in 1900. With very few exceptions, colonial buildings became fixed landmarks in the treaty ports and imperial cities, and remained long after the external powers left. For example, the grand and well-preserved architecture of Shanghai's Bund remains a living monument to the city's semi-colonial cosmopolitan past.

Technological improvements in construction methods and materials from Europe and the United States appeared in Asia after the First World War. Reinforced concrete became widely used in constructing colonial, government, and private buildings. New advancements like central heating, piped water and sewage, and electricity and telegraphs became more widespread. European-style buildings became appreciated in China, Indochina, and across Asia by the privileged; the colonial style of architecture was imitated by reform-minded officials and local elites as newly found symbols of wealth and power. For example, in colonial Hong Kong, the prominent Eurasian Robert Ho Tung was the only non-European permitted to live in the exclusive Peak District in a European-style mansion.[11] Many members of the Nationalist government in China (1928–49), despite its patriotic stance, appreciated the colonial built environment for its practical and aesthetic value. For example, Chiang Kai-shek, head of the Nationalist government in China, chose to get married and reside in Shanghai's former colonial mansions.

The Chapters

The chapters are organized geographically, moving south along the Chinese coast, from Harbin to Hanoi. Victor Zatsepine's chapter, "Russia, Railways, and Urban Development in Manchuria, 1896–1930," examines differences between Russia's civilian and military colonization projects in Manchuria, and discusses the planning and establishment of Manchuria's railways and new cities. It demonstrates that Imperial Russia's economic colonization in Harbin was more successful than its military claim over Port Arthur. Harbin became Russia's semi-colonial outpost with a flourishing urban space and a sizable Russian population. In contrast, Russia's fortress of Port Arthur did not flourish and eventually became a source of conflict with Japan. Even Russia's defeat by Japan in 1905 and its withdrawal from Northeast China did not stop Russian and Soviet participation in urban growth and industrial development in northern Manchuria, which continued after the revolution of 1917.

Bill Sewell's chapter, "Beans to Banners: The Evolving Architecture of Prewar Changchun," analyzes the emergence of Changchun, a city in southern Manchuria, as an expression of Japanese colonial ambition. Like Imperial Russia, Japan built railroads to extend its influence in Manchuria, developing Changchun as a railway town from 1905 to 1931. Sewell demonstrates that Japan saw Changchun as its own response to the European influence in Asia. Changchun's early architecture was inspired by European traditions, while its later styles incorporated Japanese nationalist ideals. From 1932 to 1945, Changchun served as the capital of the puppet state of Manchukuo, yet Japan failed to deliver the promise of modernity to the Chinese subjects there.

David Tucker's chapter, "France, Brossard Mopin, and Manchukuo," analyzes French commercial interest in the development of Manchukuo's infrastructure. Despite the fact that France did not recognize Manchukuo, French businesses were eager to invest there. French consortium Brossard Mopin, discussed in this chapter, offered to finance the construction of Manchukuo's capital in Changchun and to design some of its buildings. Japanese military and civilian authorities in Manchukuo were divided about the scope of French investment, but they used it anyway during the early years of Manchukuo.

Zhang Chang and Liu Yue's chapter, "International Concessions and the Modernization of Tianjin," studies Tianjin's foreign concessions and their influence on local municipal governance. The authors emphasize the uniqueness of Tianjin as the city with the largest number of foreign concessions in Asia. These concessions became places where the built environment and its European management served as a model for Chinese municipal authorities in their quest for reforms and self-governance. Tianjin's status as a trading hub and a fast-growing metropolis ensured a constant flow of ideas from Europe and from other treaty ports like Shanghai. Zhang and Liu demonstrate that in architecture, the dialogue between Chinese and European cultures was reflected in an eclectic style shared by both the Europeans and the Chinese. For example, after the collapse of the Qing dynasty in 1911, Chinese government officials and entrepreneurs residing in Tianjin designed their grand mansions in the European style. At the same time, however, they preserved their distance from Europeans and maintained much of their traditional way of life.

Klaus Mühlhahn's chapter, "Mapping Colonial Space: The Planning and Building of Qingdao by German Colonial Authorities, 1897–1914," describes Germany's quest to define its sphere of influence in East Asia with the occupation of the area around Jiaozhou Bay and the establishment of Qingdao city from 1897 to 1914. The leasehold, ceded by the Qing government for a period of ninety-nine years, was under the sole control of the German navy. Like Port Arthur, early Qingdao was highly militarized. From the very beginning, colonial naval commanders attempted to instate rigid control over urban space, an effort that was marked by violence and racial inequality. However, despite the demonstration of firm colonial power, Germany eventually had to accommodate a growing Chinese population and its needs.

As the chapters above illustrate, violence played a fundamental role in establishing colonial space in Asia. European and Japanese military authorities struggled to maintain their upper hand in political and administrative life in these cities. Cole Roskam's chapter, "The Architecture of Risk: Urban Space and Uncertainty in Shanghai, 1843–74," further develops this theme of violence ingrained in colonial cities, while exploring the notions of risk and uncertainty in Shanghai between 1842 and 1870 for both the colonizers and the colonized. Shanghai's foreign and Chinese communities had to deal with specific and inter-related risks, and created architectural and spatial strategies aimed at segregation, security, and stability.

The next two chapters deal with two particular buildings in Hong Kong, where colonial authority was established early and was long lasting. G. A. Bremner's chapter, "Fabricating Justice: Conflict and Contradiction in the Making of the Hong Kong Supreme Court, 1898–1912," looks at how this structure, which was meant to represent the ideas of British nationhood, identity, and justice, also became a source of conflict. Bremner highlights the political tension that existed between Whitehall and Hong Kong over its design and construction, and explores the inconsistencies of extending colonial British "rule of law" to the local Chinese population.

Peter Cunich's chapter, "Making Space for Higher Education in Colonial Hong Kong, 1887–1913," examines the arena carved out for tertiary studies in a city where land for construction was limited. He examines the local and metropolitan forces that affected its conceptualization and construction, as well as contemporary trends in establishing new universities around the world. The University of Hong Kong (1910–12) was created to act as a beacon of Western modernity for the rest of China, and was indicative of the amalgamated world created by colonialism: the project of a Parsee merchant and funded by opium money, it was located between the boundaries of the European and Chinese parts of town, delimiting geographic space and bridging two cultures. Bremner and Cunich both agree that Hong Kong's colonial authorities were often at odds with London, and attest to the real power enjoyed by the colonists, and not the metropole.

The last three chapters deal with French Indochina, in particular the capital city of Hanoi. Despite having a presence in places like Shanghai and Tianjin, the French built their Asian colonial base in Indochina — Hanoi was intended to be France's answer to British Hong Kong — and, like other colonial cities, they had to deal with similar sets of concerns. Lisa Drummond's chapter, "Colonial Hanoi: Urban Space in Public Discourse," is about French anxieties over their exotic surroundings in Hanoi. She examines the newspaper *L'Avenir du Tonkin*, which reflected French views about the city, its public spaces, and its people. She demonstrates links between the realities of living in a colonial city and the vision to transform its perceived backwardness and the practical measures to turn it into a livable European city.

Laura Victoir's article, "Hygienic Colonial Residences in Hanoi," explores how the French medical community weighed in on constructing salubrious housing in Hanoi. The threat of disease was ever-present in the colonial setting. Enormous efforts on the part of home governments and international medical communities were taken in order to reduce its incidence, as evidenced by the works of Philip D. Curtin and David Arnold.[12] Victoir's work traces the evolution of medical thought on the origins of disease and its vectors, and looks at how architecture was used as a tool to promote health. French guidebooks on tropical and colonial hygiene provide unique insight into the private, domestic space of imperial life.

The early decades of the twentieth century saw the emergence of Vietnamese and Chinese bourgeoisies, who were exposed to European culture, educated in European traditions, and worked in colonial administration and commerce. These new local elites became a new force, which demanded recognition and space. They ultimately challenged European power in colonies and treaty ports. Danielle Labbé, Caroline Herbelin, and Quang-Vinh Dao's article, "Domesticating the Suburbs: Architectural Production and Exchanges in Hanoi during the Late French Colonial Era," explores how local and exogenous housing cultures, professional training institutions, and French colonial urbanism came together in Hanoi during that period. Throughout the first half of the twentieth century, Hanoi witnessed intense cultural exchanges in the fields of art and architecture. One of Hanoi's suburbs, called the "New Indigenous Quarter," became an architectural laboratory where French-trained Vietnamese architects reinvented Hanoi's housing forms to suit the tastes of an emerging Vietnamese middle-class. This chapter reconsiders the ability of the Vietnamese to learn from the French and negotiate colonial space, and echoes Cunich's discussion of training the indigenous elite for use in the colonial administration.

This volume pays close attention to Hong Kong and Hanoi not only because they were formal colonies, but also because the lines separating European and non-European societies were more pronounced there than in other places. The case studies in the volume scrutinize and examine the built environment on both the macro and micro levels, giving not just a fuller picture of the challenges of colonialism but also the variations of experiences on the ground, which were found in the daily interactions between people who lived in particular urban settings. Both dimensions are important for a more balanced understanding of what occurred.

Furthermore, the volume moves beyond British-centered narratives of colonial presences in East and Southeast Asia by emphasizing the independent role of other European powers and Japan. British influence on China's coast was severely challenged to the north beyond Shanghai and to the south beyond Hong Kong. Just as the British, Germans, Japanese, French, and Russians competed for spheres of influence, they were in constant communication with each other and were well informed about each other's trade, diplomacy, and military activities. For example, Britain joined forces with France during the Second Opium War, while American and British interests amalgamated in the Shanghai International Settlement in the 1860s. The foreign powers became even closer when the Boxer Rebellion threatened their legation quarters in Beijing and their presence in northern China. Finally, Russian, British, French, German, and American firms co-operated very closely in their banking and financial arrangements. Our multilingual sources challenge the traditional reliance on English-language sources to paint the picture of foreign presence on China's coast.[13]

A closer look at the colonial built environment invites re-evaluation of the complex arrangements, which are often reduced to simplistic post-colonial terms of the "colonizer" and the "colonized." This volume invites further investigation of tensions and ambiguities within colonial structures and between colonial agents. It also demonstrates the ability of the "colonized" to adapt, reformulate, and, ultimately, challenge spatial arrangements imposed by the different colonial powers. Moreover, the relationship between the colonizers and the colonized was not a one-way street; it was a constant negotiation. This relationship was in constant flux and has to be understood only by paying attention to the specific historical moment, geographic location, type of colonial project, and the people involved. The advantage of focusing on the colonial built environment is that it exposes multiple layers of empire making and of conquest, both ideological and real.

Notes

1. See, for example, Johnathan A. Farris, "Thirteen Factories of Canton: An Architecture of Sino-Western Collaboration and Confrontation," in *Buildings and Landscapes: Journal of the Vernacular Architecture Forum* 14 (Fall 2007): 66–83; Gwendolyn Wright, *The Politics of Design in French Colonial Urbanism* (Chicago: University of Chicago Press, 1991); Brenda S. A. Yeoh, *Contesting Space: Power Relations and the Urban Built Environment in Colonial Singapore* (Kuala Lumpur and New York: Oxford University Press, 1996); George Steinmetz, *The Devil's Handwriting: Precoloniality and the German Colonial State in Qingdao, Samoa, and Southwest Africa* (Chicago: University of Chicago Press, 2007); William S. Logan, *Hanoi: Biography of a City* (Seattle: University of Washington Press, 2000); Edward Denison and Guang Yuren, *Building Shanghai: The Story of China's Gateway* (West Sussex, England: John Wiley & Sons Ltd, 2006); Nicola Cooper, *France in Indochina* (New York and Oxford: Berg, 2001); David Wolff, *To the Harbin Station: The Liberal Alternative in Russian Manchuria, 1898–1914* (Stanford, CA: Stanford University Press, 1999); Koshizawa Akira, *Manshūkoku no shuto keikaku: Tōkyō no genzai to mirai o tou* (Tōkyō: Nihon Keizai Hyōronsha, 1988).
2. For instance, Anthony King argued that the built environment, apart from being a representation of social order, also shaped society and its culture. Anthony King, "Urbanism, Colonialism and the World-Economy," *Journal of Interdisciplinary History* 22, no. 4 (1992): 1.
3. See, for example, James L. Hevia, *English Lessons: The Pedagogy of Imperialism in Nineteenth-Century China* (Durham, NC: Duke University Press, 2003), 26–27.
4. However, US traders did take part in the opium trade and benefited from separate unequal treaties with China, the earliest one signed in 1844. They were involved in the construction of the International Settlement in Shanghai and were part of the Eight Allied forces in Tianjin and Beijing during the Boxer Rebellion. American architects were also crucial in introducing Western architectural traditions to China. See, for example, Jeffrey W. Cody, *Building in China: Henry K. Murphy's "Adaptive Architecture," 1914–1935* (Hong Kong: Chinese University Press, 2001).
5. Wang Manjun, Huang Wei, and Feng Jieyin, *Memory of Shanghai* (Shanghai: Shanghai Jiaotong University Press, 2010), 6–9.
6. William S. Logan, *Hanoi: Biography of a City* (Seattle: University of Washington Press, 2000), 15.
7. Joseph S. P. Ting and Nai-kwan Wong, *City of Victoria* (Hong Kong: Urban Council of Hong Kong, 1994), 9.
8. Cooper, *France in Indochina*, 5.

9. For a discussion on the distinction between concessions and settlements, see F. C. Jones, *Shanghai and Tientsin: With Special Reference to Foreign Interests* (Oxford: Oxford University Press, 1940), 118.
10. Jones, *Shanghai and Tientsin*, 131.
11. Non-Europeans were excluded from living on the Peak by the Hill District Reservation Ordinance of 1904. See Jean Gittins, *Stanley: Behind Barbed Wire* (Hong Kong: Hong Kong University Press, 1982), 12.
12. Philip D. Curtin, *Death by Migration: Europe's Encounter with the Tropical World in the Nineteenth Century* (Cambridge: Cambridge University Press, 1989); Philip D. Curtin, *Disease and Empire: The Health of European Troops in the Conquest of Africa* (Cambridge: Cambridge University Press, 1998); David Arnold, ed. *Warm Climates and Western Medicine: The Emergence of Tropical Medicine, C. 1500–1900* (Atlanta, GA: Rodopi,1996); David Arnold, "Introduction: Disease, Medicine and Empire," in *Imperial Medicine and Indigenous Societies*, ed. David Arnold (Manchester: Manchester University Press, 1988).
13. For example, the most recent book by British historian Robert Bickers, *The Scramble for China: Foreign Devils in the Qing Empire, 1832–1914*, relies mostly on English-language sources to describe Western expansion in China.

2
Russia, Railways, and Urban Development in Manchuria, 1896–1930

Victor Zatsepine

When prominent Japanese poet Yosano Akiko traveled to Harbin in spring of 1928, she had mixed feelings about the city. She was impressed by its orderly layout, by its Russian-European style architecture, broad paved streets, shops, parks, and cafes. Grand Russian mansions and beautiful churches exemplified Imperial Russia's former presence in this part of the world. However, she also noticed that the Russian influence in Harbin showed signs of decay. Some of the mansions were abandoned. There were Russian beggars on the street. The vast Russian cemetery with white marble gravestones covered with flowers reminded her that at least one generation of Russians made Harbin their eternal home, and that others remained.[1] By the time of her visit, Russian Harbin was thirty years old; much of its social fabric was being replaced by a growing Chinese population. Yet, even a decade after the collapse of the Russian empire, Harbin's infrastructure and architecture remained powerful symbols of Imperial Russia's expansion into East Asia.

Imperial Russia claimed parts of Manchuria (*dong san sheng*, or "Three Eastern Provinces," as it was called during the late Qing period) as a semi-colony.[2] Like other European powers in China's coastal areas, Imperial Russia forced unequal treaties upon the frail Qing government and leased parts of Manchuria's territory, built strategically important railways and towns, utilized its natural resources, and initiated industrial development and trade on terms beneficial for Russia and its subjects. Russian urban centers in Manchuria, built by Chinese coolie labor, grew with great speed and became enclaves of Russian culture, trade, and way of life.

This chapter examines urban development as part of Imperial Russia's colonizing drive in Manchuria. It argues that in Manchuria, Russia found an ultimate expression of its European identity by building railways and towns. Russian city planning and architecture were inspired by European traditions; Imperial Russia brought its own interpretation of European style to the cities of the Russian Far East and Manchuria. The chapter analyzes how the tensions between civilian and military aspects of Imperial Russia's colonization affected the fate of the colonial built environment in Manchuria. Harbin, Port Arthur (Lüshunkou), and Dalny (Dalian) were built at the same time, but they exemplify different visions of Russian urban experiments in Manchuria. From the very beginning they served as a railway town, a military fortress, and a trading port respectively. Port Arthur and Dalny were short-lived as Russian towns: in 1905, Russia lost them as a result of its war with Japan. In contrast, Russian Harbin outlived the Romanov dynasty by more than a decade, and continued to serve as a hub of Russian/Soviet influence, trade, and culture in Republican China until the late 1920s.

"Peaceful" Railway Expansion and Harbin

The development of Russian towns in Manchuria is closely linked to Imperial Russia's two colonization projects beyond its eastern border: the construction of the China Eastern Railway (CER) (1898–1903) and leasing the southern part of Liaodong peninsula in 1898. All new Russian settlements and towns in Manchuria were linked by the CER, which crossed three northeastern provinces from east to west and extended to the south via the South Manchurian Railway (SMR) line, in the form of a capital letter T. The railway paved the way for economic colonization of China's northeastern provinces.

The railway was a pet project of Russia's Ministry of Finance, headed by Count Sergei Witte, a capable senior official who was the country's main proponent of industrialization. Russia's eastward railway expansion was approved by the Russian monarch, Tsar Nicholas II. At the beginning, this expansion was carried out peacefully. In 1891, Nicholas, while still a prince, had visited Asia and the Russian Far East. Inspired by British colonial possessions in Asia, he supported the idea of extending Russia's influence in Qing China by peaceful means. The CER served this purpose. It was to become a section of the world's longest railway, the Trans-Siberian, connecting European Russia with the Pacific Ocean. It served another purpose as well: it brought together the economies of Siberia and Manchuria, opening up the latter to international trade on Russian terms.

Imperial Russia chose a good time to negotiate this railway concession with China. In 1895, Japan easily defeated China in a humiliating war. According to the resulting Treaty of Shimonoseki, China was forced to cede Liaodong Peninsula to Japan. In the same year, Russia, Germany, and France interfered, launching the Tripartite Intervention and pressuring Japan to return Liaodong to China. By helping the Qing government negotiate with Japan for the return of Liaodong, Russia gained momentum in advancing its interests in China. In 1896, Russia invited China's senior official Li Hongzhang to the coronation of Nicholas II. During Li's trip, he signed, with Sergei Witte and Russian Foreign Minister Aleksey Lobanov-Rostovsky, an agreement of partnership between the Qing and Russian empires against a possible Japanese attack. According to this agreement, the Qing government granted railway concession rights in Manchuria to the Russo-Chinese bank, backed by the Russian government. In August 1896, a contract for the construction of the CER was signed. Russia obtained the right to build and use this railroad for transporting goods, civilians, and troops. The Russian government promised to return the railway with all property belonging to it eighty years after the railway's completion. The Chinese government retained its right to buy the railroad back after thirty years.[3]

Nicholas II's policy of peaceful economic penetration in Manchuria was short-lived. Russia's imperialist intentions became clear when two powerful lobbies—the Ministry of Finance and Ministry of War—convinced Nicholas II to go beyond Russia's prior agreements with China. In 1898, in violation of its promise not to seek territorial gains in China, the Russian Navy occupied Port Arthur and Dalny on the southern tip of Liaodong, while the Russian government negotiated with the Qing court to lease a part of the Liaodong Peninsula for twenty-five years. In the same year, Russia obtained the right to build the SMR, linking the future CER with Dalny. These agreements added a military aspect to railway expansion: Port Arthur was built to serve as a military base for the Imperial Russian Navy and to protect Russia's new territorial lease and railway concession.[4] Carried out despite Witte's disapproval of occupying Liaodong, these plans not only alienated China and Japan, but also brought Russia's Far Eastern policy to the brink of disaster.[5]

The CER was built according to the best European standards of railway construction and management. Its creation was preceded by the work of Russian topographers who surveyed the future route through the steppes of Barga, the mountains of the Great Xing'anling Range, and forests of Heilongjiang and Jilin provinces. This route was then divided into more than twenty construction districts. The CER's construction employed some of the finest engineering talent of the Russian Empire and used the most advanced railway technology and equipment imported from Britain, Germany, and the United States. The western section of the CER, running through Great Xing'anling, proved to be the most difficult because it involved the labor-intensive construction of Xing'an tunnel. Designed by the Russian engineer Bocharov with the help of Italian experts, this tunnel was three *versts*[6] (3.18 km) long. In total, including bridges and tunnels, this 2,400-verst (2,544-km) railway was built in five years.[7]

Most of Russia's construction in Manchuria was planned and executed by the CER Company. Apart from the railway line, the company built ninety-two railway stations (fifty-four along the main line from Manzhouli to Suifenhe, and thirty eight along the South Manchurian line from Harbin to Port Arthur).[8] All the major stations developed small settlements, complete with administrative buildings, inns, and markets. The company's powers in Manchuria went well beyond building a railway. It bought railway equipment; hired Chinese and Russian workers, and deployed engineers from Russia proper; as well as built railway and administrative amenities, and brick, metal-work, and equipment factories. It established its own river fleet and contributed to building several river and sea harbors in Manchuria. It provided housing to all employees, first in temporary barracks and later in brick buildings and houses (according to rank and nationality); running water and heating were available to only a privileged few. The company operated as a big conglomerate, which established its own hospitals, schools, societies, clubs, and cemeteries. It also acquired land, mining, and logging concessions, and was central in supervising the construction of Harbin and other Russian railway towns and settlements in Manchuria.

Russian settlements along the railway zone (called the "right-of-way belt," or *polosa otchuzhdenia* in Russian) and the leased territory on the Liaodong peninsula were de facto governed by the Russian administration, and had their own Russian courts, police, and military. The railway administration employed its own railway guards who protected its property and people. The Russians residing there had privileged status. They were spatially separated from the local population and were under the jurisdiction of law of Imperial Russia. Gradually, the new Russian towns in Manchuria developed their own enclaves where the subjects of the Russian empire could satisfy all their needs, be they spiritual, educational, cultural, or culinary.

Harbin became a central administrative town of the CER. During its first decade, the city's development was supervised and funded by the Imperial Russian government. Harbin's strategic location at the confluence of the Sungari (Songhua) River and the CER made it a convenient domestic and international transportation hub and distribution center for Manchuria's trade, especially in agricultural and animal products. Like the railway, Harbin was built rapidly. Long-term resident Simon Karlitsky compared the speed of its construction to that of St. Petersburg or San Francisco during the gold rush. The CER Company had acquired a considerable amount of land to secure Harbin's future territorial growth. By the time the railway was completed in 1903, central Harbin occupied approximately eight square kilometers, while greater Harbin covered nearly twenty.[9]

At the same time, early Harbin, like all pioneer towns, was not an inviting place. The railway station was built several miles from the Sungari River. The roads connecting the old town with the commercial district were not paved. There was no sewage system. Life in Harbin was expensive, as everything was imported at great cost. It was far from other Russian towns and did not have the amenities available to the Russian population in well-established Siberian settlements. In 1902, Nikolai Appolonovich Baikov, a Russian writer and an officer in the Imperial Army, described Harbin as a lonely steppe with marshes. He complained that Harbin had nothing but "wind, sand and dirt."[10]

Chinese workers and Russian railway guards lived in temporary shacks. Harbin's neighboring local settlements were sparsely populated, contributing to the overall feeling of isolation and boredom. The weather only made things worse. Cold winters and rainy summers slowed urban development and had a negative impact on the health of the newly arrived Russian settlers and Chinese migrant laborers. Harbin witnessed several outbreaks of dysentery, cholera, and plague.

Yet, over time, downtown Harbin started to show the signs of Russian modernity and of progress. Harbin's early architecture was built to satisfy the basic needs of the railway and consisted mostly of red brick one- and two-story houses of railway employees. After the first decade of the twentieth century, the city's architecture flourished. Harbin's railway station, built in art nouveau style with an enormous square in front of it, became a landmark (see Plate 1). The CER's buildings were grand and imposing, combining European architectural styles. The main administrative buildings of the CER, for instance, built by St. Petersburg architect D. A. Kryzhanovsky, stretched for 170 meters along Bolshoi Avenue and occupied 22,300 square meters of space.[11] Russian banks, schools, churches, and theaters were built in the classical Russian style. There was a Russian stock exchange as well as landowner committees, middle schools for Russian and Chinese children, chambers of commerce, a circus, cinemas, parks, cafes, and sport facilities. (Plate 2)

The Russian population of Harbin grew fast, due to the CER's increasing demand for labor, industries, and services. From 1898 to 1905, it contained 30,000 imperial Russian subjects. In 1911, when the Qing dynasty collapsed, it had more than 40,000.[12] The Chinese population also expanded rapidly, even though its seasonal migratory nature makes it difficult to provide an exact number. The CER Company employed approximately 150,000 Chinese contract workers to build the railway, of which in 1902 nearly 20,000 people were involved in the construction of Harbin. Some of these workers remained there permanently. In 1913, the Chinese population was over 23,500 people, accounting for more than 30 percent of Harbin's total population.[13] Most of the Chinese people lived in the Chinese district of Fujiadian, and were involved in construction, domestic services, shopkeeping, and small trade. Several nationalities of the multinational Russian Empire

(Tatars, Armenians, Georgians, Jews, etc.) as well as small groups of Germans, Poles, Japanese, and Koreans, settled in Harbin, adding to its cosmopolitan atmosphere. Yet the Russians and the Chinese were the two dominant groups in this rapidly expanding city. (Plate 3)

Port Arthur and Dalny as Russian Outposts

The Imperial Russian government also had high hopes for Port Arthur and Dalny to further extend its influence in China and the Asia Pacific. Yet these towns did not have the advantages enjoyed by Harbin. Both towns were built at the southernmost tip of the SMR and were even further from the towns of the Russian Far East. While Harbin's distance from major Chinese settlements provided relative security from a possible attack, Port Arthur and Dalny were exposed to the sea. Japan could easily control the sea route between Port Arthur and Vladivostok, especially the straits between the southern tip of the Korean peninsula and Japan. In addition, Port Arthur and Dalny's proximity to each other caused constant friction between different ministries and interest groups within the Imperial Russian government in St. Petersburg and their representatives in Manchuria.[14] The construction of these towns also revealed tensions between the peaceful and military methods of Imperial Russia's urban expansion in Liaodong. However, these towns relied on each other, as both of them were connected by railway to Harbin, depending on the latter for supplies and labor.

Russia established Port Arthur as a fortress and military base in 1898. It was located on the premises of the former Qing naval base built in the early 1880s by Li Hongzhang for the Beiyang Fleet, but had been destroyed in 1894 during the Sino-Japanese War. This town had a fortified coastline and several defense structures that survived the Japanese. Port Arthur fell under the jurisdiction of the Russian Ministry of War and Navy, as a strategically important ice-free port and the easternmost expansion of Russia in Asia. Military influence affected its history and its built environment. This port was restricted to other foreign powers, and the Russian civilian population there was registered with and accountable to the military authority. Port Arthur's military base and infrastructure were built by Chinese labor. Port Arthur was divided into two districts: old and new. While in the old district the Russian barracks were located near Chinese shops, the new district was planned as a European city, and the exclusive place of residence of the Russians. The Russian colonial authorities imposed new resettlement and tax policies, which alienated the Chinese population. As a result, sporadic clashes occurred, but they were immediately suppressed. For example, in February 1899, Russian soldiers shot and wounded about one hundred local farmers in a dispute near Jinzhou, located in the northeastern part of the Kwantung Leased Territory.[15] Russian military authorities attempted to dominate every aspect of daily life in the territory surrounding Port Arthur and Dalny.

In contrast to Port Arthur's role as a military stronghold in Liaodong, Dalny was designed to be a trading port, linking northern Manchuria with the Pacific. In case of war, its Russian community could be mobilized to defend the Russian-leased Liaodong Peninsula. Apart from that, it was envisioned as an international, European-styled commercial port. On an official Russian map of the city, published in 1900, Dalny looked like an orderly spider's web, with streets radiating from several plazas. Place-names were either Russian or European: Moscovsky Avenue, Krasnaya Ploshchad (Red Square), St. Petersburg Bay, and Angliisky Sad (English Garden). Dalny challenged Harbin as the most European of all Russian towns in Manchuria. By 1904 it had electricity, water, and a tramline. Its mansions were built in the European style with elements of symmetry and art nouveau, emphasizing Dalny's civilian nature and openness to international trade.[16] By 1903 a new administrative district and several impressive mansions were completed. One of them housed V. V. Sakharov, Dalny's chief city planner, who was previously in charge of building the commercial port of Vladivostok.

New Russian towns in Manchuria had much in common. They were planned and designed by Russian engineers and architects, many of whom were trained in St. Petersburg and European Russia. With lavish financial support from St. Petersburg, the new Russian towns of Manchuria overshadowed the towns of the Russian Far East, inviting both fascination and envy. Just as St. Petersburg was considered to be Russia's window to Europe, Dalny and Port Arthur were expected to become Russia's gateway and beacon to Asia. Despite the temporary nature of the diplomatic arrangements by which they were established, the Russian towns in Manchuria were built as permanent markers of Russian influence, combining the best traditions of Imperial Russian architecture and employing European styles, ranging from baroque to art nouveau.[17] These towns became an ultimate expression of Imperial Russian modernity abroad, reflecting the blend of European, Slavic, and multicultural populations, traditions, sentiments, and the built form of this vast Eurasian empire.

Moreover, the Russian Orthodox church had a strong influence in Russian urban centers along the CER. Orthodox churches were the most representative landmarks of the Russian presence. The first Orthodox church in Manchuria, St. Nicholas Cathedral, was built in Harbin in 1899. It was a wooden structure built in a neo-Russian style, and was inspired by the architectural traditions of the Russian Orthodox church dating from the fifteenth century. Compared to Protestant and Catholic churches, the leadership of the Russian Orthodox church was little concerned with spreading its Christian faith among the local population and left only a few Chinese converts. Nonetheless, the churches were central to the spiritual life of the Russian community and served multiple purposes. Besides accommodating the religious needs and boosting the morale of CER employees, Russian settlers, and soldiers, the churches also served as schools for children and were a gathering place for the Russians during weekly Sunday service, regardless of their social status.

Russian towns in Manchuria were semi-colonial in legal and spatial arrangements. Even though Imperial Russia had never formally colonized Manchuria the way it did Central Asia earlier, Harbin, Dalny, and Port Arthur were built by Chinese labor for Imperial Russian subjects who were protected by Russian law. Qing subjects had limited or no rights to purchase land, to build or buy property, or to reside in urban districts reserved for Imperial Russia's subjects. Chinese laborers and settlers provided vital services in these towns, but their private lives were spent in overcrowded and dirty quarters, which often frightened and appalled Russians. These towns, conversely, were designed to create a distinct Russian way of life (official and unofficial), where the Russians lived in privilege and protection. It is not surprising that contemporary Russian accounts mention the Chinese presence only marginally, as if it did not exist.[18] While the far corners of northern

Manchuria were sparsely populated until the early twentieth century, South Manchuria had a dense population and Chinese towns, such as Jilin and Fengtian (Mukden), with well-established local provincial administration, trade, and traditions. The vast majority of the Chinese and Manchu population in the three provinces of Manchuria did not live in towns and had only limited interaction with the Russians. In 1900, only about 6 percent of Manchuria's 12 million people lived in towns.[19] The Russian presence in new towns along the CER and SMR, apart from bringing opportunities for new jobs and trade, also invited suspicion and resentment. When pressured, the local population did not wait long to express its discontent.

Destroyed Environment and Lives

Peaceful expansion was a myth that accompanied Russian imperialist policies in Manchuria. The idea of bringing European civilization to the non-European "barren lands" was a calculated enterprise accompanied by guns and violence. Imperial Russia joined the British, French, and German empires in a scramble for concessions and spheres of influence in Qing China, fully aware of the dangers and possible local resistance. Before the construction of the CER, Manchuria's Chinese urban and rural settlements grew as a result of migration from central China and internal trade. The CER, apart from providing new jobs to Chinese migrant workers and petty traders, alienated provincial authorities and local residents of Manchuria by the sheer speed of its demand for change. In 1898, a party of Russian military topographers surveying the future route of the railway was attacked by two hundred Chinese peasants.[20] Similar attacks happened in other sections of the future railway. The CER Company's acquisition of land, forest, and timber concessions in Manchuria threatened local villages and trade. Unavoidably, the CER ran through ancestral burial sites in South Manchuria and removal of these tombs and temples invited resentment. The railway's right-of-way belt became a zone where the rights of Qing subjects were limited.

The Russian government took any threat to the CER seriously and was ready to use force to protect its new possessions in Manchuria. In June 1900, the Boxer Rebellion, which originated in Shandong and

Zhili, spread into the three provinces of Manchuria. Qing troops, hostile to Russia, and the Chinese rebels occupied all the major settlements along the railway line. For several months, construction of the CER was halted while the rebels destroyed 970 out of 1,400 kilometers of unfinished railway. The CER's western and southern branches were affected most. Telegraph lines, railway stations, and wooden bridges were destroyed.[21] Chinese contract laborers abandoned the CER, whose guards proved to be an insufficient force to protect the railway, its Russian employees, and their families. In Harbin, all Russian women and children were evacuated by several boats via the Sungari River to Khabarovsk. In June 1900, the government quickly mobilized troops from the Russian Far East. They moved to Manchuria and occupied it under the pretext of protecting the CER from the Boxers and the Qing provincial troops who sided with the Boxers.

Russia's military occupation of Manchuria was accompanied by the killing of innocent Qing subjects residing in frontier towns along the Amur River, which served as a Qing-Russian border. In July 1900, armed Russian Cossacks rounded up more than four thousand Chinese civilians in the towns of Blagoveshchensk and killed them during their "deportation" across the river to Qing territory.[22] The Blagoveshchensk massacre was followed by the burning of several dozen frontier Manchu villages and Qing military outposts in Sakhalian and Aigun. The Russian army entered Manchuria from several directions, eliminated armed resistance along the main line of the damaged CER, and by August occupied Harbin, which had been under siege for over a week. During the autumn of 1900, the Russian government sent an additional hundred thousand troops to Manchuria, removing Qing troops and rebels from the proximity of the SMR and taking control of the railway towns. It spent 71.7 million rubles to repair the damage to the railway and its property caused by the Boxer insurgency, bringing the total cost of the CER to 375 million rubles by the time it was finished in 1903.[23] Russia's human losses were minimal while the Chinese population of Manchuria was devastated and traumatized. The destruction of the Chinese settlements along the Amur, occupation of Manchu ancestral lands, and disruption of local administration ended both Witte's policy of peaceful economic penetration of Manchuria and Russia's image as China's peaceful ally. Despite the appearances of urban modernism,

Imperial Russia relied on military force and violence in achieving its goals in Manchuria.

The Fall of Port Arthur

Port Arthur appeared to be a promising naval base. In theory, its garrison and navy could protect the commercial port at Dalny, the entry to South Manchuria and the SMR. In addition, the fleet in Port Arthur and Vladivostok were intended to back up Imperial Russia's commercial interests in the Korean Peninsula. Port Arthur's history as a contested place between Qing China and Japan was of little concern to Russian advocates of military expansion—but St. Petersburg under-rated Japan's ability to build up its navy and to satisfy its own expansionist ambitions in the Liaodong and Korean Peninsulas. Ironically, Russia's own expansion in South Manchuria was challenged not by the Qing army, but by Japan, a fast-growing empire-in-the-making in East Asia. As a result of Russo-Japanese rivalry, Port Arthur became a site of the first major international war of the twentieth century, and of the first defeat of any European power by an Asian power in modern times.

Before the beginning of the Russo-Japanese War, Russia's position in Port Arthur was vulnerable, despite its existing and newly built fortifications. Port Arthur's railway link with the rest of South Manchuria could easily be blocked at the Jinzhou isthmus, a narrow land corridor connecting the Kwantung Peninsula with the southern part of Liaodong. Moreover, Port Arthur was separated by 1,000 *versts* (1,060 km) from its main supply base in Harbin. Any damage to the railway endangered Port Arthur's ability to protect itself. Port Arthur's defense facilities were incomplete, having received only one-third of the projected 15 million rubles allocated for its fortification. The War Ministry's initial request to send a 70,000-strong army to guard Port Arthur's 70-*verst* (74-km) shoreline was turned down for diplomatic and financial considerations. Instead, the Kwantung Leased Territory was left with an 11,500-strong garrison, while the line of shore defense was reduced to 22 *versts* (23.4 km).[24] Despite these shortcomings, the commander of the Port Arthur garrison, General A. M. Stessel, was optimistic about its invincibility, believing that the newly completed military brick structures and artillery were sufficient to protect it from all directions.[25] Multiple hills surrounding Port Arthur in the north provided a substantial natural barrier, while protruding *Tigrovyi Khvost* (the Tiger's Tail) Peninsula blocked the entry to the harbor, protecting Russia's armada.

Japan reserved its best forces for the assault on Port Arthur. On February 8, 1904, it attacked a Russian naval squadron in Port Arthur and blocked its exit to the sea. For the next several months, the Japanese fleet continuously bombed Port Arthur. In May, Japanese troops landed in Liaodong, occupied Dalny, and isolated the Kwantung Leased Territory and Port Arthur from the Russian forces stationed in Manchuria. During the summer and autumn of 1904, Port Arthur was again repeatedly bombed and several attempts were made to storm it. Its old town, administrative buildings, and military fortifications were either destroyed or severely damaged by Japanese artillery fire. On January 2, 1905, Russian General Anatoly Mikhailovich Stessel sent a note to the Japanese Army commander General Nogi Maresuki about the surrender of the fortress. During the next three days, the Japanese army occupied the town and imprisoned Russian forces there.[26] After the fall of Port Arthur, it took Japan two major violent battles—one over Mukden (February 19 to March 10, 1905) and another in Tsushima Strait (May 27 to 29, 1905)—to defeat Russia both in South Manchuria and at sea.

China's local population experienced the violence and cruelty of this war firsthand. The Russian military secured at least ten thousand Chinese laborers to support its operation in Port Arthur.[27] Both these Chinese laborers and those who built Dalny stayed there during the war. The Chinese population was employed in small trade and trans-portation, dug trenches, cleared the ruins, and buried the dead. Qing subjects became easy casualties of the land battles of this war: they were killed and their houses destroyed, leaving entire families without protection. Imperial Russia and Japan were too busy counting their own losses in Port Arthur, Liaoyang, and Mukden to care about the suffering of the local population.

Port Arthur and Dalny were short-lived as Russian towns. Their loss, as well as that of the SMR, marked the end of Russia's influence in South Manchuria and on the Korean Peninsula. In 1906, a diary by a Russian military doctor was published in Russia's provincial town of

Ufa. Signing his name only as N.S., he blamed the corrupt Russian government and its military for the defeat at Port Arthur, which he called the "final point in the epilogue of worldly drama." He was angered by the futility of expectations, and by the cost of the railway, Port Arthur, and Dalny, where Russia experienced enormous material damage and human sacrifice.[28] Meanwhile, Russia's loss became Japan's gain. In less than a year after signing the Treaty of Portsmouth in 1905, Japan started its own railway and urban development in Southern Manchuria on the foundations of Imperial Russia's former built environment.

Harbin's Rebirth

Russia's defeat in the war with Japan changed the fate of its expansion in Manchuria. The unpopularity in Russia of this war and, especially, Russia's shameful defeat, exposed the weakness and inadequacy of its colonial enterprise in Asia. The Imperial Russian government lost not only confidence, but also millions of rubles spent on war, military equipment, and built structures, as well as on sunken battleships and misguided investments in Southern Manchuria. The CER enterprise, perhaps for the first time since 1896, was severely criticized for its inability to secure timely supply of troops and ammunition to the war theater. However, as long as the main railway line remained in Russian hands, its future was secured as a link between Eastern Siberia and Vladivostok. Harbin remained an important railway hub, but it had to become a self-sustaining town less dependent on St. Petersburg, where the idea of further expansion in Manchuria and in East Asia found little support.

From 1905, Harbin turned into a booming transportation and trading hub. There were several forces behind this. First, the railway returned to its commercial operations, facilitating the transportation of Manchuria's agricultural goods and livestock to international markets. In 1907, Harbin gained the status of a treaty port, open for European, American, and Japanese trade and investments. A decade after the Russo-Japanese War, Harbin became an increasingly international town, home to fifty-three different nationalities, where forty-five different languages were spoken.[29] After the collapse of the Russian Empire in 1917 and two years of brutal civil war in Russia, Manchuria became home to tens of thousands of Russian émigrés and former Tsarist armies fleeing Siberia and the Russian Far East. Trade and services became major factors contributing to the further development of Harbin's built environment.

The CER management was still in the hands of the former Imperial Russian subjects, who remained beyond the reach of the Soviet authorities, because the Chinese government did not recognize the Soviet Union until 1924. Even after that, the Chinese authorities remained lenient towards the members of the CER's old administration as long as the latter was useful. During the 1920s, the CER continued to provide vital support for the city's growth. It was involved in Harbin's urban development, local and international trade, municipal government, and social organizations, despite growing challenge from more assertive Chinese and Soviet authorities. While the revolution, foreign intervention, and civil war devastated the Russian Far East, the CER administration in Harbin was content with the extent of its progress in Manchuria. In 1924, a CER publication summed up its achievements as following:

> The C.E.R. possesses an exceptionally large number of *civil constructions*, the total area of which is 8,139,929 square feet, representing more than 7,000 sq. feet per mile of the main line. There is not one railway in Russia with such a large number of civil constructions: the Russian average is approximately 2,000 square feet of dwellings and service buildings per 1 mile of main line. It is quite obvious that the upkeep of a road with such a number of constructions and buildings is a very complicated matter.[30]

The majority of these constructions were in Harbin, and were designed by Russian engineers and architects. Many of the buildings, businesses, and services in Harbin were owned by Russians and by former Imperial Russian subjects. While remaining unmistakably Russian and European in style, they served the broader interests of the Russian, Soviet, Chinese, Japanese, and Korean communities. Harbin could no longer claim to be an exclusively Russian city, as its trade, industry, and public life became as diverse as its population.

Contemporary and later references that declared Harbin to be the Moscow or Paris of the Orient were overstatements if not exaggerations, as Harbin, despite its diversity and cosmopolitan nature, also retained its provincial character. It could be more correctly compared to Samara, a provincial town located on the intersection of the Trans-Siberian railway and the Volga River. Surrounded by poor villages,

both Harbin and Samara were latecomers to the age of industrialization. For both, the railway administration was the core institution
in charge of urban development, contributing to the emergence of
modern trade and industries. Both also had populations with diverse
cultures and religions, and developed similar mixed styles of architecture reflecting the new tastes of merchants and the bourgeoisie. While
Samara's progress was interrupted by the October revolution and the
ensuing bloody civil war, Harbin prospered, while receiving a stream
of new migrants from the territory of the former Russian empire.

Very soon, however, the former Tsarist subjects and émigrés found
their position in Manchuria vulnerable. In 1920, the Bolshevik government officially ended all unequal treaties with China, ending the
privileges and the extraterritorial rights of the Russians residing there
since 1898. The Chinese provincial government resumed control over
Harbin's municipal government and administration. Imperial Russia's
successor, the Soviet Union, retained the commercial rights of the CER
for only a few years, with the Sino-Soviet agreement of 1924 limiting
its former influence in Manchuria. According to this agreement, the
railway was to be managed jointly by the Soviet Union and provincial Chinese authorities. Harbin became home to a growing community of Soviet employees, thus creating hostility between Red and
White Russians on Chinese soil. They miraculously avoided an open
confrontation, as if they subscribed to the legacy of Witte's insistence
on peaceful economic development. After 1924, the old Russian elite
started to lose its influence in the CER, in Harbin, and in Manchuria,
being forced to choose between accepting Soviet citizenship, remaining
stateless, or leaving. Well-established Russian engineers and architects
secured their position by designing the offices of Japanese and Western
firms, consulates, banks, and institutions.[31] Some of them stayed after
1935, when Japan bought the CER railway from the Soviet Union and
thus acquired one of the most valuable commercial enterprises in
Manchuria. Japan then formally replaced Russian/Soviet influence in
the region, forcing many Russians to lose their jobs.

Conclusion

Imperial Russia's military model of expansion in Manchuria was only partly successful and it contributed to the decline of Russian influence in South Manchuria, including the loss of Dalny and Port Arthur. Russian community and culture in Harbin survived the collapse of the Russian empire by engaging in international trade and taking advantage of the tensions between the warlord rule in Manchuria and the Republican government. The remaining buildings in Russian and European styles in the towns of Manchuria silently witnessed the gradual decay of Russia's political and economic power in this region. While some of the CER employees continued to enjoy comfortable lives during the 1920s, the growing Chinese, Japanese, European, and American economic presence, combined with political pressure from the government of Manchuria's warlord Zhang Zuolin and, after 1931, from Japan, forced the Russians either to adjust to international competition, accept the new regime, or to leave. Not surprisingly, many Russians chose to leave Manchuria and moved to Tianjin, Shanghai, and Hong Kong, and later crossed the Pacific Ocean. During China's War of Resistance with Japan (1937–45) and after the establishment of the People's Republic of China, colonial Russian buildings changed owners, were remodeled, abandoned, or destroyed.

Notes

1. Yosano Akiko, *Travels in Manchuria and Mongolia*, trans. Joshua A. Fogel (New York: Columbia University Press), 92–102.
2. In Imperial Russia during the late nineteenth and early twentieth century, the three northeastern provinces of China were called *Manchzhuria* (Manchuria). In this chapter I use the term "Manchuria," as it was referred to in the West, for consistency.
3. V. S. Myasnikov, ed., *Russko-Kitaiskie dogovorno-pravovye akty, 1689–1916* [Sino-Russian treaties and legal acts, 1689–1916] (Moscow: Pamyatniki Istoricheskoi Mysli, 2004), 207–10, 212–16.
4. Ibid., 221–24, 233–36.
5. Sergei Witte, *Vospominaniya* [Memoirs] (Berlin: Slovo, 1922), 119–33.

6.   Imperial Russian measurement of length. 1 *verst* = 1.06 kilometers. I use *verst*, followed by its equivalent in kilometers in brackets, every time it is mentioned in its original historical source.

7.   Ye. H. Nilus, *Kitaiskaya Vostochnaya Zheleznaya Doroga, Istoricheskii Obzor, 1896–1923* [Historical overview of the Chinese Eastern Railway], vol. 1 (Harbin: Tipografiya KVZhD, 1923), 108–23.

8.   Qu Xiaofan, *Jindai dongbei chengshi de lishi bianqian* [Historical change in the towns of the Northeast during modern times] (Changchun: Dongbei Shifan Daxue, 2001), 49.

9.   Ibid., 51; Nilus, *Kitaiskaya Vostochnaya Zheleznaya Doroga*, 148.

10. N. A. Baikov, "My Arrival to Manchuria, 1902," in *Russkii Harbin* [Russian Harbin], ed. Ye. P. Taskina (Moscow: Nauka, 2005), 12.

11. S. S. Levoshko, *Russkaya arkhitektura v Manchzhurii: konets XIX—pervaya polovina XX veka* [Russian architecture in Manchuria, from late 19th to early 20th century] (Khabarovsk: Chastnaya Kollektsiya, 2003), 75.

12. Shi Fang, Liu Shuang, and Gao Ling, eds. *Haerbin E-qiao shi* [The history of Russian emigrants in Harbin] (Harbin: Heilongjiang Renmin Chubanshe, 2003), 96.

13. Qu, *Jindai dongbei chengshi de lishi bianqian*, 64; Olga Bakich, "A Russian City in China: Harbin before 1917," in *Canadian Slavonic Papers*, Vol. XXVIII, no. 2 (June 1986): 143.

14. David Wolff, *To the Harbin Station: The Liberal Alternative in Russian Manchuria, 1898–1914* (Stanford: Stanford University Press, 1999), 58–65.

15. V. P. Kozlov, ed., *Iz Istorii Russko-Yaponskoi Voiny, 1904–1905 gg., Port Artur: vospominaniya uchastnikov* [From the history of the Russo-Japanese War, 1904–1905, Port Arthur: the memoirs of the participants], vol. 1 (Moscow: Drevlekhranilishche, 2008), 109.

16. Levoshko, *Russkaya arkhitektura v Manchzhurii*, 44–47, 166; N. P. Kradin, "Russkie Goroda v Kitae" [Russian towns in China], in *Arkhitektura Vostochnoi Sibiri i Dal'nego Vostoka* [Architecture of Eastern Siberia and the Russian Far East], vol. 1, ed. N. P. Kradin (Habarovsk: Magellan, 2002), 131–33.

17. According to Chang Huaisheng, Harbin's diverse architectural styles included art nouveau, Renaissance, baroque, classical revival, Byzantine, Russian, Judaic, "Chinese baroque," eclectic, and modern. See Chang Huaisheng, *Haerbin jianzhu yishu* [Harbin's architectural art] (Harbin: Heilongjiang kexue jishu chubanshe, 1988), 27–36.

18. For example, see Elena Taskina, *Neizvestnyi Kharbin* [Unknown Harbin] (Moscow, Prometei, 1994).

19. Qu, *Jindai dongbei chengshi de lishi bianqian*, 62.

20. Nilus, *Kitaiskaya Vostochnaya Zheleznaya Doroga*, 187.

21. N. E. Ablova, "Rossiya i russkie v Manchzhurii v kontse XIX nachale XX vv" [Russia and the Russians in Manchuria from the late nineteenth to early twentieth century], in *Russko-Yaponskaya Voina, 1904–1905: vzglyad cherez stoletie* [Russo-Japanese War, 1904–1905: an outlook a century later], ed. O. R. Airapetov (Moscow: Tri Kvadrata, 2004), 188.

22. *Vestnik Evropy* [Herald of Europe], vol. 10 (1910): 232–35.

23. Nilus, *Kitaiskaya Vostochnaya Zheleznaya Doroga*, 123.

24. A. N. Golitsynsky, "Na pozitsiyah Port-Artura: Iz Dnevnika rotnogo i batal'onnogo komandira" [Stationed in Port Arthur: the diary of the squadron and battalion commander], in *Iz Istorii Russko-Yaponskoi Voiny, 1904–1905 gg., Port Arthur: Sbornik Dokumentov* [From the history of the Russo-Japanese War, 1904–1905. Port Arthur: Collection of Documents], vol. 2, ed. V. P. Kozlov (Moscow: Drevlekhranilishche, 2008), 126–27.

25. Kozlov, ed. *Iz Istorii Russko-Yaponskoi Voiny, 1904–1905 gg., Port Arthur*, vol. 1, 132.

26. Ibid., 135–42.

27. Ibid., 124.

28. Kozlov, ed. *Iz Istorii Russko-Yaponskoi Voiny, Port Arthur*, vol. 2, 679, 708.

29. Olga Bakich, "Émigré Identity: The Case of Harbin," in *South Atlantic Quarterly* 99, no. 1 (Winter 2000): 53.

30. Economic Bureau of the Chinese Eastern Railway, ed., *North Manchuria and the Chinese Eastern Railway* (Harbin: CER Printing Office, 1924).

31. Russian architects and engineers formed their own society in Japanese-controlled Manchukuo. Among its members were such prominent Harbin architects as Mikhail Matveevich Oskolkov and Petr Sergeevich Sviridov. See Levoshko, *Russkaya arkhitektura v Manchzhurii*, 164–67.

3
Beans to Banners

The Evolving Architecture of Prewar Changchun

Bill Sewell

Spring 1937 likely represented the high point in the short history of the puppet state of Manchukuo (1932–45) and its new capital.[1] The hostilities following that summer's Marco Polo Bridge Incident inevitably required a reallocation of resources for the prosecution of war in China. And though the first five-year plan was launched that year, an array of new buildings was already completed or nearing completion, emerging amid a haven of parks, tree-lined boulevards, and modern infrastructure. The Japanese media understandably lavished a fair amount of attention on the new city and its promise, sometimes in foreign languages in an effort to sway public opinion overseas.[2] Yet even some foreign observers often critical of Japan bestowed praise. For example, John R. Stewart—economist, independent scholar, and postwar member of the Occupation authority—described the capital as "modern and attractive."[3] Étienne Dennery, then a professor at the elite École Libre des Science Politiques in Paris and a postwar director-general of France's Bibliothèque Nationale, observed that one of Manchukuo's two biggest successes was in city building, "most notably that of the capital."[4] After the war, University of Chicago professor Norton Ginsburg reported that the city offered "wide boulevards and elm-lined streets; parks dot the city and its suburbs; large modern buildings of brick, concrete, and stone rise from what was the site of soy bean farms." This he deemed "a tragic tribute to the aspirations of the Japanese in East Asia."[5]

Observations such as these are intriguing not only for their tone, but also for their topic, as prewar and wartime analyses tended to focus on strategic and economic issues. This orientation continued after the war, but other perspectives gradually emerged to provide a variety of insights, especially as to motivations and attitudes. This essay seeks to contribute to this effort by suggesting that prewar Japanese discourse regarding Manchuria—both in print and in stone—was not simply propaganda to be summarily dismissed. Although Japanese portrayals of their activities were unabashedly self-serving, the content of Japanese depictions was always contextual and a matter of choice, rendering it amenable to analysis. Therefore, in addition to the physical changes in the built environment transpiring as part of Changchun's shift from railway hub to imperial capital, the transition within the discourse about that change reveals concerns Japanese architects and planners deemed significant. These transformations can be described in part as shifts from the mundane to the exotic and from the collegial to the commanding, but they are also indicative of broader shifts apparent among Japanese regarding their country's relations with the world—from pragmatism to willful idealism and from Great Power cooperation to Axis-backed autonomous aggression. This said, a preoccupation for technical progress and a dismissive, inescapably orientalist perception of fellow Asians remained constant, betraying problematic yet enduring assumptions at the heart of the Japanese imperialist project in Manchuria.

Changchun ("Eternal Spring") developed as a farming and commercial center near a gate in the Willow Palisade, the tree-topped earthen rampart stretching from the Gulf of Liaodong that fenced off Manchu lands from Chinese encroachment. On territory assigned to Mongol allies of the Qing, China's last dynasty, the settlement at Changchun was initially illegitimate, as the dynasty initially endeavored to preserve nomadic and ancestral homelands. Having leased sections of their land to rural Chinese migrants, however, local Mongol leaders petitioned the throne to legitimize their transactions and officially recognize the town. Acknowledging the sizeable Chinese population already present by the end of the eighteenth century, the court had little choice but to agree and allowed the construction of a perimeter wall and gates. The town thereafter grew of its own accord—even relocating to better ground nearby—and assumed, roughly, the usual Chinese urban form, albeit less square and oriented on a more northwest-southeast axis. Any lingering concerns for Chinese immigration harbored by the court, however, would soon dissipate. Compelled to cede Manchuria's northern and eastern flanks to Russia in 1860, the Qing began encouraging settlement as a means of confirming sovereignty over what remained.[6] This resulted in the creation of a new frontier community, an immigrant society dependent, to a great extent, on demographic and commercial linkages outside Manchuria. These realities would continue into the twentieth century, to be exploited by whichever power dominated the region.[7]

If the distances and the relatively sparse Chinese presence in Manchuria boded poorly for the Qing, the greater distances and even sparser Russian presence hampered Russia's ambitions to integrate Manchuria into their empire all the more. Although by 1903 the population of Russia's northern railway hub of Harbin included 15,579 Russians out of a total of some 44,576,[8] Russia's southern port of Dalny (Dalian in Chinese, Dairen in Japanese) included only 2,000 Russians and 50,000 Asians.[9] Another 3,000 Russian civilians could be found nearby at Port Arthur (Lüshun), along with more than 36,000 soldiers and sailors.[10] These were Russia's main outposts in Manchuria, and even if gaining rights to construct the China Eastern Railway (CER) across Manchuria in 1896 and then a southern spur to the coast in 1898 represented major Russian diplomatic triumphs, they did not automatically result in the creation of a Russian Manchuria. The Russians were spread across the region thinly, especially in the south, and the small—only two square kilometers—Russian railway yard northwest of Changchun (at Kuanchengzi) was easy to overlook. In 1913 there "were scarcely any buildings except a few belonging to the station."[11] Perhaps unsurprisingly, the low-roofed station's style, common across Siberia, was not reproduced in non-Russian portions of Manchuria.

Not that the Russians enjoyed a large window of opportunity. The growing Russian presence induced Japanese to challenge Russia for supremacy in Manchuria and Korea, and the subsequent Treaty of Portsmouth (1905) granted all Russian holdings south of the yard at Changchun to Japan, rendering it the border between the Russian and Japanese spheres of influence in Manchuria. The Japanese thereupon built a small town between the Chinese city and the Russian settlement, integrating their town with the Chinese city and impeding Chinese connections with the Russians. Recognizing that Japanese needed to work with the Chinese and other inhabitants of Manchuria if they were to succeed, Japanese officials were from the start more open to the local population, even if they perceived Chinese as lower in status.

Table 3.1
Japanese and Chinese demographic change in Changchun and Manchuria[12]

	Japanese civilians in Changchun area	Chinese in Changchun area	Japanese civilians in Manchuria	Total population of Manchuria
1907	935	–	16,612	17,000,000
1916	4,500	91,581	–	–
1930	12,792	124,000	233,749	31,000,000
1940	114,306	359,278	1,065,072	38,000,000

The Japanese railway town at Changchun flourished (Table 3.1).[13] Before 1931 this was due to several reasons that together demonstrate the interlocking nature of the imperialist venture. As a treaty port, the town provided a base for merchants to integrate the region's fertile soybean fields into the Japanese economy as well as serving as a railway head not far from lumber and livestock resources further afield. For Japanese officials, the town offered a post from which to exercise security and consular privileges that assured Japan's local influence and facilitated further expansion of the empire, potentially into eastern Mongolia and Siberia. As Japan's most northerly outpost on the Asian mainland, Changchun was the logical site to host conferences with Russian and later Soviet officials—such as the negotiations in 1922 that more concretely delineated the Japanese and Russian spheres of influence in Manchuria and eastern Mongolia—and served as the trans-shipment point for travelers and goods changing to and from the Trans-Siberian Railway. London was only a fourteen-day rail journey via Manchuria and Siberia from Tokyo (or Shanghai) in 1913,[14] though it took three weeks for the first of the two brigades comprising what became the Russian Expeditionary Force to get from European Russia to Dalian via Changchun, and thence by sea for France.[15] Although only a little more than six thousand men, this event signified an important shift in relations. The war prodded the Tsarist government to accept Japanese military aid as well as Japan's "Twenty-One Demands" of

China, and to transform a 1910 agreement to cooperate against any third party intruding into Manchuria—meaning the United States—into a loose defensive alliance.[16]

Administering the Japanese presence in Changchun was the semi-private South Manchuria Railway (SMR), Japan's largest prewar corporation. More than simply a transport network, the SMR's responsibilities included research, education, security, and a variety of municipal concerns in the towns it managed along the railway lines. Buoyed by the rapid expansion of the soy industry, the SMR invested heavily in town building across Manchuria, the Japanese town at Changchun being the largest after those at Dalian and Mukden (also known as Fengtian or Shenyang). Indeed, because of the town's success in the collection and shipping of soybeans and their products, by 1920 Changchun earned the moniker "Bean Town" or the "City of Beans." Although the ensuing recession suppressed exports for much of the next decade, the nickname stuck.

The SMR dispatched university-trained professionals from Japan to design the railway town at Changchun in an entirely modern fashion, featuring zoning, electrical power generation, sanitation, parks, and paved roads arranged in a neat grid with rotaries to facilitate traffic flow. Buildings received similar attention, and photographs and discussion of some of the work in Changchun and elsewhere in Manchuria appeared in professional journals, most notably in the *Manshu kenchiku zasshi*, the *Journal of Manchurian Architecture*. One of the broader goals of this work—as suggested by Matsumuro Shigemitsu (1873–1937), the designer of the first structures to appear in the Changchun railway town—was to improve life in Manchuria generally through the creation of new structures designed by architects working specifically on the continent.[17] This was a view embraced generally by Japanese society in the Meiji and Taisho eras, as Japanese sought to create a modern and powerful society, one in line with the world's great powers. The slogan "rich country, strong army," popular in the Meiji era (1867–1912), identified these attitudes well and implicitly encouraged the adoption of foreign forms. More explicit was the influential journalist Fukuzawa Yukichi (1835–1901), who reported his observations from Europe and America to Japanese and eventually went so far as to recommend that the latter "leave Asia" (*datsu-A*) and join the Euro-Americans if they

42   Bill Sewell

were truly to become modern. In time, Fukuzawa also promoted the expansion of empire through jingoistic newspaper articles, adding impetus to the heady mix created by Japan's stunning military successes against China (1894–95) and then Russia.

The first Japanese structures in Changchun were historically eclectic, and in the European tradition. The post office (1910) evoked a classical air, while the police station (1910) across the street proffered a gothic turret. Centrally located on the main avenue leading south of the railway station, both were built of stone, implying stability and even permanency. Designed by Matsumuro, also the head of the Construction Department of the Kwantung (Guandong) Leased Territory, they reflected common practice among Japanese architects in Manchuria and Japan. Matsumuro had previously designed the Kyoto Prefectural Offices (1904) in a similar style, something he would use again for Dalian City Hall (1917). Reflecting contemporary structures in Europe and North America, the post office and police station demonstrated that Japanese architects were capable of expressing themselves in a manner that they thought appropriate to their nation's status. Indeed, late Meiji architecture in general favored contemporary foreign forms over anything that might be perceived as traditionally Japanese.

The buildings represented modern systems, of recent vintage in Japan as well as in Europe and North America, that had emerged along with the birth of a modern state.[18] Another modern system was the railway itself, and the three large structures facing the railway town's largest plaza served the SMR. All were designed by University of Tokyo graduate Ichida Kichijirō.[19] Changchun Station (1914), in the Renaissance style, dwarfed the nearby Russian station. Changchun's SMR office building (1910) was a large, three-story edifice with gothic spires. The third was different, because Changchun's Yamato Hotel (1909) sheltered officials and dignitaries with a most contemporary flourish—art nouveau. Constructed only six years after the first art nouveau structure in Japan, it was the only branch of this premier hotel chain to be built in this style and anticipated Nakamura Junpei's designs for the first Secession-style structure in Japan, the Tokyo-Taisho Exhibition in Ueno (1914). A natural progression from historical eclecticism, art nouveau had gained sudden popularity over the previous decade in Europe and Russia (where it was called *stil modern*). Changchun's Yamato Hotel, however, likely did not share the spirit of rebellion that infused the art nouveau movement. Columbia University-trained Ono Takeo, for example, went so far as to suggest that the style be adopted in Manchuria simply because it reflected global trends.[20] Given that Harbin—the major Russian settlement in northern Manchuria—lay only a few hours north of Changchun and included a variety of impressive art nouveau structures, it seems reasonable to conclude that Changchun's Yamato Hotel was more to demonstrate that Japanese could work in a style popular in Russia as well. Japanese architects were more generally interested in joining a global discussion as equals than in revolutionizing European aesthetics. Thus, Changchun's school (1908) was built in the Gothic style common to schools in Japan and Britain, and the Changchun hospital complex (1911) was similar to hospitals elsewhere in Manchuria. Initially, form generally followed function in Japanese Manchuria, even if somewhat loosely.

Of course, SMR architects did not design all the buildings in Changchun, nor did the railway company oversee all construction. As was the case elsewhere in the empire, the SMR—in this case functioning in effect as a government ministry—laid the foundational infrastructure as a means of promoting further activity, a strategy that proved successful. The railway town attracted businesses and people, and a Japanese community centered on a vibrant market street called Yoshinomachi soon emerged in this unlikely inland locale, comfortably ensconced in buildings not too different from any new ones in which they might have lived in Japan.

Intriguingly, some Chinese opted to build in new styles in the Chinese town of Changchun or in the mercantile district between it and the Japanese railway town. One was a Changchun magistrate, who ordered the construction of roads connecting the old city with the railway town as well as new offices (*yamen*) in 1910.[21] Another magistrate added parks, theaters, and brothels in that area. Japanese, too, built in this district, but theirs were not the only models for Chinese structures. Some five hundred Russians lived in either the Japanese or Chinese towns,[22] and the ornamented *yamen* seemed more in keeping with late nineteenth-century Russian tastes. Predating both the Japanese and the Russian presence in Changchun, moreover, were Catholic and Protestant missionaries. The latter added a medical mission in 1902, an organization that would eventually become Changchun Women's Hospital.

The Japanese town soon included a Shinto shrine, reflecting continuing connections with the home islands, and Changchun's built environment generally kept abreast of developments there and beyond. Changchun's Bank of Korea (1920), for example, was a more streamlined version of the style common to late Meiji, but it betrayed hints of an emerging innovation (see Plate 4). Sleeker lines and greater volumes, what some would come to call the "international style," were becoming commonplace, appearing in Japanese towns across the empire and evident in Matsumuro Shigemitsu's new post office in Dalian (1925). Removing anything ostentatious or frivolous, this let the structural elements themselves serve as ornamentation. One commentator noted that not only was modern industrial architecture scientific and economic, it too was inspired by technique and notions of beauty.[23] The new dormitory for the Changchun Commercial College was designed similarly to that of the Bank of Korea, but perhaps the best example of the new style in Changchun was the office of the Changchun Telephone Company (1930). (Plate 5)

These buildings demonstrate that Japanese architects in Changchun participated consciously in an international discussion, one seeking to create a shared, modern world. Another means of doing this was through residential construction. This required Japanese to fundamentally reconsider their most basic structures, as the Manchurian climate differed radically from Japan's more temperate climate. Some Japanese commentators noted that the endeavor would lead to a fundamental transformation in daily lifestyles, much as the shifts in clothing styles transpiring over the Meiji era.[24] To this end, the SMR experimented with dormitories and housing entailing different means of heating, including the use of Korean *ondul* flooring and Russian stoves (*pechka*).[25]

While some in Japan complained about relying overly on foreign practices, others spoke in defense of this. One was Matsumuro Shigemitsu, who argued that architects were in a perfect position to help devise a better and more modern society. They were not simply public officials, but crusading scientists. Matsumuro further stressed the point that Japanese as a society had the choice of being either isolated, insular, and conservative or cosmopolitan and progressive.

Cultural mixing was already a well-established Japanese path, he thought, and now it was up to architects to help lead the way to a more modern society.[26]

A later president of the association that produced the *Journal of Manchurian Architecture* expressed gratitude to Matsumuro and others for their experimentation and willingness to explore new paths.[27] This occurred, however, in a dramatically altered context, as over the 1920s Japanese came to perceive their endeavors in Manchuria imperiled. These threats included Chinese challenges to the SMR rail monopoly, massive Chinese immigration to Manchuria, rising Chinese nationalism and the installation of an anti-imperialist Guomindang (Kuomintang) government in Nanjing, Soviet military intervention in northern Manchuria in 1929, the effects of the Great Depression (on top of prior economic troubles), and the cumulative resentments of Japanese against an assortment of Euro-American policies regarding migration, trade, and finance. Some of these issues represented the problems inherent in implementing empire in an already populated country, but others represented significant changes on the global stage. Together these challenges encouraged Japanese military offi-cials to seize Manchuria by force and subsequently reorganize it in the manner they best saw fit, a *fait accompli* to which the world reluctantly acquiesced.[28] By then Manchuria was widely portrayed in Japan as an economic "lifeline," one that had been gained through the sacrifice of more than a hundred thousand lives and two billion yen. There was thus popular support in Japan for the takeover of Manchuria,[29] though it is worth noting that the Japanese military planners who executed the invasion were also acting with an eye towards revolutionizing Japanese society at home. Joined by reformist bureaucrats and a range of private individuals, their goal was a second "restoration," one that might correct the problems inherited from the Meiji and Taisho eras. In this era too, Manchuria served as a laboratory for the creation of a new and better Japan.

As part of the seizure of Manchuria, Japanese troops took control of Changchun immediately, using it as a staging ground against resist-ance to the north, but the city also quickly became a stage for another kind of contest as well. Designated the capital of the new state of Manchukuo, it was renamed Xinjing (Hsinking, as it was spelled then), read as Shinkyō in Japanese. A "New Capital" in both languages, the city became a vehicle for expressing Manchukuo's values, and its built environment was to reflect the supposedly progressive aspects of a new era. Although perhaps most popularly remembered for returning the Qing's "last emperor" Puyi (1906–67) to an imperial throne, Manchukuo also entailed state economic planning, a one-party political system, and an ideology allegedly blending Pan-Asian racial harmony with traditional Confucian morality as reformed, loosely, by none other than Sun Yat-sen (1866–1925). In so doing the new state's masters not only thought they were acting in an enlightened manner but they also reversed Fukuzawa's dictum regarding Japan's relations with Europe and Asia, for rather than leaving Asia and embracing Europe, in Manchukuo Japanese ostensibly endeavored to embrace Asia and surpass Europe. Thus, Manchukuo marked a new beginning for thirty million newly minted Manchukuoans and was not without significance for Japanese and other Asians. The sweeping nature of these changes meant that the new state's capital was directed at multiple audiences and could be used to inspire multiple aspirations.

Like the railway town, Manchukuo's capital was planned by university-trained professionals, some of whom had published in journals like the *Journal of Manchurian Architecture*, and some with considerable experience in Japan, like Sano Riki (1880–1956). In Manchukuo, however, the Japanese military also played a leading role, pressing civilian personnel to consider alternatives when it came to issues such as the design of the new capital.

Unlike the railway town, the new "imperial" capital was from the start a sprawling affair, for planners anticipated half a million residents within twenty years. It was to be a livable city though, with a lower population density and greater per capita urban green space than was typical in Asia and Europe, on par with cities in North America. Outside of parks and recreation fields, the city had tree-lined, broad boulevards, with separate lanes for slower (horse-drawn) traffic, sidewalks, and a surrounding green belt. A horserace track and hiking trails enabled leisure activities.[30] Within the city, Kentucky Bluegrass provided much of the ground coverage.[31]

Xinjing's most notable buildings were an array of stately offices (see Plates 6, 7 and 8) lining the new Xuntian ("Obeying Heaven")

Boulevard running south of the space assigned to Manchukuo's new imperial palace. All entailed features typically associated with traditional Chinese architecture. Symmetrical and emphasizing breadth rather than verticality, they suggested stability and balance, and the lack of any emphasis on the vertical helped create the effect of a floating roofline for some. Built of concrete and faced with stone outside and marble inside, they all also provided a sense of elegance. These were the new offices of the Manchukuo bureaucracy, and appearing south of the palace they replicated the layout of the Forbidden City in Beijing, theoretically enabling the cosmic force of the throne to flow south through the emperor's officials and out into the country, as Chinese had assumed was the case whenever an emperor held the mandate of heaven.

Some of this new architectural vocabulary appeared elsewhere in the city, including a large monument to the martyrs of the Manchurian Incident and the new Jianguo (Japanese: Kenkoku) shrine where Puyi might offer devotions. This style was the creation of a team led by Aiga Kensuke, who afterwards indicated that his goal had been to create "architecture for the government offices of an ideal country's national capital." Specifically, Aiga wanted something that would "show a Chinese style flavored with a modern style." The result would be a "new style inextricably woven with an Asian style."[32] The head of the capital's architecture bureau that year spoke to the significance of this endeavor, indicating that Manchukuo's "architectural culture" was without parallel, chiefly because the built environment of new countries typically favored the international style and avoided the national. As a result, he thought Manchukuo's new architecture relevant even for Japan, and might stimulate developments there.[33]

Appearing in government literature, including posters and postage stamps, the new architecture and its derivatives represented an effort to articulate pan-Asianism before the outbreak of what Japanese called the Great East Asia War, Japan's "holy war" (*seisen*) against Nationalist China and the other imperialist powers. As such, these buildings stood as testimony to some Japanese aspirations in advance of the creation of the Greater East Asia Co-Prosperity Sphere. On a theoretical level, these structures illustrate what Prasenjit Duara has intriguingly termed the "East Asian Modern."[34] Xinjing's Asian façade, however, proved ultimately more superficial than Japanese promised, as well as more

fluid and contentious—and less genuinely embraced, save by a few—
than Duara suggests. (Plate 9)

In hybridizing Euro-American and Asian forms, the capital's built
environment abstracted traditional Asian motifs to blend with contemporary building techniques, thereby attempting to show that the
puppet state represented the best of both worlds, technically proficient
yet grounded in a regional and racialized context. It was certainly
not a national context, because in abstracting Asian forms the buildings became more generically East Asian, implicitly promoting ethnic
harmony, within limits. Despite the continuing, if small, Russian
presence in the new state, there does not seem to have been any effort
to incorporate that tradition architecturally.

The result may have been pleasing to the eye, but could only go so far
as a new means of architectural expression. Using Asian motifs as ornamentation provided an Asian flavor, but nothing substantially new. In
selecting traditional elements, moreover, neither architects nor anyone
else accepted any of the assumptions that had previously imbued those
motifs with meaning. Indeed, the systems housed within these offices
were all quite modern, and unquestionably under Japanese control. As
a result, the new city's architectural message was more a cacophony
of catchphrases and platitudes rather than an articulate statement of a
new order. A similar dynamic was apparent in the "kingly way" (ōdō in
Japanese, wangdao in Chinese) that supposedly organized the new state.
Theoretically harkening back to Confucian philosophy and patrician
governance, the new regime in effect cherry-picked what it wanted from
the Chinese tradition in an effort to create an ideology that Japanese
thought appropriate for a docile populace expected to co-operate.

Thus, the biggest statement made by Xinjing's architecture had less
to do with any neo-Asian identity than with manifesting state power.
Located along broad avenues, the vistas and organization of space
involved in the placing of the state offices reflected the more total
command Japanese planners had after 1932 than to any sympathies
with Asian traditions. Other actions reinforce this view, because the
Japanese military displayed their supremacy with ideologically driven
decisions regardless of cost. For example, real estate agencies were
banned to prevent speculation, and power lines were buried so as to
not mar any views. A grand subway network was planned to avoid

the clutter associated with fixed rail networks, but also to transport the capital's citizens in a modern and efficient manner.[35]

The marginalization of tradition is underscored by the reality that the new style appeared only rarely elsewhere in the city and state, despite its being trumpeted in various media. More important to the city's designers was a continued embrace of the modern. All of the Asian-inspired official structures were faced in stone and marble, possibly reflecting the tastes of the international style, though potentially also approximating the neoclassical style which many have come to consider as defining Nazi architecture.[36] More significantly, most of the structures appearing in the new capital followed the international style, and the real heart of the city was not amid the government offices but lay a little to the northeast, at a major intersection due south of the railway station where could be found the new state bank, the state telephone and telegraph headquarters, the offices of the Concordia Society, and the new Buddhist temple (predating the creation of Manchukuo by a few years). A raft of publications also broadcast the city's technical merits. Carefully calculating water and energy resources, planners installed a sewage system and fire hydrants as well as a hydroelectric and reservoir system still in use today. Communications were also improved, including a radio station and a film studio. By 1942, non-stop air service linked the capital with Tokyo. Perhaps most telling was the extent of the planning, for, as one publication proudly noted, rather than leave the city to the vagaries of the marketplace, the new capital's development had been mapped through 1955.[37] (Plate 11)

Xinjing's basic nature, however, was impossible to camouflage, for the new capital was in many respects a Japanese city. A kind of neo-Asian architecture had emerged previously in Japan, and the roof of the Japanese military headquarters in the city was more distinguishably Japanese than generically Asian. And if people other than Japanese were not immediately aware of these realities, later propaganda would render this unmistakable. Postage stamps and posters, for example, reminded the population that "Japan's progress is also Manchukuo's." Moreover, despite the official rhetoric regarding racial equality, a repressive police system, disparate pay rates for workers, and different living conditions for not only workers but also officials and students at Manchukuo's prestigious universities specifically delineated everyone's position in the new state. While the sudden creation of a new governing infrastructure necessitated the rapid growth of the Japanese community, Chinese were primarily recruited for construction and other menial positions, and most likely not expected to remain. In order to keep the new capital's skies clear, heavy industry had been prohibited from the city. Only light industry was allowed, confined to the northeast so that prevailing winds would keep pollution out of the city center. The new capital was not to be crowded by any large laboring class. Worse, Manchukuo's opium-peddling operations were aimed at non-Japanese, and eventually the capital became home to Unit 100, one of the bacteriological and chemical weapons units known to have experimented on the city's non-Japanese residents. As a result, Manchukuo's Japanese masters quickly squandered the potential for any real collaboration.[38] (Plate 12)

Given these realities, how is one to make sense of Xinjing's built environment? Several avenues of inquiry appear useful. Perhaps most obviously, Xinjing as a national capital was exotic in an orientalist fashion. To represent their control of the city—and purported country—in a manner that might justify the Japanese reorganization of society, architects embraced supposedly timeless but nonetheless stereotypical notions of Asian architecture. However, as any student of Edward Said would say, this is a perspective dismissive of the people it objectifies. Not only were traditional and supposedly time honored-principles "improved," but beyond the new state's offices Japanese architects ultimately favored more contemporary styles to anything neo-Asian. These realities may well reflect the widespread Japanese presumption of playing a leading role in Asia, but they also point to flawed assumptions at Manchukuo's core. Condescending Japanese attitudes towards other Asians hint at the hierarchy implicit in their efforts to "liberate" the continent, and orientalist perceptions of others cannot occur without contributing to inflated self-perceptions—disastrously so in this case—as a sense of superiority and entitlement figured increasingly prominent among many Japanese of this era.[39]

At the same time, however, Japanese decisions were also self-orientalizing, introducing elements of their own architectural tradition into the city. Yuko Kikuchi has shown that in doing so with regard to crafts some Japanese attempted to establish equality with the West, but

Brian Moeran has argued that Japanese efforts of this kind were more an attempt to establish their superiority.[40] This view perhaps helps explain why Japanese could opt to follow an increasingly autonomous path over the 1930s, as perceived accomplishments in Manchukuo may well have emboldened those who deemed leading Asia was Japan's unique destiny.

The above said, Xinjing's built environment perhaps speaks also to the spiritual emptiness apparent among all imperialist societies. Like Europeans, Japanese had similarly transitioned to a modern society that was, comparatively speaking, less spiritually fulfilling than a pre-modern one. Moreover, some Japanese ideologues had also battled an array of modern art forms they found unsettling, such as futurism and cubism. It is thus understandable that Xinjing's more traditional forms might appeal to contemporary Japanese. One discussion of the new capital pointed out what the city was certainly not: "an architectural jumble deeply colored by individualism."[41]

Xinjing also represented occidentalist impulses. While the railway-era town evinced a general Japanese inclination in joining Euro-American society, the new imperial capital showed Japanese to be seeking to surpass the "West" as a matter of civilizational progress. Manchukuo's orientalist orientation assumed an occidentalized other. Retaining only the technical capabilities, the city represented an effort to beat a new path, bypassing the perceived ills of Europe and America. In this way the city's construction dovetailed with developments within Japan such as the "overcoming modernity" symposiums of 1941–42,[42] even if in reality the Japanese leaders of Manchukuo were setting themselves up as new colonial masters. In any event, the capital's built environment fetishized the "West," perhaps most notably in the building of a small European castle-like structure for the local Japanese military commandant.

Xinjing's built environment may also have been designed to encourage occidentalist views among other Asians.[43] While the Muslim presence in Changchun was longstanding—the mosque had been in operation since 1824—some Chinese and Central Asian Muslims played public roles in the puppet state's capital, and the curved rooflines and arabesque patterns in the Islamic style apparent on some of the capital's state offices perhaps represented efforts to reach out to Central Asians dissatisfied with Soviet rule.

Modernity was a useful tool for Japanese in Manchuria.[44] Modernity, however, was in some ways a mirage, an ever-shifting goal that receded into the future as the world continued to evolve. This said, while most Japanese genuinely believed in the imperialist project of the railway era, there were likely fewer genuine believers in Manchukuo. While some may have been present at the outset, with time, Manchukuo's fig leaf became increasingly tattered, especially after the military forced out of positions of influence those Japanese more genuinely committed to concepts such as ethnic harmony, or had them arrested.

Nevertheless, the new capital as a symbol was a tool of some strength. Architecture has been deeply associated with other modern authoritarian state-building enterprises, including Nazi Germany, the Stalinist Soviet Union, and the People's Republic of China. These regimes all sought to create a viable yet revolutionary alternative to the capitalist state, each offering built environments featuring large structures, people's cultures, and a timeless quality to compensate for their recent vintage.[45] As such, it is worth remembering that the new capital was not only designed to elicit support within Manchuria, but also within Japan, where 1940 was celebrated as the 2600th year of the accession of the first emperor. One aspect of this was to encourage Japanese emigration to Manchuria; another was to help foster change in Japan. To some extent both were successful, though in neither case as much as planners hoped. Migrants were few, and the anticipated "Showa Restoration" never transpired. The rhetoric did play well, however, encouraging some diasporic Japanese to come to Manchukuo and some Black intellectuals within the United States to look there for alternative global leadership.[46]

After the outbreak of the Pacific War, some Japanese cited Manchukuo as a model for the reorganization of allied regimes within the Greater East Asia Co-Prosperity Sphere, sometimes referring to gestures such as the ending of extraterritoriality and the return of treaty ports in Manchuria as emblematic of Japanese sympathies. That the puppet state only garnered limited cooperation, however, was never closely considered by officials, who elected instead to follow a logic of their own devising, creating a world on paper in which everything ought to have worked perfectly, but in reality failed completely. Japanese architects and engineers were complicit in this endeavor, designing structures for a new Asian people but ultimately following more parochial visions rather than looking over their shoulders to see if anyone was actually following their banner.

Notes

1.   I wish to thank the editors of this volume, the anonymous reviewers, and David Tucker for their comments on this chapter. I also acknowledge that Chinese and Japanese publications typically enclose the term Manchukuo ("Country of the Manchus") in quotation marks and prefix it with a Chinese character meaning "false" or "fictitious" to remind readers of the puppet state's sham nature. Following the common practice in English, this chapter does not do so for the sake of simplicity. It is also worth noting that the term Manchuria is similarly problematic but is used here for the same reason and is not intended to imply any inherent autonomy. Manchuria is taken here to mean the lands typically referred to by Chinese as the "three eastern provinces" of Fengtian, Jilin, and Heilongjiang, along with that portion of eastern Mongolia that these provinces eventually encroached upon. Manchukuo includes these lands as well as the province of Rehe.

2.   See, for example, Hajime Miura, "Hsinking, Capital of Manchoukuo," *The Far Eastern Review* 37 (March 1941): 95–98, 102.

3.   John R. Stewart, "Hsinking—Manchuria's Boom Town," *Far Eastern Survey* 6, no. 6 (March 1937): 69.

4.   The other success was in communications. Étienne Dennery, "Problèmes d'Extrême-Orient" [Problems of the Far East], *Annales de Géographie* [Annals of Geography] 46, no. 262 (1937): 346.

5.   Norton Ginsburg, "Ch'ang-ch'un," *Economic Geography* 23, no. 4 (1947): 293.

6.   The 1860 Treaty of Beijing recognized Russian authority on the left bank of the Amur and right of the Ussuri, a million square kilometers that Russia had previously recognized as part of Qing Manchuria.

7.   Thomas R. Gottschang and Diana Lary, *Swallows and Settlers: The Great Migration from North China to Manchuria* (Ann Arbor: University of Michigan, 2000) and James Reardon-Anderson, *Reluctant Pioneers: China's Expansion Northward, 1644–1937* (Stanford: Stanford University Press, 2005).

8.   David Wolff, *To the Harbin Station: The Liberal Alternative in Russian Manchuria, 1898–1914* (Stanford: Stanford University Press, 1999), 90.

9.   "Making of the Port of Dalny," *New York Times*, May 3, 1903, p. 13.

10. Evgeny Sergeev, *Russian Military Intelligence in the War against Japan, 1904–05* (New York: Routledge, 2007), 55.

11. Imperial Japanese Government Railways, *An Official Guide to Eastern Asia: Trans-Continental Connections between Europe and Asia. Vol. 1: Manchuria and Chosen* (Tokyo: Imperial Japanese Government Railways, 1913), 62.

12. Extrapolated from William S. Sewell, "Japanese Imperialism and Civic Construction in Manchuria: Changchun, 1905–1945" (PhD diss., University of British Columbia, 2000), 265–70. The 1930 figure for the number of Chinese in Changchun is one estimate; another estimate for 1913 is 130,000. Imperial Japanese Government Railways, *Official Guide*, 65.

13. Previous studies of Japanese activities in Changchun to which I am indebted are Koshizawa Akira, *Manshūkoku no shuto keikaku: Tōkyō no genzai to mirai o tou* [The Planning of the Manchukuo's Capital: An Inquiry into the Present and Future of Tokyo] (Tōkyō: Nihon Keizai Hyōronsha, 1988); Nishizawa Yasuhiko, *Umi wo watatta nihonjin kenchikuka: 20 seiki zenhan no Chūgoku tōhoku chihō ni okeru kenchiku katsudō* [The Japanese Architects who Crossed the Sea: Architectural Activities in Northeast China in the First Half of the Twentieth Century] (Tōkyō: Shōkokusha, 1996); and David D. Buck, "Railway City and National Capital: Two Faces of the Modern in Changchun," in *Remaking the Chinese City: Modernity and National Identity, 1900–1950*, ed. Joseph Esherick (Honolulu: University of Hawai'i Press, 2000), 65–89.

14. Imperial Japanese Government Railways, *Official Guide*, ii.

15. Jamie H. Cockfield, *With Snow on Their Boots: The Tragic Odyssey of the Russian Expeditionary Force in France during World War I* (New York: St Martin's Press, 1998), 34–35.

16. Russia also considered selling to Japan the northern half of Sakhalin and the rail line from Harbin to Changchun. Igor R. Saveliev and Yuri S. Pestuschko, "Dangerous Rapprochement: Russia and Japan in the First World War, 1914–1916," *Acta Slavica Iaponica* 18 (2001): 19–41; and Westel W. Willoughby, *Foreign Rights and Interests in China* (Baltimore: Johns Hopkins, 1920).

17. See the opening commentaries of Matsumuro Shigemitsu in "Manshū daigaku to kenchikuka" [Architects and the University of Manchuria], *Manshū kenchiku zasshi* [Journal of Manchurian Architecture] 1, no. 1 (March 1921): 2–4; and "Seikatsu kaizen no kenchiku" [The Architecture of Improved Living], *Manshū kenchiku zasshi* 1, no. 2 (April 1921): 2–14.

18. D. Eleanor Westney, *Imitation and Innovation: The Transfer of Western Organizational Patterns to Meiji Japan* (Cambridge: Harvard University Press, 1987).

19. In 1925, he changed his surname to Aoki.

20. Ono Takeo, "Manshū sesesshon-shiki kenchikuka no tame ni" [For Manchuria's Secession-style Architects], *Manshū kenchiku zasshi* 1, no. 1 (March 1921): 1–4.

21. Shinkyō Tokubetsushi Chōkan Shomuka, *Kokuto Shinkyō* [*Capital City Xinjing*] (Shinkyō: Shinkyō Tokubetsushi Kōsho, 1942), 18.
22. Imperial Japanese Government Railways, *Official Guide*, 65.
23. See H. H. Sei, "Shizen oyobi kōsei no biteki chūshin ten" [Key Points of Nature and the Beauty of Form], *Manshū kenchiku zasshi* [Journal of Manchurian Architecture] 8, no. 2 (February 1928): 19–24 and 8, no. 4 (April 1928): 21–40.
24. Shigemitsu, "Seikatsu kaizen no kenchiku": 2–14.
25. Mantetsu Kenchikukai, eds., *Mantetsu no kenchiku to gijutsujin* [Technologists and the Architecture of the South Manchuria Railway] (Tōkyō: Mantetsu Kenchikukai, 1976), 114–8.
26. Matsumuro Shigemitsu, "Kiro ni tatsu kenchikuka" [Architects Standing at the Crossroads], *Manshū kenchiku zasshi* 2, no. 1 (January 1922): 10–12; *Manshū kenchiku zasshi* 2, no. 2 (February 1922): 2–12; and *Manshū kenchiku zasshi* 2, no. 3 (March 1922): 2–17.
27. Oka Ōji, "Manshū kenkoku jūnen to kenchiku zakkan" [Architectural Notes on Ten Years since the Founding of Manchukuo], *Manshū kenchiku zasshi* 22, no. 10 (February 1942): 19–24.
28. Rather than confront Japan, the Chinese government opted to sign the Tanggu Truce (May 31, 1933), acknowledging Japanese hegemony in Manchuria. The policy of the United States was one of non-recognition, endeavoring to maintain the "Open Door" in Manchuria through diplomatic means. The League of Nations subsequently identified Japan as an aggressor in Manchuria, yet it too could do little. The Soviet Union responded with appeasement, selling the CER and increasing economic co-operation, but also allowing Chinese resistance fleeing Manchuria to return to China through the USSR. The Soviet Union subsequently began building up its military and economic presence in eastern Siberia and Outer Mongolia and went about improving relations with Nationalist China and the United States, gaining diplomatic recognition on December 12, 1932 and November 17, 1933 respectively. Admitted to the League of Nations on September 18, 1934, three years after the outbreak of fighting in Manchuria, the USSR increasingly represented a threat to Manchukuo (and Japan) insurmountable by Japan alone.
29. Eguchi Kei'ichi, "Manshū jihen to dai shinbun" [The Manchurian Incident and the Big Newspapers], *Shisō* [Thought] 583 (January 1973): 98–113; Louise Young, *Japan's Total Empire: Manchuria and the Culture of Wartime Imperialism* (Berkeley: University of California Press, 1998); and Sandra Wilson, *The Manchurian Crisis and Japanese Society, 1931–33* (London: Routledge, 2002).
30. Sewell, "Japanese Imperialism and Civic Construction in Manchuria: Changchun," 160–96.
31. Miura, "Hsinking": 96.

32. Aiga Kensuke, "Kenkoku zenzo no omoidasu" [Remembering the Founding of Manchukuo], *Manshū kenchiku zasshi* 22, no. 10 (October 1942): 8.

33. Makino Masaoto, "Kenkoku jūnen to kenchiku bunka" [Ten Years since the Founding of Manchukuo and the Culture of Architecture], *Manshū kenchiku zasshi* 22, no. 10 (October 1942): 17.

34. Prasenjit Duara, *Sovereignty and Authenticity: Manchukuo and the East Asian Modern* (Lanham, Maryland: Rowman & Littlefield, 2003).

35. Despite initial plans for the subway—Miura had reported that "[t]he construction of tramways has been excluded from the Capital Construction Plan in view of the noise and disfiguring effects created by tramways and their vulnerableness to air raids"—the war required officials to eventually to settle for an electric tramway. Miura, "Hsinking": 97.

36. Igor Golomstock, *Totalitarian Art in the Soviet Union, the Third Reich, Fascist Italy, and the People's Republic of China* (New York: Harper Collins 1990), 299.

37. SōA Kenchiku Renmei (Create Asian Architecture Federation), "Manshū kenchiku no tenbō" [The Prospects of Manchurian Architecture], *Gendai kenchiku* [Modern Architecture], 8 (January 1940): 2–21.

38. Rana Mitter, *The Manchurian Myth: Nationalism, Resistance, and Collaboration in Modern China* (Berkeley: University of California Press, 2000); and Yamamuro Shin'ichi, *Manchuria under Japanese Dominion*, trans. Joshua A. Fogel (Philadelphia: University of Pennsylvania Press, 2006).

39. Cf., Sheldon Pollock, "Deep Orientalism: Notes on Sanskrit and Power beyond the Raj," in *Orientalism and the Postcolonial Predicament: Perspectives on South Asia*, eds. Carol A. Breckenridge and Peter van der Veer (Philadelphia: University of Pennsylvania Press, 1993), 76–133.

40. Yuko Kikuchi, *Japanese Modernisation and Mingei Theory: Cultural Nationalism and Oriental Orientalism* (London: Routledge Curzon, 2004); and Brian Moeran, *Language and Popular Culture in Japan* (Manchester: Manchester University Press, 1989), 181–4.

41. *Shinkyō no gaikyō* [The General Situation in Xinjing] (Shinkyō: Shinkyō Shōkō Kōkai, 1942), 13.

42. Published in book form as Kōsaka Masaaki, Suzuki Shigetaka, Kōyama Iwao, Nishitani Keiji, *Sekai shiteki tachiba to Nihon* [The World Historical Position and Japan] (Tōkyō: Chūō Kōronsha, 1943).

43. Cemil Aydin, *The Politics of Anti-Westernism in Asia: Visions of World Order in Pan-Islamic and Pan-Asian Thought* (New York: Columbia University Press, 2007).

44. Bill Sewell, "Reconsidering the Modern in Japanese History: Modernity in the Service of the Prewar Japanese Empire," *Japan Review* 16 (2004): 213–58.

45. Intriguingly, Golomstock notes that "[t]he battle for architecture, like the battle for art as a whole, came to a conclusion at almost the same time in both Russia and Germany." This was in 1932, the year after the Manchurian

Incident. Perhaps also in line with the Japanese experience, he suggests that Italian Fascism, Soviet Communism, and Hitler's Nazism all exhibited religious affinities. This said, Golomstock points out that after Albert Speer's release from prison, the German architect realized his designs were "the very expression of a tyranny." See Golomstock, *Totalitarian Art*, 268–69, 285, 292–95.

46. John J. Stephan, "Hijacked by Utopia: American Nikkei in Manchuria," *Amerasia Journal* 23, no. 3 (Winter 1997–98): 1–42; Ernest Allen, Jr., "When Japan was 'Champion of the Darker Races': Satokata and the Flowering of Black Messianic Nationalism," *The Black Scholar* 24 (Winter 1994): 23–46; and Marc Gallicchio, *The African American Encounter with Japan and China: Black Internationalism in Asia, 1895–1945* (Chapel Hill: University of North Carolina Press, 2000).

4
France, Brossard Mopin, and Manchukuo

David Tucker

In September 1931, the Japanese colonial army in Manchuria, the Kwantung Army, began operations to take over Manchuria, the northeastern provinces of China. The Kwantung Army long had exercised strong influence over Zhang Zuolin, a regional military authority based in Shenyang, but had grown dissatisfied with his failure to cooperate completely and his military adventurism in North China. In June 1928, Zhang, defeated by Chiang Kai-shek's Guomindang Army, returned to Shenyang from a failed attempt to control Beijing. As his train approached Shenyang, a group of Kwantung Army officers exploded a bomb, destroying his railcar and assassinating him. Zhang's son, Zhang Xueliang, succeeded him, but instead of being the weak and pliable leader the Kwantung Army expected, he allied with the Guomindang and attempted to reduce Japanese influence. In 1931, a group of Kwantung Army officers, seeing Zhang as a fundamental threat to Japanese interests, decided it was necessary to control Manchuria directly. On September 18, they staged another bombing and used it as an excuse to attack Chinese troops in Manchuria.

Within a few months, the Kwantung Army had seized a substantial part of Manchuria, and had decided to install a new regime. Rather than allow a new warlord to take power, the army encouraged the formation of an autonomy movement, headed by local Chinese officials, that would endorse the formation of a new state. On March 1, 1932, the committee declared that Manchuria was independent of the Republic of China and the Guomindang regime, and announced the establishment of a new nation, Manchukuo. Making use of the research bureau and other resources of the Japanese colonial railway company, the South Manchuria Railway, the Kwantung Army quickly began an economic

and political transformation of the region. Japan was a signatory of the
1922 Nine Powers Treaty that guaranteed the territorial and administrative integrity of China. The Kwantung Army's seizure of Manchuria
could easily be seen as a violation of this treaty, and well as of the 1928
Kellogg-Briand, in which the signatories, including Japan, renounced
"war as an instrument of national policy." The Kwantung Army countered that it acted only in support of the wishes for good government
of the people of Manchuria who had established Manchukuo of their
own volition.

The new state of Manchukuo and its institutions then served to
extend the Kwantung Army's control over Manchuria, as a vehicle
to develop the region's resources, and as a means to deflect international criticism and to channel that criticism into acceptance or even
support. The Great Powers and the League of Nations might object to
Japanese rule of Manchuria, but presenting that control in the form of
an independent state, Manchukuo, gave them a potentially face-saving
fiction much easier to accept. Even if the United States or Britain did
not extend diplomatic recognition to Manchukuo, they might find
themselves entangled in dealing with its institutions. The Japanese
and Manchukuo governments made considerable effort to draw out
acknowledgements of Manchukuo's existence in ways used for similar
ends later in the twentieth century, such as sports diplomacy,[1] tourism,
contests, expositions, and world's fairs.[2] Even if full diplomatic recognition were not achieved, it was worthwhile to keep the Great Powers
engaged in extended negotiations and disputes, be it over the most
trivial matters.

Investment and trade were particularly important areas in which
to attract foreign acknowledgement and co-operation. They could
appeal, during the bad economic years of the 1930s, to governments
anxious about their own economies, or to interests that could pressure
those governments to relax their anti-Manchukuo stances. Rumors of
possible opportunities and deals made by rivals could attract and hold
interest, negotiations could be extended for months and years, and one
group could be played off against another—all providing reasons to
keep open the possibilities of recognition of Manchukuo and acceptance of the occupation. Foreign investment and trade also could sup-
plement scarce Japanese capital for Manchuria's development. The

Kwantung Army's plans for Manchukuo were highly ambitious and elaborate, but the army faced financial and resource constraints. On the other hand, some Japanese held that Manchukuo's development was a matter of Japanese pride, an accomplishment that should not be diluted by foreign interference, or that Manchuria's iron, coal, and other resources should be controlled completely by Japan for Japanese and Manchukuoan national security and development. This lack of unity complicated some negotiations with foreign investors.

It required considerable wooing to gain acceptance even from some sympathetic nations. Japan made extensive efforts to attain German recognition of Manchukuo, but did not achieve success until May 12, 1938. Despite considerable sympathy with Japan, Germany had large economic interests in the Republic of China—which played a major role in the global supply of the strategic materials antimony and tungsten—and gave military aid to the Chinese government. Manchurian soy oil was also an important German import, and the Manchukuo government consistently tried to expand commercial relations. A 1935 German economic mission to Manchukuo preceded a Manchukuo-German trade agreement in 1936, which the Manchukuo government claimed provided de facto recognition by Germany. Despite the November 1936 Anti-Comintern Pact between Germany and Japan, it still took another two years of effort to achieve formal German recognition of Manchukuo. Manchukuo gained Italian recognition on November 20, 1937 through a similar process of encouraging trade.[3]

Britain and the United States were, along with China, centers of determined opposition to Manchukuo, but even they were not immune to the temptations of commerce. Official British disapproval of Manchukuo did not stop British businesses from pursuing opportunities in Manchukuo. In October 1934, the Federation of British Industries (FBI) sent what it described as a "non-political" trade mission to Manchukuo. Its subsequent report praised Manchukuo's accomplishments and offered "the collaboration of British industry in the development of that State." The report argued that the best "opportunity for stimulating the sale of British products" would be found "in British participation in the development work" of Manchukuo. The Manchukuo government, even several years later, maintained that the FBI report had "rectified the errors of the Lytton Commission." This League of

Nations commission, headed by the Earl of Lytton, a British former colonial administrator, issued a report that countered Japanese claims about the Manchurian Incident, and became an important support of the non-recognition of Manchukuo by the League and by the Great Powers. Indeed, Japan withdrew from the League in objection to it. So, Manchukuo was able to use the British Federation of Industry against the British-led Lytton Commission. Furthermore, the Manchukuo government pointed out that the FBI report had discussed the "enhancement of friendly relations" between Britain and Manchukuo. Indeed, a British parlimentary question asked if recognition of Manchukuo were necessary to gain access to its market. The response was that market access could be gained without de jure recognition, through British consular representatives in Manchuria who were accredited to the Republic of China. Since any trade negotiations in Manchuria would be conducted with Japanese and Manchukuo representatives, this answer indicated the British government's apparent willingness to deal with Manchukuo for commercial benefit. Again, the promise of trade helped to keep open the possibility of British formal recognition.[4]

There were also ongoing efforts to interest the United States in trade and investment in Manchukuo. American government and business for decades had looked to Manchuria as a valuable market, and were interested in maintaining and, if possible, expanding access to it. From the beginning of the Japanese army's occupation of Manchuria, the US government was concerned that the open door of equal commercial access might close. It agreed with the Lytton Commission report which said that it was "essential" to maintain the principle of the Open Door in trade, industry, and banking, and worried that "Japanese business concerns" might take advantage of their hegemony in Manchuria. The US Department of State's January 1932 Stimson Doctrine said that the US would not recognize any de facto situation that would impair its treaty rights in China or its Open Door policy of supporting commercial access to and the territorial integrity of China. The establishment of Manchukuo violated Chinese territorial integrity and threatened US commercial access to Manchuria. Nevertheless, the US government also continued to point out commercial opportunities for American businesses which that very Manchukuo government provided. In 1933, the Foreign Construction Division of the Bureau of Foreign and Domestic

Commerce reported in *Commerce Reports* that the Manchukuo government was undertaking a ten-year $20-million program for the construction of over 200,000 miles of highways in Manchukuo. The Department of Commerce continued to report on large construction opportunities in Manchukuo, such as dams and urban construction until at least late 1940, even as US-Japanese relations continued to deteriorate. Japanese interests also attempted to attract American participation in Manchukuo during the late 1930s. Ayukawa Yoshisuke, the head of both the new Nissan conglomerate, and the Manchurian Industrial Development Corporation, through which the Manchukuo government carried out a five-year industrial development plan, made extensive efforts to bring American capital and technology into Manchukuo, including extended negotiations with Ford to set up a joint venture.[5]

France and Manchukuo

Although France also never recognized Manchukuo, its stance towards the new state was ambiguous and ambivalent. Like the other powers, France suffered from economic and political turbulence. Between the beginning of the Japanese occupation on September 18, 1931 and Japan's formal withdrawal from the League of Nations on March 27, 1933, there were five different French governments, and rapid turnover continued until 1938. As John Dreifort put it, "the chronic instability of internal conditions in France explains in considerable degree the frustrations encountered in the formulation and implementation of its foreign policy," including "toward the Manchurian crisis." Manchuria was distant, domestic issues seemed far more pressing, and French governments did not immediately produce clear policies. Meanwhile, the British and American governments were prepared to believe that the French government was uninterested in working with them to contain Japan, or even that it was supportive of Japan.[6]

Despite the domestic preoccupations of the various governments, there is evidence of considerable French sympathy for its fellow colonial power in Asia, Japan. The international law scholar, Carl Walter Young, who served as a technical aid to the Lytton Commission and wrote part of its Lytton Report, remarked that "the Chinese who had spoken" to Young about Henri Claudel, the French representative to the

Commission, claimed that the French government had appointed him "after the Japanese government, through Mr. Yoshizawa, had specifically asked that he be appointed." Those Chinese, Young said, "regard him as a type of colonial general who would naturally be *persona grata* to the Japanese." He also noted a report that Claudel "had been suggested both by the French and Japanese general staffs." Young, who was present during Commission meetings, observed that Claudel had been little interested in the proceedings until the last weeks of its investigation, when he played "his trump cards, which were evidently put up his sleeve by the French Government," and tried to "spike one or two of the major conclusions of the Report," and threatened to "submit a minority report on the section" that had assigned responsibility to "the Japanese military for having conceived, organized and supported the puppet state of 'Manchukuo.'" Claudel had "raised serious objections," which put the possibility of a "unanimous Report" in "grave doubt."[7]

Dreifort also notes Japanese efforts to separate France from Britain and the United States, as well as from the conclusions of the Lytton Report. On July 8, 1932, Koiso Kuniaki, the Japanese War Vice-Minister, told the French ambassador in Tokyo that, in order to develop Manchuria, Japan required French financial assistance. On July 9, the military advisor to Japan's Geneva delegation explained to a member of the French delegation at Geneva certain benefits of a Franco-Japanese rapprochement, and asked if the French government would instruct Henri Claudel to prevent the Lytton Report from unanimously condemning Japan. Twice later that month, the Japanese ambassador in Paris raised this subject with French Prime Minister Herriot, and other such attempts continued into the fall. Herriot, however, evaded these offers, and in September, the French Foreign Ministry argued that France, because of treaty obligations, could not recognize Manchukuo. Despite this, French businesses were eager to pursue trade and investment in Manchukuo.[8]

The Capital

Manchukuo was established on March 1, 1932. On March 10, the Manchukuo government announced that its capital would be Changchun, and on March 14, renamed it "Hsinking" or "New

Capital" (*Shinkyō* in Japanese). Changchun was a provincial town of about 130,000 near the northern terminus of the South Manchuria Railway (SMR). The Kwantung Army wanted to transform this market center for horses and soybeans into a world city—a modern, spacious, populous, and splendid city to rival the great capitals, a capital as ambitious as Manchukuo itself. Like the new state, Shinkyō was to be thoroughly planned. On December 8, 1931, well before its takeover of Manchuria was complete, the Kwantung Army produced its *Policy Draft for the Development of Manchuria and Mongolia*, which called for controlled development of Manchuria integrated with the Japanese empire. The draft proposed coordinated urban and regional planning as part of national economic development. Resources and transportation were to be developed for which appropriate facilities would be adapted. Economic development would bring with it the development of large cities, so city planning would be necessary to provide services and accommodations for residents, immigrants, and tourists. This planning would be controlled not by local, but the central government, as part of national policy.[9]

These ideas were more fully set out in the Manchukuo government's *Economic Construction Program of Manchukuo*, published on March 1, 1933. It said that the "proper adjustment of the means of transportation" was the "most important factor in the foundation work of economic construction" and made modern urban design a basic element of its transportation scheme. Shinkyō, Manchukuo's capital and first planned city, would be a model for the rest of Manchukuo's cities. The program envisioned planned cities integrated into Manchukuo's communication and transportation networks, extending national economic and land-use strategies to the local urban level.[10] This was no mere ambition: agencies began to produce new city designs for a construction boom sustained for the remainder of the decade.

Changchun presented opportunities and challenges as the site for the new capital. Surrounded by cheap agricultural land, it was on the main line of the SMR, so had good transportation to bring in construction materials and labor. But it had poor road links, few existing government buildings, inadequate electrical infrastructure and water supply, and a severe shortage of housing and even hotel rooms. The army continued counter-insurgency operations, while construction managers used firearms and barbed-wire fences to protect sites from attack. Nation, capital, and planning bureaucracy were all taking shape at the same time. In this rapidly changing and difficult environment, it was not surprising that some Japanese looked to other nations for financing and even technical assistance.

Planning bureaucracy evolved rapidly. The army made extensive use of the main research agency of the SMR—at that time known as the *Keizai chōsakai*, or Economic Research Association (ERA)—to produce a range of programs for Manchukuo's economic development. The city planning group, a small team within the ERA's Transport and Communications Section (for several months it had only two staff members), produced several drafts for Shinkyō even as it churned out plans for other cities.[11] Meanwhile, the Manchukuo government set up an agency specifically tasked with designing and building Shinkyō— the *Kokuto kensetsukyōku* or Capital Construction Bureau (CCB), which began in March 1932 as a small working group, but quickly grew to 441 employees by June 1934. The two agencies incorporated divergent interests. The SMR had extensive property and businesses in Changchun, including the railway zone, which by treaty it managed. The main SMR line also ran through the new capital's planning area. It therefore wanted to ensure ERA participation in Shinkyō's planning. Although former SMR employees were part of the CCB, the latter represented the interests of the Manchukuo government, different from those of the SMR. Two other groups participated in these early planning sessions: the Kwantung Army and Manchukuo financial officials.[12]

In a series of interagency meetings during the summer and fall of 1932, the army, the CCB, Manchukuo financial officials, and the ERA hashed out Shinkyō's initial construction plan and gave the CCB authority to administer it. Koiso Kuniaki, previously Japanese Army Vice-Minister, and recently arrived in Manchukuo as the new Chief of Staff of the Kwantung Army, chaired the first meeting. Koiso, as had other army officers, previously had tried to attract French interest in investment in Manchukuo. In this meeting, however, he and other army officers strongly criticized the proposals as too extravagant and expensive, and demanded that they be reduced. The CCB countered that a magnificent capital was vital to build the national loyalty of the population and also to show the world that Manchukuo was an advancing nation. Like the young United States, which had spent heavily on its new capital Washington, Manchukuo must also build a great city in Shinkyō. Army staff, however, remained unconvinced.[13]

Koiso, seeing a conflict between national priorities and the proposed scale of Shinkyō, demanded that construction be scaled back. He argued that costs might be more than a quarter over budget, and that Manchukuo could not afford to spend more than five percent of its projected construction expenses on Shinkyō. Despite CCB assurances that the project would become self-sustaining after two years (the CCB aimed to buy cheap agricultural land, develop, and then sell it), and that long-term bonds could finance large initial outlays, Koiso replied that such bonds diverted funding from other projects.

Sakatani Ki-ichi, chief representative of the Manchukuo government at the meeting and head of the General Affairs Board of the Manchukuo Finance Ministry and a supervisor of the Manchukuo Central Bank, then presented another plan to fund capital construction. He, together with the Japanese Consul and Manchukuo General Affairs Board Director Komai Tokuzō, one of the most influential figures in the early organization of Manchukuo, had already negotiated a French loan. This investment opportunity for French capital, he argued, would strengthen Manchukuo's claim that it adhered to the Open Door principle of equal commercial access of such concern to the Lytton Commission and the Great Powers. French financing of Shinkyō's construction also was a way of separating France from the other powers, and might bring it closer to de facto or even de jure recognition of Manchukuo.[14]

To Koiso's objections against foreign financing, Sakatani replied that 30,000 yen already had been spent to bring in French experts, and that relations with France would be damaged if this commitment were not honored. He proposed that French interest be maintained by soliciting a French plan that later could be rejected, and that negotiations be continued to learn if France wanted French engineers or construction materials used. CCB head Yuki Seitarō then interjected that France should not be brought into Shinkyō's construction. Reliance on French engineers and money would mean that Japan surrendered the development of East Asia, for which they would be criticized. Koiso also rejected Sakatani's advice and reminded him that he was able to restrict Sakatani's actions. He ended the meeting by stating that the plan and budget for the new capital were impractical and asked for a new draft.[15]

Not long after this meeting, in late October 1932, Koiso met with the French journalist Pierre Lyautey, who was the nephew of Hubert Lyautey, chief of the French protectorate in Morocco between 1912 and 1925 and noted colonial urbanist.[16] Pierre Lyautey's reports of his conversation with Koiso, and his observations of Manchukuo, confirm that the Japanese had reason to hope for French understanding and sympathy for Manchukuo, and that efforts to distance France from the United States and Britain, or even to gain open French support were worthwhile. Koiso, wrote Lyautey, had said that Japan, like France, was a force of a superior civilization, but existed in an Asia that was "gangrenous with corruption" and populated with peoples who had permitted themselves to degenerate, even while faced with the grave threat of communism. Koiso, Lyautey also noticed, was filled with his nation's civilizing mission in Asia, and envisioned Manchuria becoming an attractive model for development. Lyautey agreed that French public opinion had realized that France and Japan had the same security and moral instincts, and reciprocal "spiritual positions" on their respective continents. He proceeded to Shinkyō, and although little was built of the new capital, it reminded him of the French development of Rabat in its protectorate of Morocco, and he was impressed with the Japanese desire to build. On his return to France, Lyautey continued to promote French involvement in Manchukuo. At a March 28, 1933 meeting of the Franco-Asiatic Chamber of Commerce, he presented figures that he said showed Manchukuo's positive financial status, and urged French businesses to take advantage of opportunities to be found there.[17]

Other French journalists who reported from Manchuria during the 1930s were also impressed with the construction they saw there. In 1938, *Gringoire* correspondent Jean Douyau compared Shinkyō to Casablanca, and could not "help seeing a parallel between the task that we had in mind thirty years ago and that which is planned in Manchoukuo." Just as Casablanca demonstrated "the power of our construction work," Shinkyō showed the same supremacy in Asia. Emile Schreiber observed in 1937 that the principle which he saw in use in Shinkyō was the same as that which the French used in their territories in North Africa, building a new city outside the older one. The journal *Illustration* agreed in 1939 that in grandeur of vision and rapidity of construction, Shinkyō should be compared to Marshal Lyautey's Casablanca. They even compared it to Paris— Douyau said that a large plaza corresponded to the Étoile and he expected that after centuries of glory, an Arc de Triomphe would appear there; Schreiber wrote that the dimensions of the plaza recalled the Concorde; and Gabrielle Bertrand also remarked on this plaza. Manchukuo and its capital clearly evoked sympathetic recognition among some French.[18]

Franco-Japanese Negotiations for Contracts in Manchukuo

French investors actively sought opportunities in Manchukuo in 1932, when the Japanese ambassador in Paris approached Paul Emile Dourille about Franco-Japanese co-operation in a "great work" in Manchuria.[19] Dourille, with experience in Japan and connected to the Lyons silk industry, may have been a member of the Dourille family involved in the Yokohama silk trade.[20] On November 16, 1932, he and P. Dufour organized the Syndicat pour l'étude et la réalisation d'entreprises en Extrême-Orient to investigate market opportunities in Manchukuo.[21] Dourille and Dufour then recruited potential participants, such as the Comptoir Franco-Belge-Sarrois, and the Comité des Forges. Dourille soon left via Siberia for Japan and Manchuria, arriving on December 22. There he met with representatives of the Japanese Embassy in Shinkyō, the Manchukuo Foreign Ministry, Kwantung Army Chief of Staff Koiso, and Vice-Governor of the SMR Hatta Yoshiaki, and consulted with them about participating in Shinkyō's construction.[22] On February 28, 1933, Dourille and the SMR organized the *Syndicat pour l'étude et la réalisation d'entreprises au Mandchoukouo* (SEREM), with the Japanese name of Manshū kigyō kumiai. Yamasaki Motoki, an SMR director, served as SEREM President, and André Moyrand, an honorary deputy director of the Chemin de fer du Nord, as its vice-president. The Japanese and French sides were each to contribute a million francs of capital, which would be used for future joint ventures in Manchukuo.[23]

The enterprise proved a disappointment to the French side, which complained that the Japanese were not providing projects. Indeed, the

Manchukuo government already was negotiating with another French group, the Association nationale d'expansion économique (ANEE), formed in 1915 to research and promote markets for French businesses. It boasted excellent connections: the patronage of the President of the Republic, the Foreign Ministry, the Bank of France, and ninety Chambers of Commerce. Its president, Etienne Fougère, headed French and international silk industry organizations and was a member of the Chamber of Deputies between 1928 and 1932. In May 1933, the ANEE, in association with the Société de construction des Batignolles (SCB), dispatched André Boiscorjon d'Ollivier to negotiate investment and commercial opportunities in Manchukuo, especially public works. He brought with him documentation of SCB competence and ten albums of photographs of its projects, as well as certification, verified by the French Consul in Yokohama and the Commercial Attaché of the French Embassy in Tokyo, that he was the sole authorized ANEE representative and had no connection to the Dourille mission.[24] By the end of July, Japanese sources claimed that a Franco-Japanese Association to invest in Manchukuo had been formed with the ANEE and that French financiers were considering directing a billion francs there. In October 1933, there were reports of a deal between Ollivier and the SMR to provide for a billion-franc French loan that would finance harbor, railway, and power plant projects. Ollivier claimed that an agreement had been initialed on October 13 and would soon be signed. But by January 13, 1934, French officials were denying that there was any government support for such loans, and on January 20, Fougère said that Ollivier had gone beyond his authority, and no loans had yet been arranged. By February, Fougère denied any knowledge of a consortium of French and Japanese companies, saying that Ollivier was authorized only to research and report to the ANEE.[25]

It was not until the end of June 1934 that Ollivier succeeded. On June 30, he and SEREM president Yamasaki signed an organizational agreement for a Consortium franco-japonais pour le développement des affaires dans le Mandchoukouo. Earlier in June, Moyrand had learned of la bombe d'Ollivier, that Yamasaki and the ANEE had signed a draft contract which duplicated SEREM's contract. Moyrand continued for several months to make serious objections to this, but Yamasaki replied in September that Moyrand had misunderstood the nature of SEREM, that not all projects in Manchukuo were suitable for SEREM, which did not have monopolistic or preferential rights to them. In the fall of 1934, the two French groups associated with SEREM and the ANEE had signed contracts with the SMR, but both were unsatisfied with the lack of projects. Their solution was to combine. Near the end of November 1934, Moyrand, Yamasaki, and the ANEE agreed that the SEREM and the ANEE would establish a new group, the Société anonyme pour le développement des affaires en Mandchourie (SADAM), with Fougère as president and Moyrand as vice-president. SADAM then, with the SMR, would compose a new Franco-Japanese consortium. This arrangement, however, did not fulfill their hopes for access to more projects. What little achievement there was in this field belonged to the Brossard Mopin consortium.[26]

Brossard Mopin

The Société d'exploitation des établissements Brossard Mopin, head-quartered in Paris, established its main Asian office in Saigon by 1910, and by the 1930s had branches in Phnom Penh, Singapore, Hanoi, and Haiphong, as well as Shanghai, Tianjin, Shenyang, and Harbin in China. Brossard Mopin worked mainly in such public works as railways, bunds, bridges, docks, and waterworks, specializing in architectural design and reinforced concrete work, but also had a brickworks in Saigon, imported agricultural machinery, and even sold concrete rollers for lawn tennis courts. It soon became one of the major construction firms in Indochina—in June 1915, the United States Consul in Saigon, pointing out the necessity of bridges in the watery region, noted that Brossard Mopin seemed "to get most of the contracts in this locality"—where it built such projects as railways, the Hanoi railway station, wharves, and the main market in Saigon. In China, Brossard Mopin was most active in Tianjin, where, backed by the Banque de l'Indochine (BI), it built at least thirteen substantial buildings, including the police station and the town hall in the French Concession, the Banque Franco-Chinoise, and buildings for a Jesuit commercial school, and did concrete work for the French Bund. It also had its own dry dock in Tianjin. In Shenyang, Manchuria, Brossard Mopin had built a stadium and university accommodations, as well as the Mukden Club and private residences. It also built the Grand Hotel in Beijing.[27]

During and after the First World War, Brossard Mopin built ferro-cement ships, including a large ferry in Singapore and several ships in Indochina. It then began to build them at its Tianjin shipyard. Unfortunately, this drew it into the 1921 collapse of the Banque Industrielle de Chine (BIC). Along with other financiers, a former Tianjin officer of the BI had set up BIC to compete with the BI, and advanced Brossard Mopin forty million francs to build two ferro-cement freighters that then sank on their initial voyages. When the BIC collapsed, Philippe Berthelot, brother of BIC president André Berthelot, was forced to retire from the Foreign Office for "engaging the respon-sibility of France in the affairs of a private concern." After the BIC's failure, the Banque De Paris et des Pays-Bas (Paribas) revived it, and Georges Maspero, former Resident-Superior of Cambodia, became BIC President. Brossard Mopin then became a Paribas subsidiary.[28]

Since Brossard Mopin was already active in Manchuria when the Kwantung Army seized the region, its managers hoped to gain access to projects with the Japanese authorities there, and associated compa-nies planned to join it. In late 1932, representatives of three Paris-and Indochina-based companies—Brossard Mopin, the BI, and its sub-sidiary the Société française d'entreprises de dragages et de travaux publics—et in Paris and established the Association en participation pour l'exécution de travaux en Mandchourie to pursue opportunities in Manchukuo. The new organization was projected to continue for three years after October 20, 1932, and to pursue construction work with Japanese and Manchurian civil and military authorities in Manchuria. The headquarters would be the Brossard Mopin office in Paris. In addition to the extensive construction experience of both Brossard Mopin and Dragages, the new group had the substantial financial resources of both the BI and Paribas. Furthermore, its representatives did not have to organize expeditions of several months from Paris to Japan and Manchukuo, as Brossard Mopin already had offices in Manchuria at Harbin and Shenyang, and a regional office in Tianjin.[29]

Brossard Mopin and its associates were in a good position to observe the negotiations and lack of substantial progress between Dourille, Ollivier, and the SMR. In December 1933, the SMR asked Lucien Merlet, a Brossard Mopin engineer based in Shanghai, to come to its offices in Dairen to negotiate. Leon Ducimetière, a Brossard Mopin associate in Harbin who helped organize the negotiations, speculated that the SMR's eagerness to meet with Merlet was due to its dawning understanding that its plans with Ollivier had no serious basis, and that Ollivier had been unable to demonstrate serious French financial support. Merlet's negotiations with the SMR, however, were successful. On January 18, 1934, he signed an agreement with the managing director of the Tōa Doboku Kigyō, an SMR subsidiary which managed SMR construction. They established a joint partnership, with Tōa Doboku appointing the chief engineer who would have authority over the entire business of the joint enterprise. Brossard Mopin would appoint a treasurer to manage enterprise finances and be the assistant of the engineer. Brossard Mopin would also provide an unlimited floating capital, according to whatever projects were undertaken, and would receive ordinary bank interest for it. Profits were to be divided equally. Brossard Mopin headquarters confirmed the agreement in March 1934.[30]

Brossard Mopin's managers soon grew frustrated with the lack of projects, finding themselves waiting in the humiliating position of supplicants. But by the end of the year, they had obtained what was apparently the largest project in Manchukuo that any French firm received. This was a contract for two buildings for the Manchukuo Foreign Ministry—the Ministry building itself and the official residence of the Foreign Minister. This was not a particularly large project, as the two buildings would total only 3,500 square meters and were budgeted at 380,000 Manchukuo yen. The Manchukuo government projected spending a further 100,000 yen on furnishings. Construction was to be quick: it would begin in the spring and was to be completed by mid-December 1935. Site purification rites were held on April 5, and on May 11, the French-Japanese construction company formed by Tōa Doboku and Brossard Mopin began operations in Manchukuo. By early October, the building was nearing completion, although scaffolding was still in place.[31]

Brossard Mopin's description of the building design notes that the company constructed the Manchukuo Foreign Ministry building for the Japanese administration in Shinkyō, an indication of the Japanese control of Manchukuo's government. The client gave unusual instructions for a government ministry building. It was planned as a temporary building, to be converted into a club two or three years after construction. Brossard Mopin designed the building's left wing with temporary walls and a second floor, so that floor and walls could be easily removed in the conversion of the wing to club space. The client also specifically requested that the façade be "*ni Japonais ni Chinois, ni Européen, ni Moderne.*" The result was a three-story building with two brick wings slightly offset from a central, almost castle-like, entrance—a heavy rectangular mass of stone blocks with a deep and relatively narrow archway. It was not a building which won much architectural notice or praise outside of Japan or Manchukuo. The *Architectural Forum* published three small photographs and a paragraph saying that Manchukuo's buildings had replaced Soviet architecture as the world's worst, and describing the Foreign Ministry building as "bumbling Neo-Egyptian."

Manchukuo collapsed in the 1945 Soviet invasion of Manchuria that helped end the Second World War. Shinkyō became Changchun again. In the 1990s, new construction, often high-rise, replaced many of the deteriorating buildings left over from the Manchukuo era. One of these remaining buildings is the former Foreign Ministry, even though part of it was designed to be temporary. It has been remodeled as a club, and is hemmed by a thicket of high-rises. Much of the original façade survives.[32] (see Figure 4.1)

Although Brossard Mopin quickly completed the Foreign Ministry building, it obtained little other work in Manchukuo, and its management soon grew exasperated. At the end of January 1936, Lucien Merlet bluntly complained to the SMR about the "unacceptable situation." Brossard Mopin, he pointed out, already had fifteen years of building experience in Manchuria by the time of Manchukuo's establishment in 1932. Now, because of the "prevailing Japanese influence" in Manchuria, Brossard Mopin was unable to continue to undertake work there without new financial support. Nevertheless, its backers—the BI and Paribas—were the only French financial houses capable of executing major construction work in East Asia, so any such project involving a French firm necessarily came to them.

Dourille had attempted to obtain Paribas support, but failed, Merlet noted. Ollivier had unsuccessful appealed for BI help. The ANEE, a research group without capitalization of its own, he pointed

Department
of Justice

Department of Foreign Affairs
constructed by Brossard Mopin
Co., French Contractors

Figure 4.1

Department of Foreign Affairs building, constructed by Brossard Mopin.
Source: *Manchoukuo Illustrated* (Hsinking: Bureau of Information and Publicity,
Department of Foreign Affairs, Manchoukuo, 1936), 11.

out, had nothing to offer a bank. It was only "an agent without any
practical utility." Paribas and the BI, however, with close connections
to the French government, had no such need of intermediaries, and
one makes, Merlet continued, "a serious mistake in treating with so
little consideration these two important establishments." He finished
by asking for a definite statement of whether the SMR would require
the assistance of the BI and Paribas. If not, they would withdraw
from Manchukuo, "with the profound regret at having spent fruitless
time and money for over three years." In May, Merlet wrote to say he
decided to dissolve the joint French-Japanese enterprise. About a year
later, in the summer of 1937, Japanese forces moved into central China
and began to pressure the French and British Concessions on the China
coast. Prospects for Brossard Mopin there, and for other French firms
in China, shrank. In 1932, some French had seen the Japanese occupation of Manchuria and Japanese pressure on China as an opportunity

and as a way of protecting Indochina. As Japan occupied the China coast and then Indochina, limited Franco-Japanese cooperation became Japanese dominance.[33]

The Foreign Ministry Building and the Question of an Official Manchukuo Architectural Style

As Bill Sewell discusses elsewhere in this volume, Changchun was the site of extensive construction activity that accelerated after the foundation of Manchukuo. As he makes clear, the Manchukuo government's building program, which laid out new streets of government offices, presented an opportunity to consider and achieve a unified architectural style expressive of the new state's ideology. The massive ministerial buildings lining Xuntian Boulevard, with Japanese-or Chinese-style heavy slanting roofs that evoked both Chinese and Japanese architectural heritages, provided what has seemed a solid foundation for the discussion of the relationship between Manchukuo's city-building and architectural style. How does Brossard Mopin's Foreign Ministry building fit into this question of architectural style? The Manchukuo government presented itself to the world through its Foreign Ministry. If the Manchukuo government intended to use an architectural style to express an ideology, one might expect to find it in the Foreign Ministry building.

It is possible to see in some of Manchukuo's government buildings what Koshizawa Akira and others have called the "*Ajia-shugi* or *Kōa* style" (sometimes rendered respectively as "Pan-Asian" and "Rising Asia") or the "final elaboration of the *teikan yoshiki*" (Imperial Crown) style, and even to see this style as intended to have inspired Manchukuoan nationalism, Pan-Asian sentiment and resistance to Western colonialism.[34] Contrastingly, Nishizawa Yasuhiko has criticized the idea of a coherent Manchukuo style for government office buildings, and Brossard Mopin's Foreign Ministry, along with an annex to the State Council Building, provides some of his strongest counter-evidence. Both these buildings, he points out, lack any sort of steep, Chinese-inspired roof. If the Manchukuo government had been committed to such an ideological architectural style, an architecture of "slogans," Nishizawa argues it would have built in such a manner, and there actually is little evidence of such an intention.[35]

Brossard Mopin's Foreign Ministry was not built on the wide Xuntian Boulevard, but was located much less conspicuously to the northwest of the long-empty site of the uncompleted imperial palace. It was not a massive, square-sided, and heavy-roofed building, but might be described as rambling and asymmetrical. Both the front and back of the building were built with an attached cylindrical, flat-topped tower, but the back façade is more variegated. With porches and balustrades; a capacious, round opening reminiscent of a moon-gate; and windows of diverse size and placement, the back facade is divided into sections with varying setbacks and roof heights, and brings to mind the kind of early twenty-first century commercial architecture that presents a single building as if it were a street of adjoining shops in different styles. Curiously for a building that would receive official visitors, and unlike most of Manchukuo's government buildings, it also lacked a *porte-cochère*, described by David Stewart as a "nearly inevitable presence" in *teikan* yōshiki, or Imperial Crown Style, buildings.[36] In particular, Brossard Mopin's statement that the Manchukuo government had requested that the building be "*ni Japonais ni Chinois, ni Européen, ni Moderne*" lends support to Nishizawa's view that the Manchukuo government showed little commitment to such an official ideological style.

Yet the Manchukuo government did use the building to represent Manchukuo even before its completion, and continued to do so after the possibility of further French investment had ended. The building appeared in government-produced publicity material aimed at Japanese, Manchurian, and Western audiences to show the progress of Manchukuo and the development of a new culture. For example, a 1940 article, "Whither Manchoukuo's Architecture," declared that architecture was "the frank expression" of Manchukuo's culture. Attempts had been made to forge a suitable style by using "the Chinese decorative motif," the article continued, "and by so doing to create a new Manchurian architecture on the basis of this newly rising country, but such embellishment was found to be inconsistent with modern ideas." Indeed, some architects had "embarked on the re-emergence of Manchurian architecture in a new form, aiming to create a true culture, not a subsidiary development to the founding of the country." They provided only five buildings and a commercial street scene as examples.

One of these representative buildings was the Foreign Ministry, which does not resemble the others very much.[37] This building was the only Manchukuo government building designed by a foreigner (Japanese were one of Manchukuo's five nationalities, so Japanese architects were not considered foreigners). The government gave only vague directions for its style, and once it was built, used its idiosyncratic style as an example of Manchukuo's new culture. Brossard Mopin's Foreign Ministry lends little support to any idea of a unified Manchukuo government building style.

Notes

1. One technique was to invite foreign sports teams to compete in Manchukuo, similar to the "ping-pong diplomacy" between the United States and the People's Republic of China during the early 1970s when the US had not extended diplomatic recognition to the PRC. Another was to arrange for foreign sports teams or individual athletes to compete against Manchukuo teams or in events where Manchukuo athletes appeared.

   The Japanese government also unsuccessfully attempted to have Manchukuo accepted as a participating country in the 1936 Olympic games, and the planned, but abandoned 1940 Tokyo Olympic games would have provided a major venue for Manchukuo athletes to compete against athletes from the Great Powers.

2. At the Century of Progress Exposition in Chicago in 1933 and 1934, the SMR and Manchukuo attempted to build a joint hall. When the Exposition did not accept this proposal, the SMR arranged its own exhibit, which included exhibits about Manchukuo, such as various products, views of the capital, as well as a photographic exhibition. *Manchuria Daily News*, February 13, 1933, 4; April 4, 1933, 2; April 17, 1933, 2. "Manchuria-Graph," *International Center of Photography eMuseum*, http://fansinaflashbulb.wordpress.com/2010/02/23/manchuria-graph/.

3. Gerhard L. Weinberg, "German Recognition of Manchoukuo," *World Affairs Quarterly* 28 (July 1957): 149–64; Manchukuo State Council, *An Outline of the Manchukuo Empire, 1939* (Dairen: Manchuria Daily News, 1939), 54.

4. Federation of British Industries, *Report of Mission to the Far East, August–November 1934* (London: FBI, 1934), 3, 9–10, 34; Manchukuo State Council, *An Outline of the Manchukuo Empire*, 54; *London Times*, April 24, 1934, 7.

5. League of Nations, *Report of the Commission of Enquiry*, 125–26; US Department of Commerce, *Commerce Reports*, May 30, 1932, 514–15; Haruo

Iguchi, *Unfinished Business: Ayukawa Yoshisuke and U.S.-Japan Relations, 1937–1953* (Cambridge: Harvard University Asia Center, 2003), 31–87.

6.   John E. Dreifort, *Myopic Grandeur: The Ambivalence of French Foreign Policy toward the Far East, 1919–1945* (Kent: Kent State University Press, 1991), 48–55.

7.   Yoshizawa Kenkichi was Japanese ambassador to France at the time. Carl Walter Young, "The Manchurian Investigation of the League of Nations Commission of Inquiry: (Statement to the Board of Trustees of the Institute of Current World Affairs, New York City)," October 17, 1932; Letter from Carl Walter Young to Walter Rogers, February 21, 1932. Institute of Current World Affairs Online Archives, http://www.icwa.org/Reports.asp.

8.   Dreifort, *Myopic Grandeur,* 71–78.

9.   Katakura Tadashi, "Manshū jihen kimitsu seiryaku nisshi," in Kobayashi Tatsuo, ed., *Gendai shi shiryō 7: Manshū jihen* (Tōkyō: Misuzu Shobō, 1964), 291–92.

10. Manchukuo Government, *Economic Construction Program of Manchukuo* (New York: South Manchuria Railway, 1933), 5–8.

11. Mantetsu, *Ritsuan chōsa shorui mokuroku* (Dairen: Mantetsu, 1935), 137–39.

12. *Manshūkoku seifu kōhō niyaku,* no. 46: 1–3; no. 74: 17–18.

13. Mantetsu, *Shinkyō toshi kensetsu hōsaku* (hereinafter abbreviated as *STKH*) (Dairen: Mantetsu, 1935), 77–86. This compilation of Shinkyō's planning contains transcripts of interagency meetings.

14. Mantetsu, *STKH,* 78–85.

15. Mantetsu, *STKH,* 83–85. According to Kondō Soko, one of Yuki's coworkers in the Manchukuo government, the army and Manchukuo government had agreed to bring in French money and engineers, but Yuki's eloquent denunciation convinced them to reject French participation. Kondō Soko, "Yuki Seitarō o shinobu," Manshū kaikoshū kankōkai, ed. *Aa Manshū* (Tōkyō: Nōrin Shuppatsu, 1965), 112–13.

16. Pierre Lyautey edited several volumes of his uncle's writings and letters. For more on Marshal Lyautey and urban constructionin Morocco, see Gwendolyn Wright, *The Politics of Design: French Colonial Urbanism* (Chicago: University of Chicago Press, 1991), 75–84.

17. Pierre Lyautey, "Japon et Mandchourie, Choses Vues et Entendues," *Revue des Deux Mondes* 15 (May–June 1933): 127–29, 136; *New York Times,* March 29, 1933, 10.

18. Jean Douyau, "Impressions on Manchoukuo," Part 1, *Contemporary Manchuria* 2, no. 3 (May 1938): 124–26; Emile Schreiber, "Corée—Manchoukouo, ou le Recul des Blancs," *L'Illustration* 4823 (August 10, 1935): 477; Anonymous, *L'Illustration,* 202 (January 7, 1939): 31. Gabrielle Bertrand, *Seule dans l'Asie Troublée: Mandchoukuo-Mongolie, 1936–1936* (Paris: Plon, 1937), 80.

19. Jasper Wieck, *Weg in die "Décadence": Frankreich und die mandschurische Krise, 1932–1933* (Bonn: Bouvier Verlag, 1995), 251. Wieck points out that in June 1933, the Japanese ambassador wrote that he had been engaged in this "great work" for a year and a half.

20. The silk merchant, Paul Adrien Dourille, began his career in Yokohama by 1872, and died there in 1927. By 1903, he employed an E. Dourille as a silk inspector. Personal communication from Bernd Lebach, October 26, 2010. A Paul Adrien Dourille was the second president of the Chambre de Commerce et d'Industrie Française du Japon in 1919. *La Lettre Mensuelle: Une publication de la Chambre de Commerce et d'Industrie Française du Japon* 291, September 2008, 21. http://www.ccifj.or.jp/vie-de-la-chambre/publications/publications-periodiques/la-lettre-mensuelle.html.

21. Wieck, *Weg in die "Décadence,"* 251.

22. Ibid., 252; *Manchuria Daily News*, December 22, 1932, 1; December 23, 1932, 4.

23. Letter from André Moyrand to Yamasaki Motoki, July 13, 1934, *Archives in the Japanese Ministry of Foreign Affairs, Tokyo, Japan, 1868–1945*, Washington, DC: Library of Congress Photoduplication Service: US Department of State, 1949–51 (hereinafter referred to as *AJMFA*), Reel 214, S5110–27, frames 1144–46.

24. Desired public works included such projects as roads, rail, and tramways, canals, all sorts of urban infrastructure and utilities, electrical transmission lines, and bridges. "Mission en Mandchourie de l'Association Nationale d'expansion économique," *AJMFA*, Reel 210, S5110–26, frames 44–55.

25. *New York Times,* July 30, 1933, 10; October 17, 1933, 12; October 18, 1933, 22; October 20, 1933, 13; January 18, 1934, 11; January 21, 1934, 10; February 14, 1934, 4.

26. "Note Confidentielle," July 16, 1934, *AJMFA*, Reel 214, S5110–27, frames 1150–56; Letter from Yamasaki Motoki to André Moyrand, September 4, 1934; André Moyrand to Yamasaki Motoki, January 30, 1935, Reel 214, S5110–27, frames 1193–94.

27. "French Financial and Technical Group," *AJMFA*, Reel 214, S5110–28, frames 18–19, undated; *Commerce Reports*, vol. 3, July–September 1915, 635 (Washington, DC: Bureau of Foreign and Domestic Commerce, Department of Commerce); Hubert Bonin, "Tianjin as a French Banking Market," unpublished paper, 5.

28. "Association en participation pour l'exécution de travaux en Mandchourie," December 6, 1932, *AJMFA*, Reel 214, S5110–28, frames115–26; Nobutaka Shinonaga, "La formation de la Banque Industrielle de Chine," *Le Mouvement Social* 155 (April–June 1991): 39–65; Marc Meuleau, *Des Pionniers en Extrême-Orient: Histoire de la Banque de l'Indochine (1875–1975)* (Paris: Librairie Arthème Fayard, 1990), 269; Henri Claude *Histoire, Réalité et Destin d'un Monopole: La Banque de Paris et des Pays-Bas et son Groupe (1872–1968)* (Paris: Editions Sociales), 44; Thomas Adrian Schweitzer, "The

French Colonialist Lobby in the 1930's: The Economic Foundations of Imperialism" (PhD diss., University of Wisconsin, 1971), 61, 547; *New York Times*, August 3, 1923, 21.

29. "Association en participation pour l'exécution de travaux en Mandchourie," December 6, 1932.

30. Letter from Leon Ducimetière to Lucien Merlet, December 5, 1933, *AJMFA*, Reel 214, S5110–28, frames 30–34; "Mutual Consent," January 18, 1934, Reel S214, S5110–28, frames 137–38; Letter from Georges Maspero to Kamekishi Yagyu, March 5, 1934, Reel S214, S5110–28, frames 107–08.

31. Letter from Brossard Mopin to Paul Abry, August 27, 1934, *AJMFA*, Reel 214, S5110–28, frames 263–66; *Manchuria Daily News*, January 1, 1935, 1; January 10, 1935, 3; April 9, 1935, 3; May 16, 1935, 3; October 8, 1935, 3.

32. Letter from Paul Abry to Lucien Merlet, April 25, 1935, *AJMFA*, Reel S214, S5110–28, frame 336; Anonymous, *Architectural Forum* 67 (October 1937): 96.

33. Letter from Lucien Merlet to Matsuoka Yōsuke, *AJMFA*, Reel S214, S5110–28, frames 422–25; Letter from Lucien Merlet to Yanai Hisao, May 24, 1936, Reel S214, S5110–28, frames 507–08.

34. Koshizawa Akira, *Manshūkoku no shuto keikaku* (Tōkyō: Chikuma Shobō, 2002), 238–39; David Stewart, *The Making of a Modern Japanese Architecture: 1868 to the Present* (Tokyo: Kodansha International, 1987), 110–11.

35. Nishizawa Yasuhiko, *Nihon no shokuminchi kenchikuron* (Nagoya: Nagoya Daigaku Shuppankai, 2008), 111.

36. Stewart, *The Making of a Modern Japanese Architecture*, 110.

37. Manchoukuo, *Hsinking* (Hsinking: Manchoukuo Government, 1938), 32–33; Anonymous, "Whither Manchoukuo's Architecture," *Manchoukuo* 3 (1940): 22–25.

5
International Concessions and the Modernization of Tianjin

Zhang Chang and Liu Yue

Within Chinese scholarship on urban development, two major schools of thought stand out.[1] The first focuses on the humanities and uses historical, sociological, and anthropological approaches to understand city growth. Another school of thought mainly utilizes architectural and urban planning methodology. Both groups have been particularly interested in the treaty ports of modern China as objects of study; they have primarily focused their efforts on understanding the relationship between spatial and cultural change, including the link between urban construction and the development of social and communal life.

The most successful works to date have used Shanghai as their case study, with Shanghai studies becoming a separate discipline within urban development studies. In contrast, Tianjin has received less scholarly attention as it is a smaller city on an economic and spatial scale, its importance long overshadowed by that of Shanghai. However, before 1928, Tianjin played a more crucial political and military role than Shanghai. This pre-eminence was manifested in the physical environment of Tianjin, where nine separate international concessions set it above any treaty port city in China and in East Asia. This chapter examines how the growth of international concessions fostered change in local administration and urban planning in Tianjin.

Early Concessions and Rapid Urbanization

After the Second Opium War (1856–60), Tianjin was forcibly turned into an international treaty port by the Treaty of Peking. Following the development of foreign trade, industry, and commerce, it soon became the largest economic center in northern China and the biggest international exporter of raw materials. The development of the port rapidly accelerated the urbanization of Tianjin. As the city center expanded, numerous buildings in various non-traditional Chinese styles were erected using Western construction methods, and roads were broadened and paved. Tianjin quickly became a modern city with little resemblance to vernacular Chinese towns.

According to the conventional Chinese method of urban planning, both Tianjin and Shanghai were poorly located cities. In Chinese practice, cities could not be built along a river or the sea, as the land was often marshy, muddy, salty, and generally difficult to build upon. Such geographical characteristics were believed to foster diseases, making the land inappropriate for settlers. Both Tianjin and Shanghai's concessions were located on wasteland and marshes near rivers and thus were not considered suitable for living. The early pioneers of the Tianjin concessions described it as "the dreary grounds." According to Alexander Michie, editor of *The Chinese Times*, Tianjin's first English and foreign newspaper, "The sites of two settlements were foul and noxious swamps, and around them on the drier grounds, were the numerous graves of many generations of the people."[2] However, the British soon realized the importance of the small village Zizhulin, the name given by locals to the area three kilometers to the south of the Chinese city. Zizhulin lacked any city walls or boundaries, and the British saw great potential for growth in the small village.

Tianjin had long been an important passageway for both the water and land trade routes, as well as the most significant trading hub for Northern China. The Grand Canal connected the four major water systems—the Yangtze, Huai, Yellow, and Hai Rivers—and linked the inland river shipping route to the sea route, making it an essential part of the Chinese trade economy. Beginning at Zizhulin, the Hai River widened and it became easier for the sailing and anchoring of larger boats. Steamboats could directly maneuver into the piers constructed along the concessions and be moored easily. Across the river, and closer to the sea than Zizhulin, stood the Yuan dynasty (1271–1368) pier named Dazhigu, which had long served as the connecting point for large-scale canal shipping and mooring from the sea. The Hai River channel at Zizhulin was the only corridor to enter the confluence of the Grand Canal and the Hai River at Sanchakou, which was the key strategic point. The British and French established their concessions in this area so that they could take advantage of this convenient location, which was conducive to trade. Meanwhile, from a military sense, the position of the concessions at the river's edge gave the foreigners strong control over Tianjin, which made it easier to challenge the Qing dynasty (1644–1911) power base in nearby Beijing.

Before Tianjin was opened as a treaty port, foreign visitors such as Marco Polo (1254–1324), the first Dutch Embassy (1655), British diplomats Lord Macartney (1793), and Lord Amherst (1816), sent by the British government to negotiate trade agreements, described Tianjin as a busy port and a prominent sea town.[3] Yet, the early city was poorly developed and lacked modern infrastructure. In 1879, Constantin von Hanneken wrote,

> The whole of Tianjin had only four or five roads paved with slabs of stone. The other five or six hundred roads are all dirty and muddy … Most of these roads are no wider than ten steps across, and very narrow. Sometimes to avoid horse carriages and sedan chairs, people on the street have to press their bodies against the neighboring walls to make space.[4]

According to Sone Toshitora, a Japanese traveler, Tianjin's streets were uneven, with high edges, resembling a dry riverbed. The hygiene of the city center was very poor as well, with trash littering the streets. Toshitora wrote that during the hot months of summer, the open sewage lines became sources of epidemics, which killed many people. The land was low-lying, so once it started raining, the water flowed like a river under the city wall. At some points, the water in the roads was deep enough to reach the waist of a grown man.[5]

Following Tianjin's establishment as a treaty port, great improvements were made to the infrastructure of the city, including the expansion of the urban area and the construction of both Chinese-and Western-style buildings. With the urbanization process and migration from other parts of China, Tianjin's population increased dramatically, with an average growth of 10,000 people per year. In 1860, the estimated population was about 300,000;[6] in 1872 the population was about 400,000;[7] and by 1896, it had reached nearly 600,000.[8] Over time, Tianjin was transformed into a modern metropolis.

Like in Shanghai, the urbanization process of Tianjin was closely linked to the establishment of its concessions. The international concessions were established over three different periods: following the Second Opium War, Britain, France, and the US claimed land in Tianjin;[9] Germany and Japan built their concessions after the Sino-Japanese War (1894–95), and in 1900 the Russian, Italian, Belgian, and Austro-Hungarian armed forces established concessions in Tianjin following the victory of the Allied Forces over the Boxers. Thus, a total of nine countries built concessions in Tianjin, with Italy, Belgium, and Austria-Hungary choosing to place their only international concessions in Tianjin. These foreign neighborhoods were established on both sides of the Hai River. The western bank of the river housed the concessions established before 1900, including the British, French, American, German, and Japanese areas. The Russian, Italian, Austro-Hungarian, and Belgian Concessions were built along the eastern bank of the river. Together, the foreign areas held a combined area eight times larger than the original 1.8 square kilometers occupied by the original Chinese city of Tianjin. This vast outnumbering of foreign neighborhoods to Chinese territory is unique to Tianjin and cannot be found in any other concession city in the world. By the end of the nineteenth century, Tianjin exemplified the efforts of Western imperialism to establish their spheres of influence in Chinese port cities. (see Figure 5.1)

In Tianjin, the British Concession became the model for all later ones. The early developers made thorough plans for the concession before beginning construction. In the initial blueprint, the land was segmented into grids, while roads and plots were divided into sections and numbered. The British Municipal Council then decided on the annual rental price for each piece of land based on its size and location. The plots could be leased to both British and foreign companies, as well as to individual foreign merchants. According to O. D. Rasmussen, the annual rental of 1,500 copper cash per Chinese *mu* (with one *mu* equaling roughly one-sixth of an acre) applied to all land in the concession, although the original auction price per *mu* might have varied, depending on the location of the land.[10] Tenants were required to pay fees for the development of the concession's sewage system, road works, street lighting, recreational grounds, and police service. Because of the city's position below sea level, the early pioneers had to dredge mud

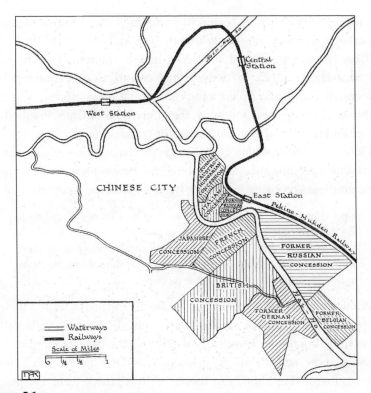

Figure 5.1

Tianjin's Concessions, 1930s. Source: F. C. Jones, *Shanghai and Tianjin*: *With Special Reference to Foreign Interests* (London: Humphrey Millford, 1940).

from the river to fill and raise the sites. The amount used was spectacular—two hundred million square feet of mud was needed to level the ground of the expanded concession area outside of the Weize canal.[11] By the 1860s, only the British Concession had established piers, warehouses, office buildings, and a consulate office. There remained very little development in the French and American Concessions during this time. Until the Tianjin Massacre in 1870, foreigners continued to live in the old Chinese city.

The massacre was a manifestation of the anti-missionary feelings of many Chinese at the time. Although Western missionary activities became legal in China as a result of the Treaty of Tianjin, which ended the Second Opium War, there were often misunderstandings and disputes between Western missionaries and Chinese in the ensuing years. The hostility of the Chinese in Tianjin was amplified due to rumors circulating around the old Chinese city that the French order called the Sisters of Charity kidnapped and harmed Chinese children. Protests were staged, and on June 21, 1870, the French consul, Henri Fontanier, fired at a crowd and nearly killed a high-ranking Tianjin official. A violent outbreak of xenophobia followed: the angry mob of Chinese killed the consul and twenty others, and burned down several churches.

Only after the incident did many expatriates move to the concessions, thus speeding up construction of the new centers for the foreign communities. According to Michie, by 1870, with the completion of

> a piled bund, the smooth road from the Old Customs Building to the Eastern Side of the Astor House Hotel; the long and straight Victoria Road, with its smooth surface and double row of elms; and the several houses of good appearance; the settlement began to assume consistence and visible form.[12]

Within the concessions, "every road was even and broad, well-lit at night; the popular hand lantern used in North China became redundant."[13]

With the booming of trade, industry, and the development of concessions, there was an influx of foreign residents moving to Tianjin. In 1861, there were only 28 of them;[14] in 1866, there were 112 people from eight countries;[15] and by 1879, there were 262 in total.[16] In 1890, the foreign population sharply increased to 612.[17] Before the Japanese established a concession in Tianjin in 1898, it was mainly Westerners who chose to live in the city. The population of Japanese in Tianjin increased from 77 in 1899 to 1,210 in 1901.[18] By 1906, the foreign population in Tianjin had reached 6,341.[19] Tianjin was transforming into an increasingly international metropolis.

The Imported Models of Urban Communities

The concept of "community" in sociology is essential to understanding the major differences between the Western city and the Chinese city. A community can be a geographical space in which people live together, or a network of social relations based on daily interactions between people. Finally, a community can be defined as a collective identity, whereby people have certain psychological attachment to the group that they belong to or where it is located. In sum, according to sociological theory of community, the city is not only a regional geographic concept, but also a concrete community organization with collective identity.

When Tianjin was first founded in 1404, its main function was to protect the capital from the sea and to guard the shipping route through the Grand Canal. Most of the city dwellers were garrison soldiers, salt merchants, or basic vendors. Tianjin, like other Chinese cities, did not have its own municipal government. Instead, the officials controlled Tianjin on behalf of the central government, giving the city no autonomous governing power. Most Chinese city dwellers hailed from rural places and belonged to their familial clan, through which they gained official residence in their village.[20] Their social network was thus based primarily on a family-kinship connection: public activities were organized around the familial unit rather than the local community of residence. Although living and working in Tianjin, they still considered their village of origin their true home and lacked an interest in establishing public buildings, parks, and other infrastructure in the city. Before the establishment of concessions, Tianjin's only public buildings were temples. Excluding the city walls and major streets, there was no urban development planning. Although there were a few spectacular private garden villas built by prominent salt merchants in the suburbs (including the Zha Family's Shuixi garden manor, once visited by Emperor Qianlong, who reigned from 1735 to 1795), the majority of people living in Tianjin were confined to small and dark mud huts.

The foreign community in Tianjin brought with them not only capital and European models of urban planning, but also the concept of creating within the city an autonomous municipal government backed by community organizations. Chinese urban residents were exposed for the first time to these new concepts of urban development. Moreover, the foreigners attempted to recreate their hometowns with familiar and comfortable lifestyles in a strange place far away from home. Yet, Tianjin's nine concessions became more than just residential areas for foreign nationals—they also provided a space for commercial and trading activities. The large number of concessions in Tianjin bred a kind of international competitiveness, effectively transforming the foreign neighborhoods into an international stage on which each nation felt compelled to demonstrate its strength. Initially, foreign consulates were in charge of the systematic land planning and civil construction for their respective international concessions. However, because each concession belonged to a different country, they failed to work co-operatively, leading to nine non-compatible neighborhoods. In this sense, Tianjin was much like Shanghai, which also had multiple international concessions. The younger Dalian and Qingdao, each occupied by a single foreign power, had a more unified city plan than either of the two.[21]

From the perspective of a city as a whole, Tianjin was very chaotic. It contained a walled Chinese city and nine autonomous international concessions. Each concession had its own road system with the main road following the zigzag of the Hai River. Straight and ordered streets, like those found in Beijing and Xi'an, were rare in Tianjin. In addition, road names in different concessions greatly varied; each concession evoked its own national identity by naming streets after its country's famous landmarks and personages. As a result, a single street running through multiple concessions often had a different name within each neighborhood. For example, the main road running through Tianjin was called "rue de France" in the French Concession, "Victoria Road" when it entered the British Concession, and was later "Kaiser Wilhelm Strasse" in the German Concession. Newly arrived visitors to Tianjin generally became quite disoriented.

At the same time, the early concessions had their own logic and order. The supreme ruling body of each concession was an elected board of directors; the executive group of the board of directors was called the "municipal council." In the Japanese case, the concession municipal council was the nominal self-governing organization, but in actuality it had to obey the orders of the Japanese consulate and sometimes even received direct commands from the Japanese Emperor and Foreign Affairs Ministry. Among the concession buildings, there were many public facilities to satisfy the social needs of the entire foreign community. For example, the shared activities held at the municipal councils, consulates, clubs, churches, and public cemeteries led not only to greater social integration between different communities, but also to enable social control and participation within each group. Schools and public libraries were loci of socialization; shops, hotels, markets, and parks facilitated social economics; while hospitals and barracks provided community members with a guarantee for social welfare and safety.

Later foreign concessions took into account plans and preferences of earlier concessions and their expatriate communities; functions were also shared across different concessions. For example, the German Concession stipulated that its land was to be mainly used for residential rather than commercial buildings, as their nationals already used the shops and theaters of the British and French Concessions. German company offices and banks were generally located in the financial and commercial districts of the British Concession.[22] Most foreign-owned factories, warehouses, and piers, were located along the banks of the Hai River. Foreign company offices were principally located in the Taku Road and Victoria Road areas of the British Concession. Banks were built around rue de Chaylard in the French concession and Asahi Road in the Japanese concession. The high-end residential areas tended to be in the newer section of the British, German, and Italian concessions. However, the Japanese nationals' commercial and daily activities were normally contained within their own concession.

In addition, each country's expatriates organized community-wide social activities at their own premises. As the largest and best-established concession in Tianjin, the British Concession—specifically Gordon Hall, the home of the British Municipal Council—acted as a central gathering point for the international community as a whole and was the venue for transnational public activities. Thus, the concessions in Tianjin were both independent and, at the same time, deeply connected.

The large-scale construction of the concessions had a significant impact on the urban planners and leaders of the old Chinese city as they began to reconstruct parts of Chinese Tianjin. They watched as Western-style villas and all the trappings of modern European life were constructed around their city. Over time, they became accustomed to this new style of architecture and living. According to Chen Xulu, the commodities representing Western culture "were not as scary as the canons, but they were more powerful than the canons; they were not like an infectious ideology, but were broadly implanted into everyone's life."[23]

Following the Boxer Rebellion of 1900, Tianjin underwent a period of immense change. The people of Tianjin had an ambivalent attitude about the dismantling of the old city wall, and accepted the substitutive circular road system and public toilets somewhat grudgingly.[24] Later, tramway transportation, street lighting, running water, and telephone system and drainage systems were built in the old Chinese city. Despite the early military nature of this occupation, the local elites started to experience the conveniences of modern life in their own homes.

Learning from the West

There were two driving forces behind Tianjin's movement towards Chinese self-governance during the late years of the Qing dynasty. The first came from pro-Westernization officials, as represented by Yuan Shikai, who actively promoted local self-governance as a foundation for constitutional reform. The second was rooted in the development of urban community and supportive social forces.

Tianjin was the source of China's Westernization movement, beginning in 1861. It was also the seat of the Zhili governors and the leaders of the pro-Westernization faction, Li Hongzhang and Yuan Shikai. The Qing government used Tianjin as a conduit to interact with foreign countries. After the Second Opium War, foreigners established consulates in Beijing, but Li was still responsible for foreign affairs from his base in Tianjin. The consuls had to travel to Tianjin to meet him, thereby limiting their presence in Beijing. Tianjin became the real diplomatic center of China; it was here that the Qing officials, many of whom were influenced by Li's diplomacy, mastered their skills in dealing with foreign officials.

With the Boxer Rebellion in July 1900, the Eight Allied Forces—composed of British, Russian, German, French, American, Japanese, Italian, and Austrian soldiers—attacked and occupied Tianjin. They soon established the Tianjin Provisional Government, which governed the city until August 1902. Although the Provisional Government was composed mostly of high-ranking military officers from each of the occupying forces, it could still be characterized as an independent decision-making body, which managed not only Tianjin's Chinese district, but also all of the foreign concessions. As a result, during this period, any municipal project had to be undertaken as a joint effort of all foreign nations. The Provisional Government held regular meetings, with topics ranging from how to tear down the city wall to buying office equipment. It had to keep in touch with foreign consulates in order to co-ordinate each urban construction project. For example, to connect and improve the individual road systems of each concession in order to facilitate traffic flow, its secretary-general asked each country's consul-general for an official map of each concession.[25] A principal goal was to promote the development of Tianjin's trading economy and to keep the Hai River shipping route open. The Provisional Government called in various people to discuss dredging the river, including the consuls of France, Germany, Japan, and Russia; the French Municipal Council and the British Municipal Council; the chairmen of the Chamber of Commerce; and the maritime customs house commissioner.[26]

The home government of each Allied power managed the concessions through consulate and military stations. Yet, public life within the foreign communities in Tianjin was not limited by national boundaries; they needed to establish their own forms of communication throughout the concessions. After the establishment of the concessions, a Board of Directors was created, which was elected by taxpayers and charged with managing the municipal council. The municipal council was responsible for routine administration, including the supervision of urban construction, ground leveling, roadworks, waterworks, street lighting, drainage, and other public utilities. It opened hospitals and medical and technical schools, and established parks, factories, and a fire brigade. It was also charged with keeping the order through maintaining police squads and voluntary corps in the concessions. Finally, the municipal council was responsible for collecting fees for municipal expenditure, including land, property, excise, and licensing taxes. The concessions could thus be considered fully autonomous in their municipal functions.

As a result of the Boxer Protocol agreed to by officials from the Qing Empire and the Eight-Nation Alliance, the Chinese section of Tianjin was returned to Qing control in 1902. Yuan Shikai, the Governor of Zhili Province, used the foreign Provisional Government as a model for administrative reforms in Tianjin. While Yuan preserved the basic structure of the original government, he altered it significantly to better fit the needs of the Chinese residents. During this period, he created the first modern court system and procuratorial institution, the first modern prison and re-education-through-labor organization, and, finally in 1907, the first modern election ever held in China.[27]

Tianjin's local government adopted the administrative models of the foreign concessions, using the charter of the Board of Directors to help set up its own government. The Tianjin County Council (with elected members) was the ruling body, which elected and supervised the Chinese Board of Directors, the managing organization. Both the Tianjin County Council and the Chinese Board of Directors adopted a collegiate system, and were independent bodies that counterbalanced each other. Voters freely elected the members of the Tianjin County Council and topics of discussion were decided by majority vote of the council members.

The foreign Provisional Government not only taught Tianjin local officials and social elites how to enhance the quality and efficiency of public services but also transferred the concept of self-determination and self-governance to the Chinese sections of Tianjin. It was the first time the democratic process was directly observed by Chinese government officials and the public, who learned how to resolve civic problems through discussions and by using such principles as the subordination of the minority to the majority. This unprecedented political participation was limited, however, to government officials and elites.

Nonetheless, these reforms contributed to Tianjin's urban growth. Foreign capital led to the economic boom and rapid development of industry in Tianjin, while the construction of the concessionary community demonstrated the obvious benefits of urbanization. The twin processes of industrialization and urbanization altered the very nature of social structure, as contemporary intellectuals trained by modern schools came forth, including journalists, editors, doctors, lawyers, teachers, as well as factory workers, merchants, and skilled workers.[28] A new urban cosmopolitan community became a reality in Tianjin; a new class slowly arose from the city's burgeoning modern economy, developing its own tastes and social groups, which challenged the exclusive spatial arrangement of the Chinese City. In part due to the support of the powerful Yuan Shikai, China's first local election occurred in Tianjin instead of Shanghai. Furthermore, the residents of Tianjin demonstrated immense social clout, quickly gaining one of the leading voices in China's modern democratic revolution. From 1905 to 1906, they organized a boycott of American goods to protest the Chinese Exclusion Act in the United States, which restricted

Chinese immigration. They also openly dissented against the restoration of Yuan Shikai in 1915 and the expansion of the French concession to include the area of Lao Xikai in 1916 without the permission of the Chinese authorities. In contrast, although many Chinese social elites lived in Shanghai's foreign concessions, they were not influential members of these autonomously run neighborhoods, and although an emerging urban class in Shanghai also demanded self-governance, it never received the support of Qing officials.

Architectural Eclecticism and Cultural Dialogue

European, American, and Japanese colonizers came to Tianjin in search of great fortune. Those who started successful ventures reinvested their wealth into the community by constructing many buildings in various styles. The development of concessions in Tianjin, Shanghai, and other Chinese cities was accompanied by the emergence of different kinds of contemporary Western architectural styles, ranging from eclecticism to modernism.

However, whether in Tianjin or Shanghai, eclecticism was always the dominant architectural style. Because the concessions enjoyed "autonomous rights" and a comfortable living environment, on top of the sharp increase of foreign nationals, there was also an influx of Chinese to the concessions during the Civil War period in the 1920s. From as early as 1905, there was a change in the general Chinese resentment against the foreigners. A letter written during this time recorded that

> there was fierce competition among the foreigners to see who could exercise most cultural influence on the natives and be closest to them personally in the hope of gaining direct advantages in the near or more distant future. Efforts to avoid emphasizing racial differences were almost embarrassingly assiduous as a part of the desire to stay in the favor of the Chinese.[29]

The number of Chinese at one point even greatly surpassed the foreign population. Those with the means built complexes of large mansions to show off their wealth and power. As Wang Shouzhi argued,

> Eclecticism is in accord with the tastes of the newly-rich bourgeoisie, it combined all their favorite designs in a single architectural decoration. They did not care about the internal logic of these

conceptions, which led to a highly conflicted, though luxurious, style. The actual demonstration of eclecticism in the treaty port cities along the coast was in the emergence of structures using both the Western and Chinese styles.[30]

Not only did the Chinese clients demand new styles when building their houses, but some foreign architects also absorbed the methods of Chinese garden construction in their works. For example, in 1943, Wu Songping, a Tianjin entrepreneur, invited Austrian architect Rolf Geyling to design his magnificent villa. The two men discussed the project for a long time and, after a few alterations, produced a house featuring a Nordic roof, large British-type windows, a southern-European-style arched gate, and a modern glass greenhouse. Geyling surrounded the building with a Chinese garden containing an artificial hill, a moon-gate, and a pond. Such eclectic structures were common to the Tianjin concessions. (see Figures 5.2–5.4)

Figure 5.2

Wu Songping's villa, photographs taken by Rolf Geyling in the mid-1930s (Tianjin Museum of Modern History)

Figure 5.3

Figure 5.4

Eclecticism represented a type of cultural transition, whereby changes in the physical environment of the city reshaped the lives of those who lived there. Among the concession communities, the British were the most powerful, thus it was British etiquette and criteria that were most imitated by non-British nationals in China. When a Prussian delegation visited China in 1861, they found that many German merchants who lived in the treaty ports emulated the British way of socializing and even spoke to other Germans in English.[31] A Russian journalist who lived in China during the Boxer Rebellion period noted that

> In the orient, some Russians wholeheartedly follow British etiquette and conduct. They are so thoroughly Anglicized that (like a real British gentleman) they speak English, read *The Times*, play tennis, wear a pith helmet, white shoes and black socks, drink whisky daily and condemn the Chinese. In short, all behaviors in line with the mission of civilized people in the East.[32]

At the early stages of interaction between the foreign nationals and local Chinese, their cultural dialogue was not evident. Take, for example, the case of language study, one of the most potent tools of cultural transmission. In order to establish a foothold when they first arrived in Tianjin, foreign nationals—especially employees serving at Qing customs houses—had to study the local language. It was essential to their career development. In 1864, Sir Robert Hart, the Inspector General of the Imperial Customs Service in Peking (1863–1908), ordered that each customs house required its foreign employees to study Chinese. Those who were unable to gain proficiency in the Chinese language could not be promoted to commissioner.[33] Gustav Detring, the chairman of the board of directors at Tianjin's British Municipal Council for thirteen years (for two non-consecutive periods between 1878 and 1893), had a high appreciation for Chinese culture and could recognize more than ten thousand Chinese characters.[34] Through language study, this ambitious customs house commissioner gained the appreciation of the Qing senior official Li Hongzhang and became the Governor's most trusted consultant. He was often called to the Governor's office for conversations that lasted the entire night.[35] Before the Boxer Rebellion in 1900, it was not common for foreigners to bring women and children to settle in Tianjin. With the increasing arrival of foreign women, however, many learned to speak Chinese through their daily interactions with their servants. Many foreign children who grew up in China were raised by amahs, and spoke Chinese as a first language. Only later in school were they forced to speak their national language.[36] Yet, with the increase of the foreign population and development of a modern educational system, all of this changed. Many schools for Chinese and foreign students were established in the concessions and in the old Chinese city. Local people also opened schools to teach Western subjects, with foreign language as a major focus. For example, at China's first public university, Beiyang University, established in Tianjin in 1895, teachers were mainly from America and Europe. Excluding Chinese literature, most of their subjects were taught in English and the textbooks were imported from Europe. Indicative of the high standards of schooling, some undergraduate students were able to enter prestigious graduate schools in America.[37] The Chinese students who mastered Western languages and returned to China after studying abroad became the social elite of Tianjin. Like many Western missionaries, these new cosmopolitan students were a major source of cultural transmission in China, one that occurred almost unconsciously during times of peace.

In semi-colonial China, this transition was not only the result of the industrialization and urbanization of Western colonizers, but also the outcome of military invasion. This point is evident when looking at the foreign barracks of Tianjin. After the Boxer Rebellion, the eight Allied powers established barracks in the concessions in accordance with the Boxer Protocol. Foreign soldiers with different nationalities could often be seen in Tianjin. A visiting soldier on temporary assignment with The United States 15th Infantry Regiment in Tianjin declared, "In one block one may see an Englishman, a Frenchman, and an Italian soldier, a dozen Japanese soldiers, a Jewish drummer, an American expatriate, and a Russian … of the lower class and a Capuchin Monk."[38] The foreign barracks in Tianjin hosted the biggest number of foreign soldiers in China, excluding Austria, as all other countries located the headquarters for their China troops in Tianjin.

Conclusion

The high tide of European imperialism and the growth of Tianjin are inter-related. European military occupation was accompanied by the creation of a modern city, which was built with Western capital and Chinese labor. Foreign concessions became a new model of urban community, aspects of which were later appreciated by the Chinese political elite. Tianjin and Shanghai both emerged as international metropolitan cities, their strategic locations near the sea transforming them into booming trade ports. Yet, Tianjin played a unique role as a gateway to the Qing capital in Beijing, at the same time as it protected both the capital and sea route shipping. In sharp contrast to Shanghai where commerce dominated, it fared prominently in the political, military, and diplomatic history of China. Tianjin was different from Shanghai in many other ways: in the use of public space, types of architecture, community construction, community organization, and cultural dialogue. Moreover, both cities were linked by political, diplomatic, financial, trading, and shipping networks, and their foreign communities did not live in isolation from each other. Tianjin's urban history thus deserves as much attention as that of Shanghai.

China did not take the traditional path to modernization; theoretically, the complementary processes of urbanization and industrialization provide the material basis of modernization, which would in turn foster political changes. In modern China, however, urbanization was not triggered by the process of industrialization, but by powerful government officials who sought to borrow from the foreign concessions in their midst. This unorthodox pattern of urbanization is evident in both Tianjin and Shanghai. The development of these two modern Chinese coastal cities is indeed the consequence of cultural changes and interactions with foreign populations. Both provided a venue for the interactions between the new and old, the traditional and the modern, and ultimately challenged the collective identity of the Chinese people.

Never

Notes

1. Some Chinese scholars have summarized the development of research on Chinese urban history. For example, Xiong Yuezhi, "Zhongguo chengshi shi yanjiu zongshu , 1986–2006" [Summary of the Chinese Urban History Studies, 1986–2006], in *Lishi xue* [Historical Studies], no. 6 (2008); Xiong Yuezhi, *Haiwai Shanghai xue* [Shanghai Studies Abroad] (Shanghai: Shangha Guji Chubanshe, 2004); He Yimin, "Zhongguo jindai chengshi shi yanjiu de jinzhan, cunzai wenti yu zhanwang" [The Development, Problems and Prospects of the Urban History Study of Modern China in the 21st Century], in *Zhonghua wenhua luntan* [China's cultural forum], no. 4 (2004); Lu Hanchao, "Meiguo de Zhongguo chengshi shi yanjiu shuping" [Review of American Scholarship on Chinese Urban History], in *Qinghua Daxue Xuebao* [Qinghua University Journal] Series on Philosophy, Society and Science, no. 1 (2008). Tianjin-based journal *The Study of Urban History* has also published many contemporary articles on both international and Chinese urban history.
2. O. D. Rasmussen, *Tientsin: An Illustrated Outline History* (Tianjin: The Tientsin Press, 1925), 9.
3. Ibid., 37.
4. Constantin von Hanneken, *Briefe aus China: 1879–1886; Als deutscher Offizier im Reich der Mitte* (Köln/Weimar/Wien: Böhlau, 1998), 38–40.
5. Sone Shōun, *Kitashina kikō*, trans. Fan Jianming (Beijing: Zhonghua Shuju, 2007), 6.
6. William A. P. Martin, *A Cycle of Cathay* (New York: Fleming H. Revell Company, 1896), 189.
7. Sone Shōun, 6.
8. Rasmussen, *Tientsin*, 18.
9. There was no construction in the American Concession after it was established in 1860. Later on, it was merged into the British Concession.
10. Rasmussen, *Tientsin*, 38, note 1.
11. Excerpt from Francis Clifford Jones, *Shanghai and Tianjin: With Special Reference to Foreign Interests*, trans. Yifan Xu, in *Tianjin lishi ziliao*, no. 3 (1964): 41.
12. *The Chinese Times*, November 3, 1888.
13. "1870 dao 1872 nian Tianjin maoyi baogao," in vol. 1 of *Jin haiguan nianbao dang'an huibian (1865–1911)*, eds. Institute of History of Tianjin Academy of Social Science and Tianjin Archives (Tianjin: Tianjin dang'an guan, 1993) (hereinafter referred to as *JHNDH*), 144.
14. Rasmussen, *Tientsin*, 39–40.
15. "1866 nian Tianjin maoyi baogao," in vol. 1 of *JHNDH*, 39.
16. "1877 dao 1879 nian Tianjin maoyi baogao," in vol. 1 of *JHNDH*, 191.

17. "Guangxu shiliu nian (1890) Tianjin kou huayang maoyi qingxing lunlue," in vol. 2 of *JHNDH*, 19.

18. "Guangxu er'shi qi nian (1901) Tianjin kou huayang maoyi qingxing lunlue," in vol. 2 of *JHNDH*, 105.

19. Chūgoku Chūdongun Shireibu, *Er shi shiji chu de Tianjinde gaikuo*, trans. Zhentong Hou (Tianjin: Tianjin Committee of Local Chronicles Compilation, 1986), 18.

20. Ibid., 584.

21. Jianhong Dong, *Zhongguo chengshi jianzhu shi* (Beijing: China Building Industry Press, 2004), 278.

22. Torsten Warner, *Deutsche Architektur in China: Architekturtransfer* (Berlin: Ernst & Sohn, 1994), 58–59.

23. Xulu Chen, *Jindai Zhongguo de xinchendaixie* (Shanghai: Shanghai People's Publishing House, 1992), 218.

24. Regarding the modernization process of Tianjin's hygiene system, see Ruth Rogaski, *Hygienic Modernity: Meanings of Health and Disease in Treaty-Port China* (Berkley: University of California Press, 2004).

25. *Baguo Lianjun shilu: Tianjin lishi zhengzhi huiyi jiyao* (Tianjin: Tianjin Academy of Social Science Press, 2004), 24.

26. Ibid., 182.

27. Shuzu Wang and Ying Hang, *Jindai Zhongguo kan Tianjin: bai xiang Zhongguo di yi* (Tianjin: Tianjin People's Publishing House, 2007), 35–46.

28. Chen, *Jindai Zhongguo de xinchendaixie*, 258–67.

29. Warner, *Deutsche Architektur in China*, 60.

30. Shouzhi Wang, *Shijie xiandai jianzhu shi* (Beijing: China Building Industry Press, 1999), 9.

31. Helmuth Stoecker, *Deutschland und China im 19 Jahrhundert*, trans. Song Qiao (Beijing: SDX Joint Publishing Press Company, 1963), 47–48.

32. Dmitry Yanchevetsky, *Russkie Shturmuyut Pekin*, trans. Chongxin Xu (Fuzhou: Fujian People's Publishing House, 1983), 39.

33. "1864 nian 6 yue 21 ri haiguan zong shuiwu si shu di 8 hao tongling," in *Jiu Zhongguo haiguan zongshuiwusishu tongling xuanbian*, ed. Huang Shengqiang (Beijing: China Customs Press, 2003), 31.

34. Based on Ying Hang's interview with Carl Lange, the descendant of Gustav Detring, in Germany, September 12, 2000.

35. Paul King, *In the Chinese Customs Service: A Personal Record of Forty-Seven Years* (New York: reprint, 1980. First published in 1924), 88.

36. *Jiu Zhongguo haiguan zongshuiwusi shu tongling xuanbian*, 33–34.

37. Beiyang Daxue, Tianjin Daxue jiao shi bianji shi, eds., *Beiyang daxue, Tianjin daxue jiao shi ziliao xuanbian (1)* (Tianjin: Tianjin University Press, 1991), 3–15.

38. Alfred E. Cornebise, *The United States 15th Infantry Regiment in China, 1912–1938* (Jefferson, N.C.: McFarland & Co., 2004), 15.

6
Mapping Colonial Space

The Planning and Building of Qingdao by German Colonial Authorities, 1897–1914

Klaus Mühlhahn

Mathias Erzberger (1875–1921), a member of the German Reichstag representing the Catholic Centre Party, delivered a speech in the budget talks in the German Reichstag in 1908, in which he sharply criticized the expenditure of a total of 110 million Reichsmark for the German leasehold in Kiaochow China in 1897.[1] He said, "I believe that if that 110 million had been spent in Germany, one could make the finest garden in the world even out of the Mark of Brandenburg."[2] At that time he could not know that the final bill for developing Kiaochow would run much higher, in fact almost double the amount he had discussed in 1908. Six years later, when Kiaochow was surrendered to the Japanese Imperial Army in 1914, the German Reich had spent at least 200 million Reichsmark in Kiaochow, more than in any other German colony. The actual expenses for the seventeen years of German rule over Kiaochow were probably even higher, although Kiaochow was not only many times smaller than the African colonies, and the African colonies existed much longer, that is, since the 1880s. Kiaochow was distinct in other respects too. The most expensive but short-lived German colony was also the only one not controlled by the regular colonial administration, but was instead independently run by the German imperial navy (*Reichsmarine*). It was the only German colony that had a colonial college (*Hochschule*). Suffice to say here, that Kiaochow testifies to the different kinds of German colonialism and, more generally, the variety of imperial or colonial forms in the nineteenth and twentieth centuries.[3]

Unique localized forms were the rule rather than the exception in the history of colonialism and imperialism. Ann Stoler and Carole MacGranahan argued that "imperial formations neither imagined uniform sorts of rule nor subscribed to uniform vocabularies."[4]

Differentiation, distinct forms, and blurred categories resulted from efforts of active realignment and attempts of continuous reformation and adaptation. Colonial "governmentality" was a complex and constantly evolving assemblage of institutions, procedures, analyses, and reflections aiming at erecting dynamic differences between the colonizers and the colonized, and maintaining the colonial state's control over a dependent society. Contemporaneous sources indeed contain an abundance of references to the importance of technologies such as education, medicine, and science in this endeavor. A later German colonial minister in Berlin, Bernhard Dernburg, called science and education "the most important auxiliary field of learning (*Hilfswissenschaft*) for the colonizer,"[5] surpassing military training and technology.

The case of Kiaochow is well suited to demonstrate that nineteenth-century colonialism thus was a multifarious, diverse, and variable enterprise. Colonial states were not steady states, but "states of becoming,"[6] where constant formation and flexible adaptation was based on ongoing transfers of ideas, practices, and technologies between the metropolitan regions and their far-flung colonies across fixed boundaries and political forms. Colonies were terrains where projects of power and concepts of superiority were not only imposed, but also engaged and contested by the colonized. Colonialism was equally challenged at home by anti-colonial parties and movements.[7] In fact, political activism within, about, and against colonial rule has also led to reinterpretations and modification of the meanings of basic colonial concepts such as race, difference, and hierarchy, both in the colonies and in the metropolitan areas.[8] Circuits of ideas and rhetoric that either upheld or subverted colonial rule connected European societies to the colonies. Alan Lester points to the existence of a metropolitan-colonial network of linked sites across which "colonial discourses were made and remade."[9] The effects of imperial rule were thus felt in the European societies as well as in the colonies themselves, albeit to varying degrees and in divergent ways. Global modernity would be unthinkable without the imprint of colonialism; colonialism in various forms has become an integral element and international experience.[10]

The paper will explore the spatial order of the German colonial city of Qingdao the principal town in Kiaochow. In a survey ranging from street planning to legal regulations, sanitation to prostitution, the paper discusses the dual spatial and social order of the colonial project. In this new and somewhat artificial city, a political rationality was at work, predicated on a new spatial order, which enabled the possibility of an enclosed, rational, organized colonial modernity. The project, however, was increasingly challenged by forms of anti-imperialist activism among the indigenous Chinese population. Those forces were eventually successful in permeating the spatial and social boundaries erected by colonial authorities and thus started to reclaim the city center. This was also reflected in the appearance of Chinese architectural elements in urban Qingdao. Starting from about 1908 onwards, the rigid, predominantly military form of colonial rule gave way to a more flexible one allowing more contacts and exchanges with local traders and elites.

Semi-Colonialism at the China Coast

Since the 1860s the German Reich was seeking to obtain a naval base on the China coast. The base was envisioned to serve as a coaling station for German warships and as an entry point for German businesses to expand into inland China. During the late nineteenth century a number of European nations such as Great Britain (Hong Kong, Singapore), Russia (Port Arthur, Dalian), or France (Indochina) had managed to establish colonial outposts on the China coast and in the greater East Asian region. These bases speak of the variants of nineteenth-century colonialism. In East Asia, port colonies or colonial bases were perhaps the most prevalent form of imperial rule. European powers soon realized that the conditions for maintaining control in this part of the world were markedly different from Africa or the Americas. Here, most of the regions were densely populated and for centuries governed by indigenous, non-European empires that promoted their own civilizing missions, social and racial hierarchies, and diverse forms of rule. European adventurers, merchants, or officers encountered sophisticated forms of indigenous governance, highly developed economies, and complex societies that were difficult to penetrate and to control. Any territorial settlement by Europeans and long-term direct rule over large regions were quickly deemed unattainable and also undesirable. European powers also confronted determined and successful efforts of defending East Asian empires that in many cases succeeded

in retaining a core of sovereignty and holding foreign powers at bay—
despite some signs of weakness and internal crisis that empires in East
Asia may have shown in the nineteenth century.

But small and secure colonial possessions were still useful and
perhaps indispensable to European powers as logistical bases for the
operation of mercantile fleets and military warships. In East Asia,
European powers mainly aimed at obtaining harbor colonies or
colonial bases along the seacoast and the major rivers.[11] These were
usually located in small territories that were geographically suited
for maritime ship traffic; ideally they had a meager local population,
which could serve as a workforce, and were close to resources in the
hinterland and important domestic and international trade routes.
Foreign powers sought to establish so-called urban settlements or
urban colonies in order to have a permanent presence in major Chinese
cities and in treaty ports. These were clearly defined residential areas
under foreign administration that were leased to an overseas government for a restricted time.[12] Foreign powers operated approximately
twenty settlements in China, the best-known example being the international settlement in Shanghai. The classical colony, that is the unlimited and unconditional cession of a relatively large territory, was rather
an exception.[13]

Settlements, leaseholds, and colonial bases were means, rather than
ends, towards creating larger political, economic, and cultural dominions. Western imperial powers made use of so-called spheres of interest
or spheres of influence that gave them clearly defined economic,
cultural, and often also military privileges in a certain region. Being
under the influence of a foreign state meant that the Chinese government typically retained full sovereignty over Chinese subjects, but
otherwise had obliged itself to lend preferential treatment to a foreign
government and its nationals. In treaties with the Chinese government, European powers forced it to guarantee that their own businesses would be favored in providing provincial governments with
capital, receiving concessions for the construction of railway links,
or for setting up educational projects. In the late nineteenth century,
China was, as nationalist historians pointed out later, "carved up like a
melon" and divided into several spheres of influence. By the turn of the
century, a unique imperial formation had emerged on the China coast.

Colonial ports under foreign control along the coast served as bases for the economic, cultural, and military penetration of a large region, which remained outside of direct colonial control.

Western historians of colonialism have rarely discussed the historical specifics of colonial bases or harbor colonies in China and beyond.[14] But Chinese scholars have argued as early as in the 1920s and 1930s that the existence of particular colonial forms was indicative of a special manifestation of colonial rule they called semi-colonialism.[15] For them, semi-colonialism described a transitional state in which various forms of hegemony (political, economical, and cultural) by a foreign power coexisted with remnants of formal political sovereignty of the dominated country. Chinese theorists stressed the unevenness or imbalance that was produced by such conditions: global colonialist and capitalist practices were said to collide with indigenous local practices, creating a transitory social formation that was caught between different conflicting forces in the global, national, and local realm. But Chinese thinkers also stressed that the outcome of the transition was open and could lead to either independence or full colonization.[16] Rather than being a mere step to full colonization (as Lenin would have described it), the term "semi-colonization" in China was meant to refer to possibilities of resistance and thus to mobilize the intelligentsia in defense of the nation.

The multitude of colonial formations in China indicates the degree to which colonialism was both flexible and opaque; semi-colonialism was simultaneously diffuse and tangible. It oscillated between secretive, visible, and ambiguous structures of control and sovereignty, and underlined what Stoler concluded about imperial formations in general: they were "supremely mobile polities of dislocation, dependent … on shifting categories and moving parts whose designated borders at any one time were not necessarily the force fields in which they operated."[17]

The German Colonial System in Kiaochow

The murder of two German missionaries in the prefecture of Caozhou, west Shandong, in November 1897 gave Germany the long awaited excuse for the military occupation of Kiaochow. In March 1898 a treaty with China was signed that gave Germany a ninety-nine-year lease of the territory. German interests in China were by no means limited to the small territory directly ruled by German colonial authorities. With this treaty, Germany also secured rights in Shandong province to build railways, start mining operations in a corridor along the railway lines and deploy troops.[18] Shandong province thus became Germany's primary "sphere of influence" (*Einflußsphäre*) in China. The construction of the Qingdao-Jinan railway and the opening of coalmines along this railway were considered to only be the beginning of greater German economic, cultural, and political domination of the province. The development of Shandong as a market for German products and ideas was also planned.

Kiaochow was formally a leasehold, but German authorities treated it as nothing less than a colony. Since one of the main goals of the occupation was to give the navy a repair and coal station on the Chinese coast, it was relatively undisputed that the colony in China should be governed by the navy; Kiaochow became the only German colony ever run by a branch of the military. Normally then, Kiaochow was under the responsibility of the commander-in-chief of the German navy. In a very unusual step in mid-January 1898, Wilhelm II placed Kiaochow under the jurisdiction of the naval ministry (*Reichsmarineamt*)—which was thought to be a purely political office that was supposed to represent the navy's interests and financial claims in the Reichstag.[19] During the whole time of Qingdao's existence as a German colony, the influential secretary of state of the naval ministry, Admiral Alfred von Tirpitz, made sure that no other government agency would get authority over Kiaochow, and maintained a leading role in all major policy decisions concerning Kiaochow.

In a note from January 1898, Tirpitz emphasized the importance of Kiaochow for the navy. He wrote, "If the navy is on the top of the colonial movement, the colonial successes as well as the results will benefit the navy."[20] He hoped that the possession of a well-managed colony would mobilize popular support for the navy and thus also help to realize his far-reaching ambitious naval plans. In the whole duration of Kiaochow's occupation, the political situation in Germany was as important to him as diplomatic or colonial strategies. Tirpitz's political calculations were right. In March 1898, a German newspaper commented, "The events in Kiaochow and the new hopes for commerce and the missions increased the willingness of German Naval Cabinet to make sacrifices for the navy."[21] One month later, the Reichstag approved the so-called Tirpitz Plan, which envisioned the building of a large technologically advanced German naval force. Eventually, this decision triggered an arms race with the leading sea power Great Britain, which was one of the most important long-term factors leading to the outbreak of the First World War.

If Tirpitz's overall naval plans loomed very large in his China policy, he also pursued broader goals. In 1896, during a year in China as commander of the German Squadron in East Asia, he became convinced that it was time to make a move if Germany wanted to be an actor on the global stage. In private correspondence with his family he wrote,

> The accumulation of giant nations like Pan America, Greater Britain, the Slavic race or the Mongolian race under the leadership of Japan will destroy or almost extinguish Germany ... in the course of the next century, if Germany does not become a great power outside the borders of the European continent. The imperative basis for that ... is a fleet.[22]

Like many other contemporaries, especially in the military, Tirpitz had a Darwinistic understanding of international relations in the modern age, seeing it as a fight for survival between nations. He was clearly convinced that colonial bases in combination with a worldwide operating and powerful fleet formed the condition *sine qua non* for the global projection of power. This alone could guarantee the survival of the German "race" in the long run. Not economic or diplomatic, but above all, military considerations were at the very center of Tirpitz's colonial ambitions for China.

The German colony in China was of highest priority for Tirpitz. From his one-year stint in China, he had a clear understanding of the unique semi-colonial formations there. He viewed these not as limitations or concessions to Chinese sovereignty but rather as innovations for a new, reformed, and advanced form of imperial expansion. It allowed the metropolitan authorities to avoid the unnecessary costs associated with the maintenance of large regional dependencies, such as territorial defense, upholding security over a huge indigenous population, dealing with potential rebellions and upheavals, and expenses created by large administrations and infrastructure. By limiting itself to a small territory, colonial rule could be intensified, and become more efficient and more pervasive. The hinterland remained outside of direct colonial control, but was secured and accessible to colonial agents for their economic, political, and cultural projects of domination.

From these considerations, Tirpitz was eager to forestall any possible disruption by local colonizers or domestic political groups. His overpowering role greatly limited the powers of the governors of Kiaochow.[23] The governor, who had to come from the ranks of the navy, had to issue a monthly report about important developments within the colony. Every ordinance issued by the governor had to be countersigned by Tirpitz.[24] When governors failed to carry out the policies expected by Tirpitz, they were dismissed. This happened to Governor Carl Rosendahl in 1898, because Tirpitz felt that Rosendahl had neglected the colony's economic development.[25] It also happened to Governor Oskar Truppel in 1910, when he failed to support the establishment of the German-Chinese College, which was one of Tirpitz's pet projects.[26] By declaring Kiaochow an imperial "protector-ate" (*Kaiserliches Schutzgebiet*) in April 1898, German parliament was barred from legislation for Kiaochow. Unlike the British crown colony, Hong Kong, Kiaochow was under tight supervision by the authori-ties of the motherland, with little room left for self-governance or self-administration.[27]

The colonial system that emerged in Qingdao consistently empha-sized the importance of the metropolitan state in supervising and steering the development of its territory. In building up the economy, Tirpitz and the various governors favored a corporate system. Like Hong Kong, Kiaochow was set up as a free port; duties were only charged for goods that passed through it and entered Chinese territory or were exported abroad. Private firms and enterprises were welcome to open local branches or factories, but had to apply for various conces-sions before being allowed to go into business. There were a number of guidelines and detailed regulations for companies operating in Qingdao. In addition, the government actively sought to persuade large German corporations to become investors in Kiaochow. Since Krupp and Siemens, two of the biggest German corporations, were unwilling to make large investments, because of dim prospects for profits, the colonial authorities ended up running most of the key industries:[28] the naval shipyard, harbor operations, and power generation. Such state initiatives often operated to the detriment of small businesses owned by local German entrepreneurs, which were eventually forced to go out of business.

The role of the state was particularly prevalent in setting up the two key industries that were, time and again, described as the most important economic motive for the occupation of Kiaochow: railways and coal mines. To establish these industries, the government in Berlin and colonial authorities in Kiaochow formed two major syndicates that comprised of large banks, heavy industries, shipping companies, and trading houses. These syndicates raised capital for two companies that were established in 1899: the Shandong Railway Company—charged with building the railway from Qingdao to Jinan, the provincial capital of Shandong—and the Shandong Mining Company, to exploit the mineral resources along the railway. Both companies had to apply for government concessions and were also obliged to use German supplies, technologies, and standards, as well as to co-ordinate their pricing with the colonial authorities and yield part of their profits to the German government.[29] This economic conception can best be described as bureaucratic capitalism, in which the state maintains a decisive regulatory role[30] in mobilizing, organizing and protecting capitalist interests. In this case, it was not so much capitalist interests that drove colonialism as much as the interests of the colonial state that nurtured capitalism.

The colonial system in Qingdao was unique in many ways. The military played an exceedingly important role in Kiaochow, not only because the navy was in charge of the colony and military personnel made up the vast majority of the German population. More significant was the fact that the military apparently served as a model for the entire social organization of the colony. Stress was put on asserting control from top to bottom, improving general cleanliness and public health, upholding an efficient and friction-free social order, and erecting spatial and social hierarchies.

Ordering Space and Society in Qingdao

Constructing and upholding difference between the colonizers and the colonized has long been identified as an important tenet of colonial rule. Colonialism was contingent on discourses that create otherness and identify various differences between Europeans and Chinese. Those differences were turned into a political, legal, and social hierarchy between colonizers and the colonized. Colonial rule therefore implied inequitable treatment, hierarchical relations, and unequal governance. Efforts by authorities in Qingdao to enforce and sustain differences between Europeans and Chinese populations were multifold and complex, entailing scientific epistemologies, spatial segregation, and the development of a dual legal system.

In order to make room for the new colonial city, the authorities started to buy land in February 1898. Chinese landowners received monetary compensation, although many considered it too low and protested that the German authorities unilaterally set the prices. After Germany acquired the land, the local population of approximately 4,500 people was ordered to leave and six villages in the area were razed.[31] The authorities developed specific building regulations.[32] According to them, the new colonial city Qingdao was to have various zones or sectors, whereby each zone would have a different function and be occupied by different social groups.[33] Within the urban area there were three zones: a European residential and commercial area (*Europäisches Wohn-und Geschäftsviertel*), a residential zone with single-family homes (*Villenviertel*), and the Chinese city (*Chinesenstadt*)—Dabaodao. The *Chinesenstadt* had the highest building density (75 percent) and the most urbanized character, whereas in the *Villenviertel* and the *Europäerstadt* (*European town*), more space was set aside for streets, walkways, parks, and public space. Chinese workers had to settle in two special worker towns (*Arbeitersiedlungen*)—Taidongzhen and Taixizhen—located outside of Qingdao. (Plate 14)

The first big projects were to improve the city's infrastructure. The harbor and streets were built, and a sewage system and water pipes laid. This phase was followed by the construction of public buildings, including the hospital (*Gouvernementslazarett*, completed in 1904), public school (*Gouvernementsschule*), administrative offices (*Gouvernementsdienstgebäude*, completed in 1906), governor's mansion (*Gouverneurswohnhaus*, built in 1905–07), as well as police station (*Polizeistation*), prison (*Gefängnis*), court house (*Gerichtsgebäude*), and the Sino-German College, the last big public construction project in Qingdao.[34]

The public buildings were designed and built by German architects and construction companies, and most building materials were imported from Germany. The objective was to develop a specific German colonial architecture. Popular architectural forms and structures from Germany were modified to fit the local climate. Sanitation, pest control and air circulation were main concerns for the architects. Efforts were made to use the most advanced technologies and materials.[35] A specific Qingdao architectural style emerged, which was heavily dominated by glass porches and balconies.

For office and administrative buildings, the architects liked to use rough granite or bricks for columns, bow windows, and walls. It gave some of the buildings a fortress-like look, which was softened a little by porches and open corridors. In contrast, classicist elements found in other treaty ports such as Hong Kong or Shanghai played almost no role in Qingdao. In the early years, the administration faced few financial constraints: the amount spent on most public buildings was several times higher than on comparable projects in Germany. For the administration, it was a matter of prestige to build public buildings that were supposed to represent the prowess and technical capability of the German Reich.

From the very beginning, the colonial administration also attempted to segregate colonial space in Qingdao. One of the most important goals was to avoid any uncontrolled mingling of different races or social groups (such as soldiers and civilians). The European district was home to the colonial administration, European businesses, and the residences of German and European settlers. It was made up of European-style buildings and villas on the south shore of the bay.[36] The streets were wide and lined with trees and other plants. Many of the buildings were luxurious and lavishly appointed. A total of 2,069 Europeans, among them 1,855 Germans, lived here in 1913.[37] The area where well-to-do Chinese lived was called Dabaodao, adjacent to the European town. The streets were smaller and the houses less luxurious. After the 1911 Chinese revolution that brought down the Qing dynasty, segregation policies were relaxed and some German businesspeople settled down here as well. Workers and poorer Chinese resided in the new towns of Taidongzhen and Taixizhen that were intended for Chinese residents exclusively. Regulations for Dabaodao, Taixizhen, and Taidongzhen allowed for higher building density; the plans in these areas followed a checkerboard pattern with all constructions having the same height and width. In 1913, 53,312 Chinese lived in these districts. There was also the harbor district consisting of functional and industrial buildings as well as dormitories for workers and apprentices.

The colonial society in Qingdao, which emerged under the circumstances described above, was distinct. Unlike German colonies in Africa, Kiaochow was never considered to be a colony for German settlement, but rather, served primarily as a colonial outpost for the navy. Whoever came from Germany and wanted to settle in the colony had to apply to the governor of Kiaochow first,[38] and only those with special skills and experiences in trade, engineering, or construction were allowed to move to Qingdao. The German community within the colony, therefore, consisted mainly of soldiers, merchants, professionals, and specialists who were charged with specific tasks; there were few families or women. The Chinese population was mostly male too.[39] Merchants and workers lived only temporally in Qingdao. As a result, prostitution was rampant throughout the whole period of German rule.[40] Within a short time, a large Chinese pleasure quarter came into being. In general, the social universe of the colony seemed artificial. This was due to the fact that the colony was not organic, but created by foreign intervention. There were, of course, also contact and interaction between Chinese workers and German businessmen, students, and teachers, as well as officials on both sides, but all these interactions unfolded within a framework of difference and asymmetry.

The civilian administration of Kiaochow was organized into three separate structures.[41] The governor's office (called *"Gouvernement"* in German) was responsible for the general administration of the colony, excluding affairs that involved the Chinese population, which was organized separately. In Qingdao (Dabaodao, Taidongzhen, and Taixizhen), the administration of the Chinese population was carried out by a district office (*Bezirksamt Tsingtau*), while the district office in Licun (*Bezirksamt Litsun*) was in charge of Chinese living in the rural areas outside of Qingdao. Both offices were headed by a commissioner who was appointed by the governor. While in rural areas, the district commissioner tried to avoid any changes in jurisdiction and administration, therefore often co-operating with traditional community leaders, the Qingdao district office took active command and issued a whole set of new regulations for the urban Chinese population. The relationship between the colonial government and the Chinese subjects in Qingdao was specified in the "Ordinance for Chinese Living in the Urban Area" (*Verordnung betreffend Chinesenordnung für das Stadtgebiet,* often called "*Chinesenordnung*")[42] created on June 14, 1900. Part B of the ordinance, entitled "Maintenance of Public Order and Security," set forth that Chinese living in Qingdao had to register with the Commissioner for Chinese Affairs (*Chinesenkommissar*).[43] §5 ordered that after 9 p.m. every Chinese had to carry a lantern while walking on the street. §6 stated that all public proclamations written in Chinese had to have official approval by the colonial administration. §7 forbade any gathering without approval from the administration. The most important instruction, however, is found in part C: "General Regulations for the Maintenance of Public Health," of which §10 forbade any Chinese to settle in the European section of Qingdao, supposedly for sanitary reasons.

The specific administrative regulations for Chinese, the building regulations, as well as the land system (with the monopolization of land by the colonial administration) together produced one of the essential features of society in Kiaochow: the division of colonial space. The separation of Chinese and Europeans into segregated areas was justified as a "sanitary measure." In German medical publications from 1911 to 1913, Chinese were described as "unclean" and "infectious" because of their "promiscuous" and "unhealthy" way of living.[44]

Fundamentally based on the perceived differences between Chinese and Europeans, the legal system reflected the same strict dualism.[45] The "Governor's Order on the Legal Affairs of the Chinese" from April 15, 1899 created distinct civil and penal laws for Chinese and for Europeans.[46] §17 (in the part of the civil code) ruled that local common law should be applied to "natives" in the rural district. The district commissioners therefore had to explore Chinese common law and codify it for use by the German administration. Lesser litigation cases were also to be settled in the traditional way by the village heads. Only if no solution were found through traditional Chinese proceedings would the case be brought to the district commissioner who was then authorized to make a final decision. The part on penal law (§5) ruled that the Qing code had to be applied for the Chinese population.

For that reason, the district commissioners, who were Sinologists but had no judicial training, made various translations of the Qing code;[47] they dealt with most of the cases involving the Chinese. The judges at the court of Kiaochow only dealt with European and mixed European-Chinese cases, as well as appeals against the sentences of the district commissioners. In 1908 a full appeals court was established, which handled all appeal cases thereafter.

The directives about penal law were vague and ambiguous. For example, in §5 it was stated that all actions "which constitute an offense" are punishable—but there was neither a definition nor an enumeration of what would be considered an offense. This paragraph is an obvious violation of an essential principle of European law of *nulla poena sine lege* (no punishment without law). One has also to note that there is no enumeration of what kind of offense would result in what form of punishment. In practice, this meant that even for a minor offense, one could have severe penalties. Lashing was the most frequent form of punishment for the Chinese, but not for Europeans. For minor offenses like spitting or urinating on the street, a policeman could impose a punishment of ten strokes on the spot without a trial. Moreover, the district commissioner was not required to record minutes of proceedings or explain his legal reasoning; he only recorded the sentences in a verdict book.[48]

The High Judge of Kiaochow was Georg Crusen.[49] He wrote several essays on the legal system in Kiaochow, explicating and justifying it. One of the important questions was, who, in a legal sense, should be considered to be natives in Kiaochow. Since the colonial legal system was based on the distinction between natives and Europeans, this was a very practical problem. In a speech at the Colonial Institute in Hamburg in 1912, Crusen defined natives as "Chinese in an ethno-logical-cultural sense."[50] He went on to explain that the reason for not applying German law to the natives rests with the cultural difference: "It had to be avoided that German law was applied to people who lack the basis for such an appliance." Crusen stressed the role of culture, which, in his view was closely related to law. He noted that law is the outcome of the cultural standards and values of a people and reflects their beliefs and ethics. Only after a modernization of Chinese culture could the "natives" qualify to be legally treated like Europeans. Crusen therefore compared Chinese law with medieval European law, yet by stressing culture, he did not exclude the possibility of development for China. The colonial power bestowed upon itself the mission to help China slowly modernize her culture and law. Parallel to the development of the colony and the improvement of its education, modern law, it was seen, needed to be incrementally introduced to the Chinese population.[51] Yet, colonial society in Qingdao and Kiaochow was fundamentally dependent on postponements and deferrals; it delayed granting rights and equality to the Chinese, promising them for the future. The emerging legal and social order created scales of differentiation, gradations of rights, and declarations of emergency in times of crises and rebellion.

Qingdao as a Colonial Contact Zone

Colonies were not simply constructs of power projected unilaterally on a local population, but also became "zones of contact" between the colonizers and the colonized. Although colonies were sites of asymmetrical relations, they hosted widely divergent local arrangements whereby different strategies were promoted by various social groups. Tensions and conflicts emerged not only between the colonizers and colonized, but also within the German and Chinese communities.

For Chinese authorities, the violent conflicts between the local population and the foreigners represented a crucial factor for the rapid spread of social instability during the Boxer movement. After 1900, Chinese officials pursued a strategy of de-escalation. Yuan Shikai, the governor of Shandong Province, and his most important successors Zhou Fu and Yang Shixiang developed a "new policy" to establish communications in order to deal with the German colonial administration and to avoid further conflicts. Besides solving disputes arising from the railway construction or mining operations, a central focus of the governors of Shandong was to take care of the political interests of the Chinese population in Kiaochow. Starting in 1902, the Governor of Shandong paid regular visits to Kiaochow.[52] Lower civil and military officials were even more frequent visitors in the territory. Zhou Fu, who was the first Chinese governor to visit Kiaochow, described the construction projects under way and the enormous amount of money the German administration was investing in a memorial to the emperor.[53] Like him, many other officials expressed admiration for the large scale of the German plans and carefully investigated the German system on their visits to Qingdao. Another equally important goal was to take care of the Chinese population in the territory. In 1902, Zhou Fu reported that he had sent agents who tried to reorganize the *baojia* system, a community-based structure of law enforcement and civil supervision that dated back to the Song dynasty (960–1279). The Chinese authorities hoped that this would give them a greater degree of control: on the one hand, it could be used to protect the Chinese population in Kiaochow; on the other, the Chinese governor could try to avoid spontaneous and violent conflicts or popular actions, such as the ones associated with the Boxer movement, which were both feared by and were neither in the interest of Chinese nor of German officials.

When the German authorities noticed these efforts to establish informal structures to protect Chinese interests, Governor von Truppel was alarmed. He stated the German position that the Chinese population was subject to the German colonial authorities alone. However, Zhou Fu contradicted this, saying that the "Chinese people in Qingdao still belonged to their families and clans, they therefore were still under Chinese law, and should and must seek help from there."[54] He went on to demand the presence of an official Chinese agent in Qingdao, who would both represent Chinese interests and deal with the Germans. Zhou's proposals were of course not acceptable to Truppel, who held the view that this would be a severe limitation to German sovereignty in Qingdao. The question of who asserted control over the population in Qingdao remained a continuous source of conflicts between German and Chinese authorities in later years.

Despite German objections, Chinese officials continued to take care of the Chinese population in Qingdao. Excellent relations existed between the Chinese merchants in Qingdao and the officials in Jinan. In particular, after the completion of the railway in 1904, there was an increasing influx of well-educated, well-off local Chinese businesspeople who came to the colony in order to take advantage of the facilities build by the colonial government.[55]

The Chinese merchants in Qingdao soon demanded some form of participation in affairs that concerned them. After lengthy discussions,

Governor Truppel approved the demand by Chinese guilds to form a committee in 1902.[56] The so-called "Chinese Committee," whose members were elected by merchants through the guilds, was permitted to comment on specific economic questions and was heard by the Governor. Over time, the committee became powerful and self-confident. In 1908, it felt strong enough to organize boycotts and protests against the colonial administration due to the rise of depot tariffs in the harbor, whereby they succeeded in mobilizing almost the entire Chinese population of Kiaochow. The well-managed boycott shocked the colonial administration. Only after essential concessions by the administration did the committee agree to end the boycott. Recapitulating the conflict of 1908, Truppel stated with disappointment, "The population still feels and thinks like Chinese."[57] Because of these events, the Chinese Committee was dissolved and replaced in 1910 by Chinese counselors who were selected by the governor.

After 1905, relations between Germans and Chinese became more co-operative and constructive. A jointly operated German-Chinese College, with a German director and a Chinese inspector, was founded in 1909. This was the only foreign-led educational institution ever to be cosponsored and officially acknowledged by the Qing government. Students were chosen by the Chinese government, and Western-style education by German teachers in the morning was supplemented by teachings in the Confucian classics in the afternoon by Chinese instructors. A factor in the establishment of the school was the changing political climate in China. As the influx of new and radical ideas grew stronger, many elite members of Qing society looked favorably toward the German Reich and saw it as a partner for co-operation. After the revolution of 1911, many high Qing officials fled to the German leasehold and purchased houses there.[58] Even earlier, they had begun to send their sons to Kiaochow to attend the German schools.

As a result, the architectural appearance of Qingdao changed too. With the influx of wealthy Chinese homeowners, more Chinese-style residential buildings were constructed after 1908. Chinese-style roofs began to appear in Dabaodao and other places of the colony, with the exception of the European quarter. Colonial builders started to change their style as well, experimenting and integrating Chinese ornamentation and décor into their buildings, exemplified by the Laoshan resort and the German-Chinese Seminary. An architectural syncretism emerged that reflected the cultural hybridity of the colonial world.

In the beginning, the occupation of Kiaochow was met with fierce Chinese resistance. Boycotts, protests, as well as violent upheavals in the surrounding areas all document the resentments against foreign occupation in the first years of German rule. In later years, relations with the Chinese population improved somewhat as the colonial authorities became more flexible. After the completion of major infrastructure work for the city and the hinterland (railway, mines, harbor), an economic surge began around 1907 that transformed the colony into a busy marketplace connecting the hinterland to national and international markets that reached Europe. By 1914, Kiaochow had indeed become a "contradictory formation,"[59] where segregation and discrimination were practiced in the legal, administrative, and spatial order of the colony, but where at the same time, contacts, co-operation, and exchanges started to undermine the barriers erected by the colonial state.

Conclusion

Kiaochow was acquired from China for ninety-nine years, but the grand colonial project ended much sooner than that. The rising imperialist power in Asia, Japan, used the opportunity of World War I to declare war on Germany in August 1914. The following month, Japanese ships and troops attacked the colony and overwhelmed the German station after some fighting. Yet the brevity of Kiaochow's colonial history has led historians to overlook the particular and significant historical place of Qingdao.

Colonial Studies has produced an image of empire that seems to be fundamentally based on territory and bounded space;[60] more flexible and less visible forms of control have been overlooked. One could argue that the conventional approach does little justice to the complexities of the German imperial system in Kiaochow, which is an example of a form of colonialism that largely worked outside the framework of the classical model. Instead of control over a large dependent territory, colonial authorities in Kiaochow limited their efforts to building a base in Qingdao from which a larger sphere of influence in the hinterland was established and maintained. This form of colonialism was less expansionist and territorial than intensive and pervasive. Prasenjit Duara described this phenomenon as "new imperialism," to be distinguished from classical nineteenth-century colonialism of European provenance. Duara wrote,

> While new imperialists maintained ultimate control of their dependencies or clients through military subordination, they often created or maintained legally sovereign nation-states with political and economic structure that resembled their own. ... This new imperialism reflected a strategic conception of the periphery as part of an organic formation designed to attain global supremacy for the imperial power.[61]

This describes well the overall function of a colonial base within a larger imperialist design.

The architecture in Qingdao reflected the peculiarity of the colonial order. The combination of massive granite sidewalls and its ruptures by front porches and balconies created a colonial style that, while representing the power and superiority of the colonial center, appeared flexible, pragmatic, and almost playful. Moreover, the European villa quarter displayed an almost idyllic small-town feel projecting the image of a modern, prosperous, yet tiny and caring community. In all cases, the functionalism and pragmatism reflected a colonial project that was not only invested in the demonstration of power and might but also developed forms of accommodation to local conditions.

At the same time, Qingdao also serves as an example for possibilities of profound transformations in a colonial space. Here, society continued to emerge and change through migration, exile, and trade, to become a complex, highly diffuse zone of contact, within which colonial agency was produced, attracted, contended with, and negotiated among various Chinese social groups and networks. A zone of contact connotes an area where "foci of cultural contact in a zone of dispute" can stimulate "cultural dissonance"[62] as well as more open forms of conflict and co-operation. The semi-colonial situation produced a broad range of liminal identities and collaborations that thrived in such ambivalent circumstances. Qingdao for sure was a colonial base for the projection of German power in East Asia, but it also became a fluid zone of contact between cultures, and a place where experiments in making money, creating revolutions, and "constructing" a new nation across boundaries of various kinds evolved. These developments challenged the colonial power to move beyond the formal colonialism of the previous century, as the German Reich competed with other European powers to control global resources.

Emphasizing diversity and contingency, Frederic Cooper advocated thinking about multiple colonialisms—as opposed to a one-size-fits-all model—in conceptualizing colonial situations, so as "not to diminish the importance of the specific forms of colonization" and to enable precise analysis of colonial processes.[63] The specific semi-colonial condition in China challenged German authorities to rethink and reform policies. An "enlightened" form of the imperial project emerged that was designed to be more efficient, more flexible, and less openly violent than the classical nineteenth-century model. Kiaochow can be interpreted to mark the transition from old to new imperialism, from colonial control over territory to a de-territorialized, adaptable form of domination that created and maintained semi-colonial subjects in ambivalent and opaque circumstances.

Archives

BAarch/MA Bundesarchiv/Militärarchiv (German Federal Archives /Military Archives)
1)   RM 2 Reichsmarine/Marinekabinett (Naval Cabinet)
     Nr. 1835–41 "Erwerb und Verwaltung des Kiautschou-Gebietes" (acquisition and administration of the Kiaochow territory)
2)   RM 3 Reichsmarine/Reichsmarineamt (Naval Ministry)
     Nr. 6699–6707, Organisation des Schutzgebietes, 1897–1923 (organization of the leasehold)
     Nr. 6714 Verordnungen für das Schutzgebiet (ordinances for the protectorate)
     Nr. 6717–24 Allgemeine Gouvernementsangelegenheiten (general matters of the governor)
     Nr. 6778–85 Unruhen in China—Ganz Geheime Angelegenheiten (unrests in China—secret matters)
BAP Bundesarchiv, Abteilungen Potsdam (German Federal Archives, Potsdam)
     DBC Deutsche Botschaft China (German Legation China)
     Nr. 1238–47 Pachtgebiet Kiautschou (Kiaochow leasehold)
FHA First Historical Archives, Beijing.
     5012/0–2, Nr. 292. Shandong xunfu dang (files of the governor of Shandong)

AS/JYS Academia Sinica/Jindaishi yanjiusuo (Institute for Modern History, Academia Sinica, Taiwan)
02–11 Zudi zujie (leased territories and leaseholds)

Notes

1. "Kiaochow" (or "Kiautschou" in German and "Jiaozhou" in Chinese) was the administrative name of the colony, which consisted of the city of Tsingtao ("Qingdao" in Chinese), a large rural area, and several islands. The seat of the colonial administration was in Qingdao. The whole territory covered approximately 552 square kilometers.
2. Quoted in John E. Schrecker, *Imperialism and Chinese Nationalism: Germany in Shantung* (Cambridge: Harvard University Press 1971), 220.
3. George Steinmetz, *The Devil's Handwriting: Precoloniality and the German Colonial State in Qingdao, Samoa and Southwest Africa* (Chicago: University of Chicago Press, 2007), 5–7, 19–17.
4. Ann Laura Stoler and Carole MacGranahan, "Refiguring Imperial Terrains," in *Imperial Formations*, eds. Ann Laura Stoler et al. (Santa Fe and Oxford: School for Advanced Research Press, James Curry, 2007), 23.
5. Bernhard Dernburg, *Zielpunkte des deutschen Kolonialwesens* (Berlin: E. S. Mittler, 1907), 11.
6. Ann Laura Stoler, "On Degrees of Imperial Sovereignty," *Public Culture* 18, no. 1 (2006): 125–46.
7. See Frederick Cooper, *Colonialism in Question: Theory, Knowledge, History* (Berkeley and Los Angeles: University of California Press, 2005), 3–32.
8. See James Epstein, "Politics of Colonial Sensation: The Trial of Thomas Picton and the Cause of Louisa Calderon," *The American Historical Review* 112, no. 3 (2007): 712–41.
9. Alan Lester, *Imperial Networks: Creating Identities in Nineteenth-Century South Africa and Britain, London* (London: Routledge, 2001), 5–7.
10. Gyan Prakash, *Another Reason: Science and the Imagination of Modern India* (Princeton: Princeton University Press, 1999).
11. Jürgen Osterhammel, "Konzessionen und Niederlassungen" and "Pachtgebiete," in *Das große China-Lexikon*, ed. Brunhild Staiger (Darmstadt: Wissenschaftliche Buchgesellschaft, 2003), 394–97, 551–53.
12. Five leaseholds were established by European powers: 1896, Dalian, and 1898, Port Arthur/Lüshun (Manchuria) by the Tsarist Empire; 1898: Guangzhouwan (Guangdong Province) by France; Weihaiwei (Shandong Province) by Great Britain; Jiaozhou (Shandong Province) by the German Reich; Kowloon/Jiulong (incorporated into Hong Kong) by Great Britain.
13. There were only two instances where this occurred: Hong Kong was ceded to Great Britain in the Treaty of Nanjing (1842) and Taiwan went to Japan in 1895.

14. Jürgen Osterhammel, *Kolonialismus: Geschichte, Formen, Folgen, 4. Aufl.* (Beck: München, 2003), 7–17; Jürgen Osterhammel, "Semi-colonialism and Informal Empire in Twentieth-Century China: Towards a Framework of Analysis," in *Imperialism and After: Continuities and Discontinuities*, eds. Wolfgang Mommsen and Jürgen Osterhammel (Boston: Allen and Unwin, 1986), 290–314.

15. The term goes back to Lenin's *Imperialism: The Highest Stage of Capitalism* from 1916 writing where semi-colonialism is explained a step towards full colonization.

16. On the Chinese discussion of semi-colonialism see Rebecca Karl, "On Comparability and Continuity: China, circa 1930s and 1990s," *Boundary* 32, no. 2 (2005): 169–200.

17. Stoler and MacGranahan, "Refiguring Imperial Terrains."

18. There is a number of studies on Kiaochow: Schrecker, *Imperialism and Chinese Nationalism*; Dirk Alexander Seelemann, "The Social and Economic Development of the Kiaochou Leasehold (Shantung, China) under German Administration, 1897–1914" (PhD diss., University of Toronto, 1982); Shouzhong Wang, *Deguo qinlüe Shandongshi* [The German expansion in Shandong] (Beijing: Renmin chubanshe, 1987); Hans Christian Stichler, "Das Gouvernement Jiaozhou und die deutsche Kolonialpolitik in Shandong 1897–1909. Ein Beitrag zur Geschichte der deutsch-chinesischen Beziehungen" (PhD diss., Humboldt Universität zu Berlin, 1989); Mechthild Leutner and Klaus Mühlhahn, *"Musterkolonie Kiautschou." Die Expansion des Deutschen Reiches in China. Deutsch-chinesische Beziehungen 1897–1914. Eine Quellensammlung* (Berlin: Akademie Verlag, 1997); Klaus Mühlhahn, *Herrschaft und Widerstand in der "Musterkolonie" Kiautschou: Interaktionen zwischen China und Deutschland, 1897–1914 (Studien zur Internationalen Geschichte 8)* (München: R. Oldenbourg, 2000); Annette S. Biener, *Das deutsche Pachtgebiet Tsingtau in Schantung, 1897–1914. Institutioneller Wandel durch Kolonialisierung* (Bonn: W. Matzat, 2001); Steinmetz, *The Devil's Handwriting*, 433–508. Shorter overviews are Yufa Zhang, "Qingdao de shili quan" [The sphere of influence of Qingdao], in *Jindai Zhongguo quyushi yantaohui lunwenji* [Essays of the conference on regional modernization in modern China], ed. Institute of Modern History, Academia Sinica (Taibei, 1986); Horst Gründer, *Geschichte der deutschen Kolonien* (Paderborn: UTB, 1991), 188–205, W. O. Henderson, *The German Colonial Empire, 1884–1919* (London: F. Cass, 1993).

19. See Documents 42 and 43 in Leutner and Mühlhahn, *"Musterkolonie Kiautschou,"* 181–84. In 1889, the Emperor reorganized the commanding structure of the navy. He created three institutions of equal standing: the naval cabinet (led by the adjutant Gustav von Senden-Bibran) was responsible for all affairs concerning naval officers, the naval ministry (directed by the naval minister Alfred von Tirpitz) protected the political affairs of

the navy, and the high command (with a commander-in-chief at the top) was in charge of all naval units.

20. Note written by Tirpitz, January 1898, BArch/MA, RM3/6699, Bl. 1–11.
21. Centrumskorrespondenz, March 2, 1898, quoted in Konrad Canis, *Von Bismarck zur Weltpolitik. Deutsche Außenpolitik 1890 bis 1902* (Berlin: Akademie, 1997), 273.
22. Quoted in Wilhelm Deist, *Flottenpolitik und Flottenpropaganda. Das Nachrichtenbureau des Reichsmarineamts 1897–1914* (Stuttgart: Deutsche Verlagsanstalt, 1976), 111.
23. Kiaochow had four governors: Oskar Truppel (1897–99 and 1901–11), Carl Rosendahl (1898–99), Paul Jaeschke (1899–1901), and Alfred Meyer-Waldeck (1911–14).
24. According to the imperial order of March 1, 1898, the naval minister had the authority of a commanding admiral over all military personnel (including the governor) in the colony (BArch/MA RM 31/513, fol. 150). Steinmetz (*The Devil's Handwriting*, 437) has a different take: citing two pieces of secondary literature, he maintains that prior approval from Berlin was requited only for the most important regulations. Formal prior approval was indeed unnecessary for most decisions, but all regulations had to be signed by Tirpitz to enter into force. In practice, that of course meant that the governor had to consult with Berlin in advance. See Mühlhahn, *Herrschaft und Widerstand*, 204.
25. Letter from Tirpitz to Wilhelm II, October 7, 1898, BArch/MA, RM2/1837, Bl.126–28, in Leutner and Mühlhahn, "*Musterkolonie Kiautschou*," 352–53.
26. See Lewis Pyenson, *Cultural Imperialism and Exact Sciences: German Expansion Overseas, 1900–1930* (New York: Peter Lang Pub Inc., 1985), 258.
27. Local colonizers and business people criticized that they were not even able to participate in decisions concerning local affairs. Before 1907, three elected civil representatives could comment on current affairs. After 1907, there were four of them. In later years, criticism by the civilian population on this grew stronger. See Otto Hövermann, *Kiautschou. Verwaltung und Gerichtsbarkeit* (Tübingen: J. C. B. Mohr, 1914), 29; Biener, *Das Deutsche Pachtgebiet Tsingtau*, 209, 213ff.
28. See Mühlhahn, *Herrschaft und Widerstand*, 143–46.
29. See Vera Schmidt, *Die deutsche Eisenbahnpolitik in Shantung, 1897–1914. Ein Beitrag zur Geschichte des deutschen Imperialismus in China* (Wiesbaden: Harrasowitz, 1976), 65–66. The concession can be found in Leutner and Mühlhahn, "*Musterkolonie Kiautschou*," 395–99. See also BArch, kl Erw. 623, Bd. 2.
30. See Hans-Ulrich Wehler, *Deutsche Gesellschaftsgeschichte. Dritter Band: Von der "Deutschen Doppelrevolution" bis zum Beginn des Ersten Weltkrieges, 1849–1914* (München: Beck, 1995), 550, 662–80 on the characteristics and origins of organized capitalism in Germany after 1873.

31. See Seelemann, "Social and Economic Development," 13.

32. See "Vorläufige baupolizeiliche Vorschriften für die Stadtanlage im Gouvernement Kiautschou," in Friedrich Wilhelm Mohr, *Handbuch für das Schutzgebiet Kiautschou* (Qingdao: Deutsch-Chinesische Druckerei und Verlagsanstalt, W. Schmidt, 1911), 206–09.

33. On the building plans see Bökemann, "Die Stadtanlage von Tsingtao," in *Koloniale Monatsblätter,* Vol. 15 (November 1913): 465–87.

34. There were also fortifications and underground defensive tunnels, the construction of which was very costly.

35. Hans-Martin Hinz and Christoph Lind, eds. *Tsingtau Ein Kapitel deutscher Kolonialgeschichte in China, 1897–1914* (Berlin: Deutsches Historisches Museum, 1998); Bökemann, "Die Stadtanlage von Tsingtao": 480–87.

36. See Torsten Warner, "Der Aufbau der Kolonialstadt Tsingtau: Landordnung, Stadtplanung und Entwicklung," in *Tsingtau,* eds. Hinz and Lind, 84–95.

37. Throughout the period from 1897 to 1914, the German population of Qingdao remained relatively small. The whole German military personnel amounted to 2,400. See Mohr, *Handbuch für das Schutzgebiet Kiautschou,* 442, and Leutner and Mühlhahn, *"Musterkolonie Kiautschou,"* 238.

38. In a letter to the chief of the Naval Cabinet Senden-Bibran, secretary of state of the Naval Ministry Alfred von Tirpitz stressed that everybody had to make an application before settling in Qingdao. Letter from Tirpitz to Senden-Bibran, June 2, 1898, BA/MA, RM 2/1836, fol. 237.

39. This is of course not true for the peasants living in the rural regions. In 1914, Kiautschou had a Chinese population of 187,000 people. Of these, approximately 55,000 lived in urban quarters. They were mostly workers, who lived in Kiautschou only periodically. See Leutner and Mühlhahn, *"Musterkolonie Kiautschou,"* 238.

40. See Wolfgang Eckart, *Deutsche Ärzte in China 1897–1914. Medizin als Kulturmission im Zweiten Deutschen Kaiserreich* (Stuttgart: Steiner 1989), 31–33. The colonial authorities tried to cover up this aspect of colonial society. See letter from Truppel to Tirpitz, December 12, 1903, in Leutner and Mühlhahn, *"Musterkolonie Kiautschou,"* 220–22. Despite censorship, prostitution was occasionally mentioned by German newspapers. See, for example, *Tsingtauer Neueste Nachrichten,* March 9, 1911, p. 9, which reported that "in the large pleasure quarter" many children and young girls had been forced into prostitution.

41. Ralph A. Norem, *Kiaochow Leased Territory* (Berkeley: University of California Press, 1936), 107ff, and Schrecker, *Imperialism and Chinese Nationalism,* 70, were among the few who paid attention to this feature of Kiaochow.

42. See text in Leutner and Mühlhahn, *"Musterkolonie Kiautschou,"* 213–18.

43. There was in fact only one "Commissioner for Chinese Affairs"—the translator and Sinologist Wilhelm Schrameier (December 1897 to January

1909). After his departure, the tasks were given to the civil commissioner (*Zivilkommissar*). See Biener, *Das deutsche Pachtgebiet Tsingtao*, 216.

44. See Walter Uthemann and Karl Fürth, "Tsingtau. Ein kolonialhygienischer Rückblick," *Beiheft 4 der Beihefte zum Archiv für Schiffs- und Tropenhygiene* 15 (1911): 35–36; Franz Kronecker, *15 Jahre Kaiutschou, Eine kolonialmedizinische Studie* (Berlin: Goldschmidt, 1913).

45. The legal system is discussed by Seeleman, "Social and Economic Development," 76–96. While not being identical, it is comparable to that of other German colonies. See Udo Wolter, "Deutsches Kolonialrecht - ein wenig erforschtes Rechtsgebiet, dargestellt anhand des Arbeitsrechts der Eingeborenen," *Zeitschrift für Neuere Rechtsgeschichte* 17, no. 3/4 (1995): 201–44.

46. Ordinance Concerning the Legal Position of the Chinese Population, April 15, 1899, in Mohr, *Handbuch für das Schutzgebiet Kiautschou*, 72–77.

47. See Emil Krebs, "Chinesisches Strafrecht," in *Die Strafgesetzgebung der Gegenwart in rechtsvergeleichender Darstellung*, eds. Franz von Liszt and Georg Crusen (Berlin: International Association of Penal Law, 1899).

48. On the legal system, see Steinmetz, *Devil's Handwriting*, 452, and Klaus Mühlhahn, "Staatsgewalt und Disziplin: Die chinesische Auseinandersetzung mit dem Rechtssystem der deutschen Kolonie Kiautschou," in *Kolonialisierung des Rechts. Zur kolonialen Rechts- und Verwaltungsordnung*, eds. Rüdiger Voigt and Peter Sack (Baden-Baden: Nomos, 2001), 125–56.

49. Georg Crusen (1867–1949) studied law in Lausanne, Berlin, Leipzig, and Marburg from 1886 to 1889. Afterwards he worked in various positions in the court of justice in Berlin. From 1889 to 1899, he published several works on penal law in non-European countries and became an expert in comparative penal law. In 1899 he was appointed a judge in Frankfurt. In the same year he was sent to Tokyo, where he taught at the police academy. In 1902 he was transferred to Kiaochow and in 1903 was appointed as High Judge at the Imperial Court of Law. He remained in this position until 1914. See Hermann A. L. Degener, ed., *Wer ist's?* (Leipzig: Verlag von H. A. L. Degener, 1912), 269.

50. Georg Crusen, "Die rechtliche Stellung der Chinesen in Kiautschou," *Zeitschrift für Kolonialrecht* 15, no. 2 (1913): 4–17; 15, no. 3 (1913): 5.

51. Georg Crusen, "Moderne Gedanken im Chinesenstrafrecht des Kiautschougebietes," *Mitteilungen der Internationalen Kriminalistischen Vereinigung* 21, no. 1 (1914): 134–42.

52. The visits were an initiative from China. German authorities could hardly believe it when they learned that the Chinese wished to send a delegation to Qingdao.

53. Memorial of Zhou Fu to the Grand Council, December 31, 1902, AS/JYS 02-11-13 (1).

54. Letter from Truppel to Tirpitz, December 30, 1903, in BArch/MA, RM3/6718, Bl. 71–74.
55. The Chinese merchants in Kiaochow had formed several guilds to represent their interests. The Jiyan guild represented merchants from Tianjin and Shandong, the Sanjiang guild was organized by merchants from the Lower Yangzi, while the Guangdong guild was formed by merchants from Canton. In 1913, two more guilds were added: the Changyi and the Haiyang. Both had members who undertook international trade. On the guilds, see Zhang, "Qingdao de shili quan," 801–38.
56. See Leutner and Mühlhahn, *"Musterkolonie Kiautschou,"* 179–80.
57. Letter from Truppel to Naval Ministry, November 4, 1908, BA/MA, RM 3/6721, fol. 220–23.
58. In 1912 there were twelve Qing governors and general-governors living in Qingdao. See letter from Alfred Meyer-Waldeck to Naval Ministry, February 24, 1912, BArch/MA, RM3/6723, fol. 84–85.
59. Steinmetz, *Devil's Handwriting,* 506.
60. Stoler and MacGranahan, "Refiguring Imperial Terrains," 15.
61. Prasenjit Duara, The Imperialism of "Free Nations": Japan, Manchukuo, and the History of the Present, in Stoler et al. 2007: 212.
62. Eric R. Wolf, "Cultural Dissonance in the Italian Alps," *Comparative Studies of Society and History* 5, no. 1 (October 1962): 1.
63. See Cooper, *Colonialism in Question,* 52–53.

Plate 1

Harbin's Railway Station, postcard, author's collection.

Plate 2

Harbin's Kitaiskaya Street, postcard, author's collection.

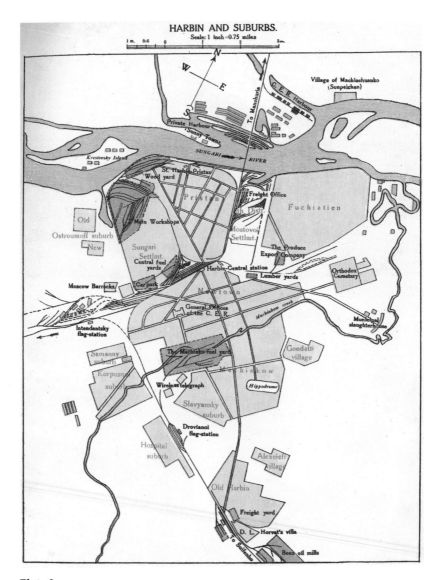

Plate 3

Russian map of Harbin, showing its major districts: Old Harbin, Majiagou, New Town, Pristan, and Fujiadian. Source: Economic Bureau of the Chinese Eastern Railway, ed., *North Manchuria and the Chinese Eastern Railway* (Harbin: CER Printing Office, 1924).

Plate 4

Bank of Korea, 1920

Plate 5

Changchun Telephone Company

Plate 6

State Council

Plate 7

Public Security, later Manchukuo Military Headquarters

Plate 8

Supreme Court

Plate 9

Jimmu Den

Plate 10

Bank of Manchukuo

Plate 11

Daikyō Building

Plate 12

Tokyo Kaijō Building

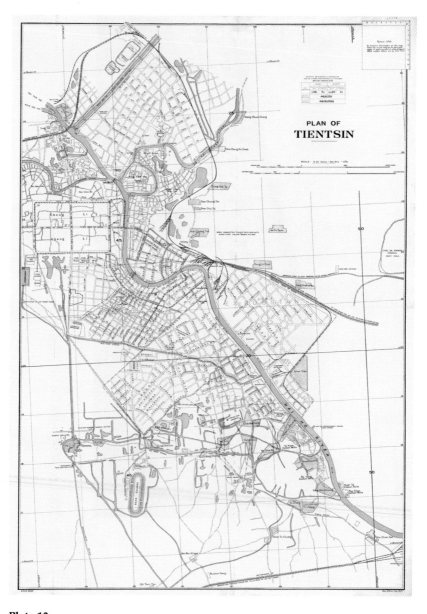

Plate 13

Tianjin map by War Office of British Government, 1927. Source: The National Archives in London.

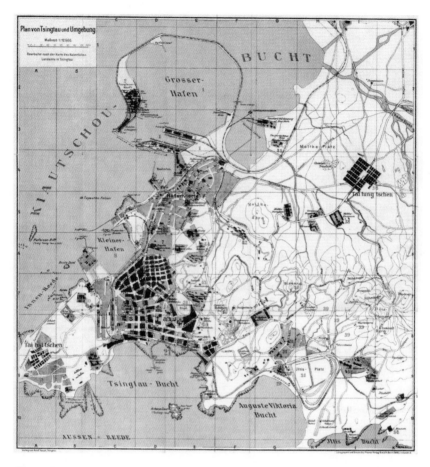

Plate 14

Map of Qingdao, Qingdao, 1911. Published by Adolf Hauft. Courtesy of Wilhelm Matzat.

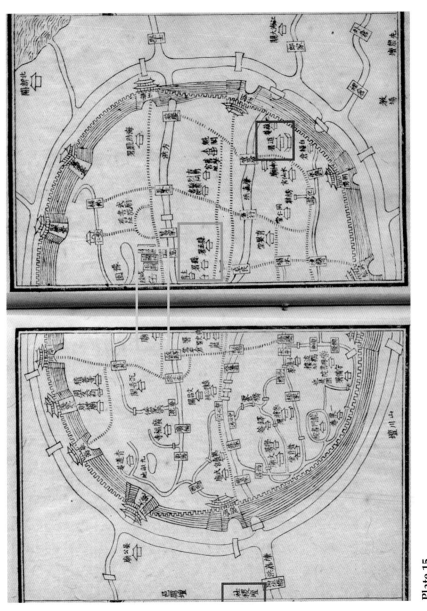

Plate 15

Shanghai, 1870 (*Chong xiu Shanghai xian zhi*, 1882)

Plate 16

Shanghai, 1855 (J. W. Maclellan, *The Story of Shanghai: From the Opening of the Port to Foreign Trade,* 1889)

Plate 17

Russell and Company compound, Shanghai, 1870s (Peabody Essex Museum, Salem, MA)

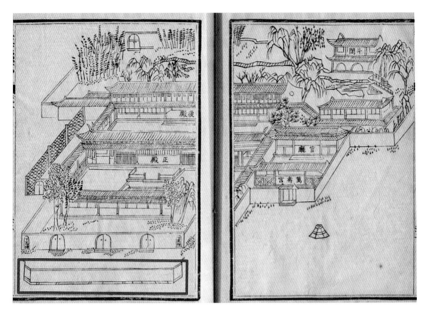

Plate 18

Guandi Temple with *zhaoqiang* fender, Shanghai, 1870 (*Chong xiu Shanghai xian zhi*, 1882)

Plate 19

The Shanghai Bund, 1860s (Peabody Essex Museum, Salem, MA)

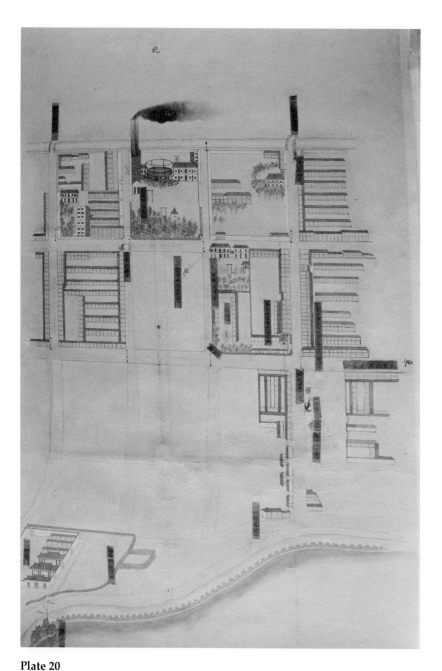

Plate 20

Plan of the Ningbo pagoda district in Shanghai, undated (Archives du Ministère des Affairs étrangères, Nantes, 635PO/B/63)

Plate 21

Plan of the Ningbo pagoda district in Shanghai, undated (Archives du Ministère des Affairs étrangères, Nantes, 635PO/B/63)

Plate 22

Central Criminal Courts, Old Bailey, London (1900–06), by Edward Mountford

Plate 23

The Victoria Memorial, Kolkata (1904–21), by William Emerson

Plate 24

The tower of the University of Hong Kong's Main Building as originally designed with its elaborate scheme of decoration. It was emblematic of the University's role as a beacon of Western modernity for China. (HKU, University Archives)

7
The Architecture of Risk

Urban Space and Uncertainty in Shanghai, 1843–74

Cole Roskam

In 1842, Great Britain and China signed the Treaty of Nanjing, ending the First Opium War, redefining five cities along the Chinese coast as treaty ports, and creating urban spaces of indeterminate cultural and political identity within which international trade could legally proceed within and adjacent to Qing imperial boundaries.[1] The creation of such cities, lying as they did beyond the bureaucratic reach of any formal, colonial administrative authority, coupled with the unwillingness of foreign representatives to expose themselves or their constituents to Qing rule of law, necessitated the establishment of a new system of extraterritoriality whereby foreign residents remained subject to the legal codes of their own respective national governments represented by locally-based consular authorities.[2] Of the hundred ports eventually opened within China under the treaty system, Shanghai became the largest and most commercially successful example. An American mercantile presence was subsequently established there in 1845, followed by the founding of the French Concession in 1848.[3]

The obvious and critical impact of extraterritoriality upon everything from the city's physical fragmentation to its unique cultural development from 1843 to 1943 has been well documented, as has the particular commercial bravado and peculiar cultural exceptionalism it engendered within the foreign community.[4] Indeed, as a well-worn quote from a British merchant in the early 1850s attests:

> It is [our] business to make a fortune with the least possible loss of time, by letting my land to Chinese, and building for them at thirty to forty per cent interest, if that is the best thing I can do with my money. In two or three years at farthest, I hope to realize a

fortune and get away and what does it matter to me, if all Shanghai disappears afterwards, in fire or flood? You must not expect men in my situation to condemn themselves to years of prolonged exile in an unhealthy climate for the benefit of posterity. We are money-making, practical men. Our business is to make money, as much and as fast as we can; and for this end, all modes and means are good which the law permits.[5]

Although it is the statement's unadulterated greed that has been routinely noted by numerous scholars as worthy evidence of Shanghai's commercially exploitative *raison d'être*,[6] the admission also suggests an important if relatively unexamined aspect of the extraterritorial Shanghai experience: the profound uncertainty, of both a spatial and temporal nature, that undergirded the entire enterprise.

This chapter explores notions of risk and anxiety embedded within early treaty-port era architecture, urban space and its visual representation in Shanghai between 1843 and 1874. The speed and haphazardness with which Shanghai was economically and physically reconfigured and the lack of any initial overarching local municipal authority within the city left a series of daunting and unanswered challenges for Chinese and foreign residents alike. These questions were further aggravated by the physical obstacles posed by the place itself, the cultural unknowns that came with Shanghai's new bifurcated urban composition, and the significant financial risks associated with expanding influential international trading networks. Most importantly, perhaps, was the lack of insight regarding just how long such a treaty port might be able, and allowed, to operate. In the absence of swift diplomatic resolution, the employment of particular spatial and architectural strategies within both the Chinese city and foreign settlements emerged as a means of both adjusting and adapting to the perceived precariousness within which all sides found themselves intertwined.

Initial Interactions, 1842–53

Understanding the uncertainty involved in Shanghai's redefinition as a treaty port first requires a contextualization of the city's physical composition prior to foreign arrival. Geographical risks had long played a fundamental role in Shanghai's urban and architectural history, as emblematized by the presence of a city wall, first built in 1554, to limit exposure to the dangers of both the surrounding countryside as well as the sea.[7] Lacking any substantial hills to its north, Shanghai was considered to be more susceptible than other parts of China to the whims of spiritual forces believed to exist within the natural environment, the effective control of which is generally known as *fengshui* or *kanyu*. Any disturbances caused by the erection of new houses, high towers with pinnacles, the planting of poles for scaffolding, the cutting down of trees, or the building of houses too near to graves carried with them the potential for misfortune within a local community if not countered by proper *fengshui* practices. As a result, Shanghai's major streets extended east-west, with few continuous north-south corridors, lest they invite malevolent northern forces into the city. Each of the city wall's main guard towers were also bestowed with names that evoked positive *fengshui* connotations.

Within the city, a sizable network of ceremonial, imperial, educational, and religious spaces existed that collectively may be said to comprise a kind of civic sphere bound by communal beliefs in *fengshui* and a predominance of courtyard constructions, known as *li*, the form of which suggested a carefully choreographed mediation between private and public space within the city.[8] (Plate 15) The City God Temple complex constituted the city's physical and spiritual center. Constructed between 1403 and 1425, it represented the home of Shanghai's magisterial deity, a figure whose jurisdiction included the city's dead. Just south of the temple sat the city's district magistrate's main *yamen*, or residential compound. The district magistrate represented the emperor in all of Shanghai's daily bureaucratic operations, including tax collection and local adjudication. Together, the two structures formed the locus of imperial power within the city, a matrix that extended from its earthly territory into its spiritual dominion. From them radiated the city's other, lesser political and religious monuments.[9]

As recent scholarship has indicated, Shanghai had begun to experience a rise in regional trading activity years prior to foreign arrival as evidenced by the construction of semi-public monuments devoted to the city's *huiguan*, or native-place organizations.[10] Many were initially established by sojourning workers keen to associate themselves with other residents from their native locale upon arriving in the city. In Shanghai, where more than half of its population consisted of immigrants from other parts of China by the late nineteenth century, *huiguan* became critical forces in the preservation of native-place identities within the city. *Huiguan* construction clustered around the city's Small East Gate, where Chinese customs was headquartered, or in the east and west gardens of the City God Temple. Their presence began to redirect both cultural and commercial activity in the walled city towards the east. Functioning as community centers, the compounds incorporated *yamen*-like as well as temple-style architectural compositions, with multiple courtyards housing altars for local gods, and stages for theatrical performances that created spatial nodes of professional and personal communal interaction.[11]

These shifts in Shanghai's pre-existing urban order were further aggravated by the subsequent construction of the city's first foreign mercantile compounds, each built with the goal of "rendering houses and property insurable, and to afford lasting peace and comfort to the mercantile community."[12] British consular authorities, eager to avoid the isolation of the Canton system, in which foreign merchants had found themselves ostracized to an adjoining island outside Guangzhou, initially insisted on maintaining a presence within the Chinese walled city. Chinese officials, however, hoped to limit Shanghai Chinese population's exposure to unwanted foreign influence, a point underscored by the "severe wounding" by gunshot of a Chinese boy by a British merchant just days following the port's official opening.[13] After a reconsideration of the spatial limitations imposed upon them by the cramped, seemingly unhygienic quarters of the walled city, Great Britain consented to the creation of an independent foreign concession located just north of this with the understanding that Chinese residents would be prohibited from residing there.

Chinese officials and residents alike struggled to frame and position themselves in relation to their foreign cohabitants through an array of linguistic, spatial, architectural, and pictorial strategies. On one hand, increased foreign trade came with obvious commercial and material benefits. Foreign goods were seen as exotic, dazzlingly modern, and in many ways superior to Chinese products.[14] At the same time, the seductive allure of the foreign triggered deeper anxiety among some Chinese residents with respect to China's cultural and political autonomy, giving rise to simultaneously dissociative and associative impulses within the Chinese city towards the foreign community's presence. From their inception, the foreign concessions were referred to by Chinese residents as *yichang*, or Barbarian Quarters, and over the course of the 1850s and 1860s, the construction of the foreign settlement itself within proximity of numerous ancestral graves began to represent an intervention into the city's perceived spatial balance.[15]

Geomancy emerged as a key mediating device between these competing interests used to alleviate general public unease by limiting the alleged destabilizing effects of the growing collection of large and monumental Western buildings to the Chinese city's north without fundamentally disrupting commercial contact between the two areas. The unexpected death of Shanghai's district magistrate, Wang Shaofu, within months of his taking office in 1849, for example, prompted Chinese protests over the recently completed construction of the Southern Baptist church within the Chinese city north of the magistrate's compound. Local authorities demanded that the church's minister, Matthew T. Yates, pull down the tower, an order with which he refused to comply. A local geomancer was subsequently called in to examine the situation and determined that if the magistrate's compound was rebuilt on its original lot but employed an axis other than north-south, any objectionable spirits would pass by the corner of the compound's wall and miss the magistrate's *yamen*.[16]

As Chinese residents came to terms with the spatial, commercial, and political implications of the foreign settlements through increasingly defensive geomantic posturing, foreign residents grappled with the Chinese city through a series of rhetorical and architectural strategies of their own. Collectively, Shanghai's Chinese and foreign communities may be considered the spatio-economic product of what Jonathan Simon has characterized as the world's first "risk society"; namely, a Victorian-era combination of widespread industrialization, the emergence of global financial markets, expanding international opportunities for travel, and a burgeoning insurance market brought risk into wide public consciousness for the first time, compelling the state and legal system to address the creation and distribution of risk as a subject of public policy.[17] A comparable spirit helped to shape both the French Civil Code, enacted in 1804, as well as American geographic, economic, and political expansion westward over the course of the mid-to late nineteenth century.[18] Each would subsequently influence economic, political, and social development within Shanghai's Chinese and foreign communities.

Along with the financial risks of international commercial expansion came equivalent cultural and social uncertainties. Like their Chinese equivalents, many of Shanghai's foreign residents were both intrigued and threatened by the physical insularity and spatial inscrutability of the Other, namely, the Chinese city, and they quickly challenged its presence through culturally constructed claims of Western aesthetic and architectural superiority.[19] Catherine Vance Yeh, for example, has used the representational development of Shanghai maps to explain how the Chinese city's existence was ignored and visually denied by the foreign community.[20] (Plate 16) Similarly, Chinese civic architecture was depicted by foreign observers as structurally weak and temporal; Walter Medhurst, a British missionary and member of Great Britain's initial negotiation party with Qing officials in Shanghai following the Opium War, described the country's political architecture to be "never of much moment: those in Shanghai are particularly insignificant … They procure the smallest sized timber, and the most fragile materials, so as to run up sheds of a given size in the cheapest manner."[21]

At the same time, foreign associations linking the Chinese city to death and decay over-rode the recognition of any perceptible Chinese public spatial order. Robert Fortune, for example, an American entrepreneur traveling through and around Shanghai just prior to its opening as a treaty port, noted on his 1846 travels there that

> a very considerable portion of the land in the vicinity of the town is occupied by the tombs of the dead. In all directions large conical shaped mounds meet the eye, overgrown with long grass, and in some instances planted with shrubs and flowers. The traveler here … constantly meets with coffins placed on the surface of the ground.[22]

Rhetorical and visual renderings of Shanghai's Chinese built environment as an obsolete, historical footnote allowed foreign residents and visitors alike to confidently position themselves and their countrymen as key to the city's future development. Initial foreign planning efforts subsequently reinforced this distinction by attempting to limit their exposure to the Chinese city and countryside. By the end of 1843, the British Settlement's first riverside lots had been quickly claimed by the first foreign merchants there, forming a roughly partitioned grid around which roads and paths followed, the construction of which was deemed the individual responsibility of each mercantile house. As Alexander Michie, biographer to Rutherford Alcock, Shanghai's British Consul between 1844 and 1846, noted,

> Not only did friendly relations exist, but a wonderful degree of confidence was established between the natives and foreign tourists. But although the foreigner in his proper costume moved freely within the prescribed area, it was considered hazardous to venture beyond these limits.[23]

The Settlement's first compounds represented relatively self-sufficient spaces designed, in the words of Shanghai's merchants, to "protect life and property from causes of national disturbance in the country where they were located."[24] (Plate 17) Consisting of a simple, utilitarian comingling of professional and private spaces and buildings hierarchically ordered within its walls, compounds typically included a merchant's main house and office, housing for visiting staff as well as Chinese staff, and godowns (an English neologism borrowed from Malay terminology for "warehouse," or *gudang*). While the main residence and office tended to be built within prominent view of the compound's boundaries, the kitchen and Chinese servants' quarters lay behind both main structures as a means of both protecting the main house from the risk of fire and limiting the presence of Chinese staff within the house.

As architectural projections of a hopeful but unfounded commercial optimism, Shanghai's compounds fulfilled several functions. For one, they offered their inhabitants a "delicious sense of safety."[25] The durable, self-contained nature of the structures as depicted in images, plans, and elevational drawings also suited the growing demands of the burgeoning international fire and marine insurance industries.[26] More generally, they operated as architectural nodes of contact literally and figuratively situated between China's domestic market and the global network of commodities trading represented by the Huangpu River itself.[27] Their physical construction, in fact, often depended upon such commercial and social connections—extending from India to Singapore to Hong Kong, Guangzhou, and Shanghai—along which technological advancements, architectural templates, and building expertise could flow. Besides enabling the city's swift physical construction, pre-established social networks also helped in connecting the foreign settlement to other foreign communities in Asia and around the world. British-born Freemasons, for example, were a critical if previously unexamined force in the settlement, helping to fuel early British dominance of Shanghai's commercial and building activity while also facilitating transfers of knowledge, construction techniques and forms, as well as skilled labor.[28] The influence of these globally-connected organizations could be seen in the settlement's architecture itself, with many structures appearing reminiscent of other cross-cultural international building types such as the bungalow in India or colonial mercantile constructions in the West Indies.[29]

Managing the Risks of Coexistence

As the city's foreign population grew from approximately 100 residents in 1843 to 175 in 1850, steps were taken to establish some type of broader, extra-consular foreign civic administration. A committee devoted to obtaining space for a foreign cemetery was founded in 1844, followed by a Roads and Jetties Committee in 1846. Both may be seen as representing a collective desire for what Timothy Mitchell has described as "the appearance of order" sought by colonizing enterprises in an attempt to rationalize and control the unknown.[30] Too often, however, Shanghai's semi-colonial status left its foreign residents without the systematic and organizational means of achieving it. These administrative shortcomings would become painfully apparent on September 7, 1853, when the Chinese city of Shanghai found itself occupied by a group of Cantonese triad-affiliated rebels identifying themselves as the Small Swords Society.[31] The occupation coincided with an attack on Nanjing that same year by another southern Chinese regional faction known as the Taiping Rebellion.[32] Its supporters would eventually invade Shanghai in 1863 and occupy it for two years, capping a ten-year period of intermittent bloody civil regional warfare between Chinese rebels and Qing imperial troops with occasional involvement from foreign military representatives.

The violence resulted in the influx of thousands of shelter-seeking Chinese refugees into the foreign areas, quickly rendering null a pre-existing policy agreed upon by Chinese and British officials prohibiting Chinese inhabitants from the Settlement.[33] Acting against British consular instructions, foreign entrepreneurs responded by constructing makeshift housing they rented out to the settlement's new Chinese residents, expanding its population exponentially and necessitating the creation of a more sustainable municipal authority. Such actions dashed consular expectations for official settlement neutrality in the conflict while irreparably blurring the once ostensibly clear physical, political, and social boundaries separating the city's various ethnic inhabitants.

Over the course of the Taiping Rebellion, geomancy continued to play a significant role in the spatial and psychological adaptation to the Chinese city's dramatic population shifts both into and out of the foreign settlements. The depreciation of business that occurred within Shanghai's Chinese quarters over the course of the 1850s and 1860s, for example, was blamed not on the disruptions caused by its occupation by various rebel forces but rather on the unfortunate redirection of positive *qi* from the south without obstruction into the foreign settlements.[34] The Chinese city's Little North gate, with its lack of a side entrance or *fengshui* fender, was seen as the specific source of the outflow of rich, southerly spirits through the Chinese city into the foreign districts. A screen wall, or *zhaoqiang*, was subsequently constructed in front of the gate, to little eventual effect on the city's economy. This was coupled, in 1870, by the construction of a more substantive *zhaoqiang* in front of the Guandi Temple, located in the city's westernmost quadrant adjacent to the French Concession, as a similar means of warding off evil spirits. (Plate 18)

The impact of the war upon the foreign settlement and its trade was equally significant, albeit for different reasons.[35] The influx of Chinese refugees into the area, and the ad-hoc building boom it triggered, convinced foreign officials that cross-cultural interaction was inevitable and ultimately beneficial to the foreign settlements' long-term prospects. In response to both the unpredictability of China's civil war, the settlements' new Chinese population, and the increasing geopolitical and territorial opacity which foreign residents found themselves struggling against, each of the city's three major foreign powers agreed to form a shared municipal council in 1854. Eight years later, the British Settlement renamed its main streets in 1862, employing the names of Chinese cities for all east-west arteries and those of Chinese provinces for its north-south roads in an effort to provide greater accessibility to more Chinese merchants and residents.[36] This was followed in 1863 by American-led efforts to open a new gate along the eastern section of Shanghai's existing city wall. A French gate had already been constructed in an effort to delineate, and control access to, French-controlled territory from the Chinese city. Edward Cunningham, American Consul and Director of the Russell and Company's Shanghai offices, proposed creating a street, twenty-four feet wide, that would extend from the International Settlement's riverfront due west into the heart of the Chinese city, "an avenue for air and health which would be invaluable in giving the Chinese authorities a direct and dignified access to the foreign settlement."[37] Although the plan was abandoned in part because it required the partial demolition of the city wall, it heralded a plethora of new public and semi-public building proposals within the foreign settlements between 1865 and 1874, indicating growing foreign commitment to the Shanghai enterprise.[38] "There is no doubt that more attention is now being paid to matters of purely local interest," reported the *North China Herald* in 1867.[39]

Gradual acquiescence to the realities of cross-cultural co-existence can also be detected in architectural changes related to form and scale undertaken within the Chinese city's Daotai compound at the time. The changes initially wrought by foreign arrival and subsequent internal Chinese conflict had represented a direct and immediate spatial affront, not only to the city's well-being, but to its pre-existing governing spatial authority. The city's Daotai, representing an intermediary official position between the district magistrate and provincial authorities, had occupied his own official *yamen* in Shanghai's southeast quadrant since the post was first established in 1645. The subsequent imposition of foreign mercantile operations and the construction of the British Settlement increased his civic and diplomatic responsibilities, which were expanded to include the mitigation of the city's foreign influence. As a result, the Daotai emerged as a far more powerful figure than the district magistrate, regardless of the ancillary position his compound historically held within the city's spatial hierarchy.[40]

With greater commercial and diplomatic contact came growing awareness on the part of Chinese officials to the cross-cultural power of verticality, itself a Western-orientated signifier of spatial and, by extension, political authority. Around 1867, for example, Shanghai's Daotai Ding Richang added an extensive garden to the property. This included the construction of a three-story pavilion from which one could now "look down upon" clouds and mist collecting along the Huangpu River, as was subsequently reported to the Emperor in Beijing.[41] The completion of two new literary institutes within the city at approximately the same time, known as the *Ruizhu* and *Longmen* institutes, represented an improvement of higher learning opportunities in Shanghai, reinforcing the new Qing emphasis upon higher education in an attempt to counter perceptions of Western scientific and technological superiority.[42] A gradual embrace of Western-introduced technologies by Chinese authorities followed, and by the early 1870s, growing evidence of foreign building décor, styles, and ornament within the Chinese city reveals the extent to which imported architectural elements had become legible, rather than merely threatening, aspects of its own built environment.

Often lost within the broader dynamics of Chinese-foreign tension of the time is the presence of internal conflict within both the foreign and Chinese communities themselves. Increasingly intense, nationalist-driven competition within the foreign Settlements threatened to hamper any prospects for any type of foreign-led, cosmopolitan municipal infrastructure. The British Consul's continued position as main arbiter in all land-related cases involving the Settlement, for example, left non-British foreign merchants increasingly upset over alleged improprieties on the part of British officials towards non-British subjects living there.[43] American officials continued to express outrage over Britain's handling of the Opium War, while Great Britain scoffed at America's indignant attitude in light of their willingness to take full advantage of England's wartime efforts in China. France's late entry into the city, meanwhile, left it at a distinct disadvantage in relation to either country. With war between each country seemingly and perpetually possible, tensions began to manifest themselves almost immediately through a growing divergence of both opinion and vision with regard to the Settlement's future.[44] In 1863, France would extricate itself from the arrangement, creating the French Municipal Council and leaving the city governed by a tripartite municipal structure until 1943.

In the Chinese city, too, distinctions based on migrant laborers' respective hometowns continued to impact the spatial development of particular neighborhoods. Workers from Guangdong, Ningbo, and Shanghai each competed with each other for commercial influence; in 1868, for example, disagreement broke out among the city's Shanghai, Shaoxing, Ningbo and Suzhou construction workers over the issue of salary standards within each building guild. An agreement and merger was subsequently brokered by official Qing carpenter Zhu Bingshi, who became chairman of the newly combined guild, though it would not eventually last.[45]

Representing the City

As the risks posed by cultural cohabitation as well as the ebb and flow of ethnic, national, and commercial pressures wove themselves into the city's architectural, urban, and administrative fabric, visual representations of Shanghai revealed the changes in differing and occasionally contradictory ways. The majority of early pictorial depictions of the city were oil paintings intended for foreign audiences in China and abroad.[46] Most tended to isolate the Settlement's Bund within a single, unobstructed view that emphasized only the cohesion of the foreign community and the regularity with which it had been created. (Plate 19)

Individual architectural monuments are rendered in tiny but crystalline detail, with primary attention paid to the positioning of individual compounds, conveying the sense of a modest but established community. Capturing the perspective of the settlement from the Pudong side of the Huangpu River also provided observers with a view as one might acquire upon approaching the city by boat, imparting an idealistic faith in the enterprise's prospects as an international destination within proximity to Europe and the United States while suggesting a spatial order and lucidity the settlement did not necessarily possess.

Scenes of the Shanghai waterfront, like those from each of China's early treaty ports, stand as supremely optimistic manifestations of foreign expansion onto Chinese soil. Pains were taken to obscure and otherwise remove signs of any potential disturbances. Little to no further depiction of natural landscape within the images exists, echoing early foreign distrust towards the unknowns of the surrounding countryside. The Settlement's natural Chinese context has been cleanly cropped from the images. The Customs House and occasional sampans stand as the only evidence of any Chinese presence within the city, and they sit isolated, surrounded by monuments to Western ingenuity and initiative. The images leave an impression of the Settlement as a static and stable entity, perched upon the edge of a vast unknown but firmly situated along the Huangpu. Even the bustle of marine activity dominating each artwork, which underscored the river's vital role in the Settlement's economic and physical development, conveys a strict horizontal and vertical gridding of ship masts, lines, and rigging whose orthogonality suggests that most efficient of capitalist spatial systems: the grid.

An 1874 Chinese representation of violent Chinese protests in the French Concession triggered by French efforts to build a road through the Ningbo guild's ancestral cemetery also highlights the systematizing of space within the city, though to very different effect. Presenting a far more conflicted, complicated, and equivocal view of the city than foreign-commissioned export paintings, the map depicts both the imposition of a new physical order within the city by the foreign settlements as represented by the street grid as well as the culturally contested areas in which the feared risks of racial cohabitation occasionally made themselves tragically tangible. (Plates 20 and 21)

The rationality of the street system belies chaotic contents. Extensive documentary evidence captures and preserves the memory of the protests, and their victims, for historical record. Six Chinese bodies are depicted strewn upon the streets, though foreign press reports of the incident listed four.[47] Besides the locations of their death, the ages of the victims have been noted. They range from a seventy-year-old man—the victim of a French bayonet—to an eighteen-year-old male. Twisted and crumpled, the corpses have been depicted in excruciatingly precise detail. They awkwardly straddle the careful lines demarcating street and compound property, each seeming to defiantly reject the concession's spatial rigidity and, by extension, the municipal authority of the place itself. One diagonal in particular violently mars the scene's overarching orthogonality: a bullet line stretching from the verandah of M. Percebois, who ultimately opened fire from his compound in self-defense, leading to the body of a sixty-year-old Chinese man, his head haloed in blood.

Conclusion

The contrast between the two visual representations of Shanghai—the placid and orderly facades of the International Settlement versus the bloody aftermath of civil unrest evident along the French Concession's contested boundaries—underscores the respective limits of foreign and Chinese strategies to impose their own contradicting "systems" of architectural and urban order upon the city's spaces.[48] Despite pre-existing processes of economic and cultural change underway in Shanghai prior to foreign arrival, the physical establishment of the British settlement and the eventual founding of both the French Concession and the International Settlement by 1863 tore a particularly significant and disruptive fissure in Shanghai's urban composition and orientation that would linger well into the early twentieth century. Increasingly aggressive and intrusive foreign insertions such as railroad tracks, telegraph lines, and public monuments into the Chinese landscape extended throughout all levels of Chinese society, from the village level to Beijing.[49] These were often met by *fengshui*-related protests fanned by growing Chinese recognition that foreign settlements were not, in fact, temporary insertions that would vanish over time as mercurially as they had arrived continued well into the late nineteenth century throughout the country.[50]

Both the Chinese city and foreign settlements responded to the inherent cultural, economic, and political uncertainties posed by the treaty port experience, though neither was particularly well-equipped to adequately resolve them. New spatial and architectural strategies were needed to compensate for the fundamental flaws in the city's fragmented municipal organization and social structure. These would come, over the course of the early twentieth century, in the form of physically symbolic but theoretically more inclusive civic architectural and urban projects within the city, including the decision to tear down the Chinese city's wall beginning in 1912 and the construction of new International Settlement Municipal Council offices beginning in 1914.

Unlike earlier architectural and urban experiments with containment and isolation, each made an effort to bridge the various cultural, ethnic, and social gaps existing in Shanghai. In doing so, they offered some indication that uncertainty in the city was increasingly becoming perceived as a collective civic experience wrought by mutual exposure to the risks of intensified international contact and the shared prospects of an indeterminate future.

Notes

1. The history of China's treaty ports has long occupied a key position in modern Chinese history. See, for example, John K. Fairbank, *Trade and Diplomacy on the China Coast: The Opening of Treaty Ports, 1842–1854* (Cambridge: Harvard University Press, 1953); Fei Chengkang, *Zhongguo zujie shi* (Shanghai: Shanghai Shehui Kexueyuan Chubanshe, 1991).

2. Extraterritoriality's existence in China may be traced to the tenth century, when Song officials bestowed extraterritorial status upon traders from the Middle East and Europe. It subsequently formed the procedural basis for the legal presence of foreign communities within China. See Yuan Jicheng, *Jindai Zhongguo zujie shi gao* (Beijing: Zhongguo Cai Zheng Jingji Chubanshe, 1988), 1–20.

3. In Shanghai, a settlement consisted of land rented to individual foreigners by Chinese landowners. A concession, by contrast, was defined as an area at a treaty port leased in perpetuity to a foreign government for occupation by its nationals. See Irving Sigmund Friedman, *British Relations with China: 1931–1939* (New York: International Secretariat of Pacific Relations, 1940), 4.

4. See, for example, Robert Bickers, "Shanghailanders: The Formation and Identity of the British Settler Community in Shanghai, 1842–1937," *Past and Present* 159 (1998): 161–211; Leo Ou-fan Lee, *Shanghai Modern: The Flowering of a New Urban Culture in Shanghai, 1930–45* (Cambridge: Harvard University Press, 1999); Kerrie MacPherson, "Designing China's Urban Future: The Greater Shanghai Plan, 1927–1937," *Planning Perspectives* 5 (1990): 39–62; Frederic Wakeman, *Policing Shanghai, 1927–1937* (Berkeley: University of California Press, 1995), 13–14. In 1927, British journalist Arthur Ransome coined the term "The Shanghai Mind" to define the peculiar psychological disaffection displayed by many within the Shanghai foreign community with respect to the broader economic, political, and social context of China. See Ransome, *The Chinese Puzzle* (London: George Allen & Unwin, 1927), 29–30.

5. Rutherford Alcock, *The Capital of the Tycoon: A Narrative of a Three Years' Residence in Japan* (New York: Harper & Brothers, 1863), 38.

6. See Lai Delin, *Zhongguo jindai jianzhu shi yanjiu* (Beijing: Qinghua Daxue Chubanshe, 2007), 41, note 4; John King Fairbank, *Trade and Diplomacy on the China Coast*, 161; Edward Denison and Guang Yuren, *Building Shanghai: The Story of China's Gateway* (West Sussex, England: John Wiley & Sons Ltd, 2006), 43–44; Samuel Liang, "Where the Courtyard Meets the Street: Spatial Culture of the *Li* Neighborhoods, Shanghai, 1870–1900," *Journal of the Society of Architectural Historians* 67, no. 4 (December 2008): 485.

7. The city wall was constructed in 1554 after several attacks by Japanese pirates. See Francis Wood, *No Dogs and Not Many Chinese: Treaty Port Life in China 1843–1943* (London: John Murray, 1998), 19.

8. For an analysis of *li* construction in Shanghai, see Liang, "Where the Courtyard Meets the Street." A discussion of the role of ritual as pertaining to urban space in late Qing society may be found in Richard J. Smith, "Ritual in Ch'ing Culture," in *Orthodoxy in Late Imperial China*, ed. Kwang-Ching Liu (Berkeley: University of California Press, 1990), 281–310.

9. A. R. Zito, "City Gods, Filiality, and Hegemony in Late Imperial China," *Modern China* 13, no. 3 (1987): 333–71.

10. See, for example, Linda Cooke Johnson, *Shanghai: From Market Town to Treat Port, 1074–1858* (Stanford: Stanford University Press, 1995). Also, Bryna Goodman, *Native Place, City, and Nation: Regional Networks and Identity in Shanghai, 1853–1937* (Berkeley: University of California Press, 1995), 48–50.

11. Several foreigners, for example, Medhurst included, deemed the city's *huiguan* to be more impressive than its government buildings. Cited in Elizabeth Perry, *Shanghai on Strike: The Politics of Chinese Labor* (Stanford: Stanford University Press, 1993), 34. See also Goodman, *Native Place, City, and Nation*, 18–20.

12. "Collection of Pamphlets Relating to Land Tenure in the Foreign Concessions, 1845–1883," Land Regulations, November 29, 1845, Special Collections, University of Hong Kong, Hong Kong.

13. Notification, General George Balfour to population of the British Settlement at Shanghai, November 24, 1843. In *Shanghai: Political and Economic Reports, 1842–1943, Volume 1, 1842–1846* (Slough: Archive Editions, Ltd., 2008), 559.

14. See Frank Dikötter, *Exotic Commodities: Modern Objects and Everyday Life in China* (New York: Columbia University Press, 2006), 155–87.

15. By the 1870s, following foreign complaints over the term *yi*, Qing officials encouraged residents to use a new term for the foreign districts: *shili yangchang*, or "ten miles of foreign settlements." Some residents, however, continued to use and justify the use of *yi* in reference to the city's foreign inhabitants. See Yu-chih Lai, "Remapping Borders: Ren Bonian's Frontier Paintings and Urban Life in 1880s Shanghai," *The Art Bulletin* 86, no. 3 (2004): 550–72.

16. In fact, the original design of the church and its spire, which had been intended to rise 160 feet in height, had already been altered when no willing Chinese worker could be found to build the church according to its original specifications. It was replaced by a Gothic construction reaching 80 feet tall. Yates, a Southern Baptist minister from Wake County, North Carolina, moved to Shanghai in 1847 and took a leading role in Shanghai's Western-led debunking campaign against what he saw as the "cruel bondage" geomancy represented to many Chinese adherents. Yates was an extremely influential figure within the Settlement; in 1862, was offered a position on the Shanghai Municipal Council as an interpreter and superintendent of Chinese taxes. One merchant was quoted as believing Yates to have more influence over both the city's Chinese and foreign populations than any other person in Shanghai. See Charles Taylor, *The Story of Yates the Missionary, as Told in His Letters and Reminiscences* (Nashville: Sunday School Board, Southern Baptist Convention, 1898), 61.

17. Jonathan Simon, "Edgework and Insurance in Risk Societies: Some Notes on Victorian Lawyers and Mountaineers," in *Edgework: The Sociology of Risk-Taking*, ed. Stephen Lyng (London: Routledge, 2005), 208–26. See also Elaine Freedgood, *Victorian Writing about Risk: Imagining a Safe England in a Dangerous World* (Cambridge: Cambridge University Press, 2000).

18. See, for example, François Walter, Bernardino Fantini, and Pascal Delvaux, *Les Cultures Du Risque: XVIe–XXIe Siècles* (Genève: Presses d'Histoire Suisse, 2006). See also Gunther Peck, "Manly Gambles: The Politics of Risk on the Comstock Lode, 1860–1880," *Journal of Social History* 26, no. 4 (1993): 701–23.

19. In 1844, for example, George Smith, a British citizen traveling through China on behalf of the Church Missionary Society and in obvious ignorance of the history of the city's walled fortifications, observed that "Like most Chinese cities, [Shanghai's] exterior appearance is not calculated to impress the approaching traveler with the wealth or grandeur of the place." See George Smith, *A Narrative of an Exploratory Visit to Each of the Consular Cities of China, and to the Islands of Hong Kong and Chusan: In Behalf of the Church Missionary Society, in the Years 1844, 1845, 1846* (London: Seeley Burnside & Seeley, 1847), 137.

20. Catherine Vance Yeh, "Where Is Shanghai? Maps and the Struggle to Define the Image of the City between 1860 and 1930," in *Peking, Shanghai, Shenzhen*, eds. Kai Vockler and Dirk Luckow (Frankfurt: Campus Verlag, 2000), 506–11.

21. W. H. Medhurst, *A Glance at the Interior of China* (Shanghai: Mission Press, 1849). See also Taylor, *The Story of Yates the Missionary*, 64. Such language echoes what Gregory Clancey has studied with respect to the interaction of Western and Japanese building cultures in nineteenth-century Meiji Japan, where certain construction materials were considered to be

more exemplary indicators of "civilization" and progress than others. See Gregory K. Clancey, *Earthquake Nation: The Cultural Politics of Japanese Seismicity, 1868–1930* (Berkeley: University of California Press, 2006). In fact, significant environmental degradation over the course of the Qing dynasty had led to increased material conservation throughout the country, producing less substantial building material. See Mark Elvin, "The Environmental Legacy of Imperial China," *The China Quarterly [Special Issue: China's Environment]*, no. 156 (1998): 733–56.

22. Robert Fortune, *Three Years' Wanderings in the Northern Provinces of China: Including a Visit to the Tea, Silk, and Cotton Countries: With an Account of the Agriculture and Horticulture of the Chinese, New Plants, Etc.* (London: J. Murray, 1847), 127. Another early foreign visitor remarked that during his 1847 visit through the Chinese city, he saw no less than "six or seven dead bodies," two of which were found lying at the entrance of a temple. See Smith, *A Narrative of an Exploratory Visit*, 153. Between 1857 and 1858, the only architectural feature George Wingrove Cooke, a special correspondent in China for *The London Times*, noted in his travels through Shanghai was the Chinese city's twenty-foot-tall "baby tower," within which families abandoned unwanted children. See George Wingrove Cooke, *China: Being "The Times" Special Correspondence from China in the Years 1857–58* (Wilmington: Scholarly Resources, 1972), 99.

23. Alexander Michie, *The Englishman in China during the Victorian Era as Illustrated in the Career of Sir Rutherford Alcock, K.C.B., D.C.L., Vol. 1* (Edinburgh: W. Blackwood, 1910), 127.

24. "Minutes of Public Meeting of Foreign Renters of Land, July 11, 1854," Collection of pamphlets relating to Land Tenure in the Foreign Concessions, 1845–1883, Special Collections, University of Hong Kong Library, Hong Kong.

25. See "The S.V.C. Parade," *North China Herald*, December 28, 1870.

26. In 1847, Arthur Dallas, Shanghai representative for Jardine Matheson, was asked by the Alliance Fire Assurance Company to provide sketches of his newly constructed compound for the purposes of fire insurance. In response, Dallas promised that "I beg to acknowledge receipt of your favor of the 18th ultimo requesting ground plan and description of the buildings occupied by foreigners. With regard to the ground plan, I have been long promised one by HM's Vice Consul, and I shall now press the matter and endeavor to procure one. The buildings are all detached of solid brick work with tiled roofs and generally in spacious compounds, some few of the buildings have wooden pillars built in the walls. I look upon both houses and godowns in Shanghai as safe risks." See letter from A. G. Dallas to Alliance Fire Assurance Company, September 9, 1847, Jardine Matheson Company Archive, Cambridge, England.

27. Mercantile compounds became known as "compradoric" architecture in reference to the Chinese compradors who had first facilitated foreign trade in Canton. See Johnson, *Shanghai: From Market Town to Treaty Port, 1074–1858,* 195–96, 250–51; 387, note 53.

28. For a full discussion of the Masonic network as a component of British formal and informal empires, see Jessica Harland-Jacobs, *Builders of Empire: Freemasons and British Imperialism, 1717–1927* (Chapel Hill: University of North Carolina Press, 2007), 10. A number of those present at the Settlement's founding were Masons, as were two of the three founding members of the city's Committee of Roads and Jetties. The city's first Masonic lodge was founded in 1849. See Frederick M. Gratton, *Freemasonry in Shanghai and Northern China* (Taipei: Ch'eng Wen Publishing Company, 1900), 305.

29. Shared features included flat or gently sloping roofed structures and over-hanging, shuttered verandahs, located on either the first or second floors and often supported by decorative, neoclassical orders in an attempt to shield the structure's windows from the sun. See Thomas W. Kingsmill, "Early Architecture in Shanghai," *North China Daily News & Herald*, July–December, 1911, p. 30.

30. See Timothy Mitchell, *Colonising Egypt* (Cambridge: Cambridge University Press, 1988), 32. See also Bernard Cohn, "The Census, Social Structure, and Objectification in South Asia," in *An Anthropologist among the Historians and Other Essays* (Delhi: Oxford University Press, 1987), 224–54.

31. Composed of triad secret society members, the Small Swords Society has been connected to the simultaneous civil unrest perpetrated by the Taiping Rebellion, though they were not directly related. See Earl Cranston, "Shanghai in the Taiping Period," *The Pacific Historical Review* 5, no. 3 (1936): 151.

32. The Taiping Rebellion was launched by Hong Xiuquan, a failed civil service candidate, or *shengyuan*, from Guangxi who believed himself to be the younger brother of Jesus Christ. Beginning in 1847, the movement spread throughout southern China, and a Taiping capital was established in Nanjing from 1853 to 1864. They would approach Shanghai in 1863. A history of the Taiping Rebellion may be found in Thomas H. Reilly, *The Taiping Heavenly Kingdom: Rebellion and Blasphemy of Empire* (Seattle: University of Washington Press, 2004.)

33. Though British officials supported the official prohibition of Chinese residents, American representatives found it unnecessary and counter-productive to America's long-term interests in Shanghai, which US Consul Humphrey Marshall predicted would become "the greatest city of Eastern Asia." Foreign exclusion of Chinese residents "exercised exactly the spirit of exclusivity towards them, which we [the US] now complain of when exercised towards ourselves. It cannot be sound policy to segregate the

populations, and instead of prohibiting the settlement of Chinese among the foreigners, it should be invited." At the same time, Marshall doubted that any Chinese would actually exercise the privilege unless he was "some man of fortune," noting that one wealthy Chinese merchant had already rented a foreign-styled residence within the settlement's boundaries. Letter from Humphrey Marshall to Secretary of State W. L. Marchy, July 26, 1853, "Despatches from U.S. Ministers to China." National Archives, College Park, MD.

34. Matthew T. Yates, *Ancestral Worship and Fung-Shuy [Read at the Missionary Quarterly Meeting, Shanghai, September 16th, 1867]*, 22.

35. *The British Shanghai Trade Report and Returns for 1865* begins with the admission that "probably no year ever opened on the trade of this port with gloomier prospects than 1865. The vast exodus of Chinese after the defeat of the rebels had left stranded in serious difficulties many traders ... The effect upon the state of business at his port was striking." See *Shanghai Political and Economic Reports, 1842–1943: 1863–1866, Volume 5*, 504–6.

36. Consulate Road, for example, became known as Beijing Road, while Park Lane was renamed Nanjing Road, Rope Walk Road became Jiujiang Road, and Custom House Road was now to be known as Hankou Road. Bridge Street was renamed Sichuan Road, Church Street became known as Jiangxi Road, and Barrier Road became Henan Road.

37. Letter from Anson Burlingame to George Seward, June 25, 1863, "Despatches from U.S. Ministers to China." Burlingame, the American Minister to China stationed in Beijing, asked Qing officials about opening the wall. Beijing deferred the decision to local authorities, who ultimately decided against it.

38. These structures included the new Masonic Lodge, the foundation stone for which was laid in 1865; the new Trinity Cathedral, designed by Sir Gilbert Scott and completed by William Kidner in 1869; the new Oriental Banking Corporation building, designed by Kidner in 1870; new proposed municipal council offices in 1873; improvements made to the pre-existing French Consulate and the construction of a new British Consulate that same year; and unrealized plans for a new American Consulate, first announced in 1874.

39. "Shanghai," *North China Herald*, July 5, 1867.

40. Yuansheng Liang, *The Shanghai Taotai: Linkage Man in a Changing Society, 1843–90* (Honolulu: University of Hawai'i Press, 1990), 46–66.

41. See Yue Yu, *Chong xiu Shanghai xian zhi*, 1871.

42. Liang, *The Shanghai Taotai*, 157.

43. Johnson, *Shanghai*, 243–45.

44. A November 1845 dispatch from Jardine Matheson offices in Hong Kong stated that "In the event of war with America, there is no doubt that—Bills drawn by Americans in China under letters of credit from authorized agents

in America of English houses, and negotiated previous to the outbreak of war to a British subject could not be refused payment or acceptance upon any plea whatever if clean bills. And even if conditional on the ground of security from shipping documents under ordinary circumstances the bills could not be refused." See correspondence, Jardine Matheson Offices, Hong Kong to Shanghai, November 1845. Jardine Matheson Company Archives, Cambridge, University, Cambridge, England.

45. See Xue Liyong, *Shanghai tan diming zhanggu* (Shanghai: Tongji Daxue Chubanshe, 1994), 330.

46. For a history of these paintings, see Carl Crossmann, *The Decorative Arts of the China Trade* (Woodbridge, Suffolk: Antique Collectors' Club, 1991).

47. *North China Herald*, June 26, 1852.

48. Henri Lefebvre, *The Production of Space* (Cambridge: Blackwell, 1991), 16.

49. See, for example, the circumstances surrounding the construction, purchase, and subsequent destruction of the Wusong Railway by Chinese officials. David Pong, "Confucian Patriotism and the Destruction of the Woosung Railway, 1877." *Modern Asian Studies* 7, no. 4 (1973): 647–76. See also Erik Baark, *Lightning Wires: The Telegraph and China's Technological Modernization, 1860–1890* (London: Greenwood Press, 1997).

50. On June 21, 1870, for example, a group of seven thousand Chinese residents attacked the Catholic Church and French Consulate in Tianjin, a treaty port located north of Shanghai. The mob looted both buildings and brutally killed twenty foreigners found within them, including the French Consul, a monk, and ten nuns. See "The Tientsin Massacre," *Shanghai Evening Courier*, July 4, 1870. Wrote the Shanghai Chamber of Commerce to Earl Granville in 1870, "Ever since the opening of the various ports of Nanking, the security of foreign life and property has been practically, though tacitly, guaranteed by the presence or near proximity of one or more of Her Majesty's vessels-of-war. The mass of the people, both at the open ports and in the interior, have always been well-disposed towards foreigners … For various reasons, which it is unnecessary here to recount, this conviction has been rapidly dying out, and within the last two years many outrages have been committed on Europeans. See letter from Shanghai General Chamber of Commerce to Earl Granville, September 30, 1870, "Consular Dispatches, 1847–1906," RG 59, General Records of the Department of State, 1756–1999, National Archives, College Park, MD.

in a number of [illegible] a congratulatory [illegible] to the outbreak of [illegible] should not be allowed [illegible] Not [illegible] on the ground [illegible] and shipping [illegible] make [illegible] the [illegible] could not be [illegible] (in the [illegible]) [illegible] Peking to Shanghai, [illegible] 1863 [illegible] Maritime Customs [illegible]

8. See [illegible] Young, *Shanghai* [illegible] Chinese [illegible] (1861), 38.

9. For a history of the [illegible] see [illegible]

10. [illegible] *North-China Herald* [illegible] 1862.

11. [illegible]

12. See, for example, the circumstances surrounding the construction, [illegible] and destruction of the Woosung Railway [illegible]

13. On [illegible], for example, a group of seven [illegible] consul [illegible] north of Shanghai [illegible] Shanghai [illegible] July [illegible] the [illegible] since the [illegible] security [illegible] guaranteed by the presence of [illegible] the [illegible] many [illegible] letter from [illegible] Consul [illegible] Shanghai [illegible] 1870 [illegible] Department of State, [illegible] National Archives [illegible]

8
Fabricating Justice

Conflict and Contradiction in the Making of the Hong Kong Supreme Court, 1898–1912

G. A. Bremner

Erected nearly a century ago, the old Hong Kong Supreme Court (1898–1912) still stands proud on the eastern perimeter of Statue Square, Central. Dwarfed by commercial skyscrapers which have since risen all around, including the HSBC headquarters by Sir Norman Foster, it is one of very few historic buildings left on Hong Kong Island dating back to the heady days of British imperial rule. Even the harbor's edge, which it once graced, greeting visitors as they arrived by boat, has almost disappeared from view. Indeed, it is no longer even a court of law, having been the offices of the Hong Kong Legislative Council since 1985.

Despite these developments, the old Supreme Court building has an important story to tell. At the time of its completion the building was understood to signify something noble and inspiring in the minds of Hong Kong's governing elite. Located in one of Britain's most geographically isolated and politically tenuous colonies, this building, with its bold and explicit references to the English classical tradition, emerged to become not only a conspicuous statement of British colonial rule but also a clear allusion to the imperial metropolis and its cultural authority. (see Figure 8.1)

But appearances can be deceiving. The facts surrounding the building's design and construction reveal the very complex, tense, and, at times, dysfunctional relationship between Whitehall and the colonial government in Hong Kong. This concerned not only the imposition of directives from London and their interpretation "on the spot" but also the involvement of the local Chinese. As a key administrative institution, the Hong Kong Supreme Court was a symbol of a very particular

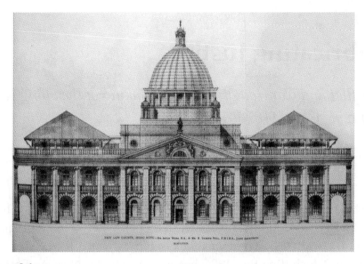

Figure 8.1

Final design of the Hong Kong Supreme Court by Aston Webb and E. Ingress Bell exhibited at the Royal Academy in 1908. Source: *The Builder*, May 1908.

discourse regarding British imperial government: the rule of law. This is important because there was no more fundamental or significant set of ideas in the British popular imagination than those of liberty and justice.

As quite a lot of documentary evidence still survives on the Hong Kong Supreme Court, it provides an excellent case study for a close reading of primary source material concerning the relationship between architecture and colonial culture in late nineteenth- and early twentieth-century Hong Kong. In what follows, every aspect of the old Supreme Court will be explored. Beginning with the issue of style (central to the articulation of identity and imperial power), the essay will move on to consider the design process itself and the problems that emerged as a result of a misunderstanding over who was in control. The wider cultural and political context will then be examined, looking at how anxieties over the transposition of British law and order in Southeast Asia affected perceptions of the new building and the urban context in which it was situated. Finally, the essay will conclude with a discussion on the involvement of the Hong Kong Chinese in the building's construction and what a foreign code of law and its representations signified to that community.

Edwardian Baroque: Style and Empire in Early Twentieth-Century Hong Kong

In order to appreciate the wider resonances of a building such as the Hong Kong Supreme Court, it is necessary to consider the architectural context from which it emerged. This is especially important with respect to public building projects in the British Empire. Anyone who has studied the history of architecture in Britain's former colonial empire will be aware that key institutional buildings relating to imperial governance were designed to project notions of identity and power.[1] To be sure, the nature and degree of this projection changed over time, having much to do with anxieties concerning Britain's apparent economic, cultural, and political superiority in the world. Nevertheless, appearances mattered. This idea was doubly important with respect to a court of law.

The case of the Hong Kong Supreme Court refers to a specific time and place: Southeast Asia during the late Victorian and Edwardian period. This period witnessed the emergence of a particular mode of formal expression in British architecture known as the "Grand Manner" or Edwardian Baroque. This style was neither formally homogenous nor particularly long-lived. Although "baroque" is the moniker that has now attached itself to this movement, in reality the sources from which it drew inspiration extended well beyond the seventeenth century to include Anglo-Palladian models and motifs. Indeed, it would be difficult to find a more self-consciously "national" and therefore narrowly representative style than the Edwardian Baroque in the history of British architecture. It came closer perhaps than any other style in modern British architecture to realizing a form of expression that was not only identifiably "English" but also sufficiently imposing for a nation that was experiencing unprecedented growth, both at home and abroad.

As Alistair Service has observed, the Edwardian Baroque style was forged in an atmosphere of high patriotic and imperial fervor. With the diamond jubilee of Queen Victoria (1897), the Second Anglo-Boer War (1899–1902), and the coronation of Edward VII (1902) all in quick succession, this was a time in which the "moneyed public" in England were demanding an architecture that represented British might and that was able to communicate the feelings they had towards their monarch, their country, and the empire.[2] It is precisely these national and imperial connotations that gave Edwardian Baroque architecture its vitality. Among the distinguishing features of this style were references to London and the buildings of Sir Christopher Wren, in particular St. Paul's Cathedral (1675–1710), Hampton Court Palace (1690), and the Royal Naval Hospital at Greenwich (1696–1716). St. Paul's especially was considered by many to be the noblest and most original work of architecture in England.[3] Moreover, it was the great monument of the metropolis, of London, a city that was by the late nineteenth century not only the cultural, political, and economic epicenter of British national life, but also the capital of a worldwide empire.[4]

As interest in Wren and English Baroque (or "Renaissance" as it was known at the time) architecture continued to grow into the first decade of the twentieth century, an identifiable trend emerged in which overt reference to prominent metropolitan buildings became increasingly common in new public architecture.[5] This was also the case in the colonies. Being a mode of expression that appealed to notions of British heritage and identity, the Edwardian Baroque style was naturally appropriate for such contexts. Indeed, several of Britain's most prominent architects of the period, including William Emerson, Aston Webb, Herbert Baker, and Edwin Lutyens, had all designed monumental public buildings abroad in this style.[6] Emerson's Victoria Memorial in Calcutta (1904–21) and Baker's Union Buildings in Pretoria (1910–13) have come to exemplify this tradition and its imperial connotations, culminating in Lutyens' magisterial Viceroy's House in New Delhi (1912–31).[7] (Plates 22 and 23)

The Hong Kong Supreme Court is part of this tradition. It is, in short, an intelligent and knowing amalgam of late seventeenth- and early eighteenth-century English models. Indeed, as the architects were keen to point out, the dome of the building was based directly on that of St. Paul's.[8]

Webb and Bell's design, however, is much more austere, even solemn, than Wren's masterpiece. Its cool simplicity is closer to examples such as John Webb's King Charles Block at Greenwich (1662) or even James Gandon's Four Courts building in Dublin (1776–1802) (see Figure 8.2). These similarities are most apparent in the way the architects have accommodated both levels of the building within a long colonnaded range fronted by a giant hexastyle portico screen, flanked by double-height pavilions at either end. Notwithstanding the verandah space, these features also associate the building with mid-eighteenth-century English country house design.[9] (see Figure 8.3)

Figure 8.2

King Charles Block, Royal Naval Hospital, Greenwich (1662), by John Webb

Figure 8.3

Original design for Houghton Hall, Norfolk (1722), by Colen Campbell from *Vitruvius Britannicus* (1715–25)

This broadly Palladian theme was carried through in the planning of the building (see Figure 8.4). The rather simple, geometrically pro-portioned layout is based on a series of intersecting rectangular spaces that culminate in the central or "large" court space situated directly beneath the dome. The secondary courtroom spaces are double height and amply proportioned, while the main space is distinguished by its hemispherical ceiling, oculus, and large thermal window, recalling well-known Palladian and Anglo-Palladian prototypes.[10]

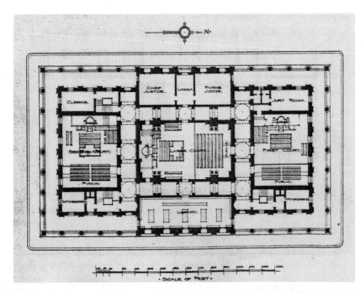

Figure 8.4

Webb and Bell's plan for the Hong Kong Supreme Court (1908). A centralized plan based around the "large" courtroom. Source: *The Builder*, May 1908

This hankering after a distinctive national style in British architecture was nothing new. It had been an element of architectural debate in Britain (and elsewhere) for much of the second half of the nineteenth century, and was part of that process of national self-examination and wider social transformation that resulted from Britain's changing political constitution and rise to world power. What the idea of Sir Christopher Wren had come to mean by this time may be gleaned from the thoughts of one of the Edwardian Baroque movement's earliest and most vociferous exponents, the Scottish-born architect John Brydon (1840–1901). Speaking at the Architectural Association in April 1889, Brydon praised what he saw as the self-reliance and originality of Wren in forging an architecture that was unique and "civilized." "It had been a wonderful century," he declared:

> the country had made advances in all that makes for the greatness of a nation. It was no longer a question of England and Scotland, but of Great Britain … The East India Company had been incorporated, and made great progress in the formation of what ultimately became our Empire in the East. England's Colonial Empire had been

founded by the settlements in the Carolinas and the New England
States—the beginning of that Greater Britain which has come to be
such a factor in the civilization of the world. ... In Literature we
have the immortals Milton, and Bunyan, and Dryden; in Science
the mighty Newton, and Harvey, and Flamstead, the founding of
the Royal Society and the Royal Observatory. ... Through sixty
years of it all, Wren worked away at his architecture. ... Wren
may be said to have closed the Early English Renaissance, which
had lasted about one hundred years. It had now become firmly
established as the national style—the vernacular of the country. ...
We must recognize that we are here in the presence of an English
Classical style as truly the embodiment of civilization ... a living,
working, architectural reality, as much a part of England as its literature or its great school of painting ... the nearest to us in time
and in similitude of requirements.[11]

In this passage Brydon draws a parallel between late seventeenth- and
late nineteenth-century British history. In his view, the age of Wren,
much like his own, was a period of unity, prosperity, and unfettered
expansion. The "high ideal" of "vigorous manhood" that Brydon so
readily associates with English architecture of the period was considered commensurate with the bold and adventurous spirit of the nation
itself. It was for this reason he considered late seventeenth-century
English architecture to be the most appropriate and fitting model for
modern British architects.[12]

With this in mind, the design for the Hong Kong Supreme Court
can be seen as a species of a movement in British architecture that had
already begun to gain momentum by the 1890s. Thus, Webb and Bell's
new building was an exercise in the imposition of metropolitan taste.
It had all the requisite adaptations for a tropical climate, but was based
on formal design initiatives that were clearly contemporary in character and British in origin.

This is important because it tells us something about how Edwardian
Baroque architecture found its way to the colonies, reflecting Webb's
own thinking on the role of public architecture. Like his contemporary
William Emerson, Webb shared an enthusiasm for the idea of "Greater
Britain."[13] He had hoped that a closer union might be forged between
Britain and its colonies in the future, leading to the development of
an architectural style that would be appreciated "all over the world as
representing this wonderful empire."[14] In this respect the Hong Kong

Supreme Court is linked to Webb's proposal to redevelop The Mall
in London as a showcase of imperial solidarity following the death
of Queen Victoria in 1901, thus establishing a formal dialogue that
attempted to unify the empire architecturally through time and space.[15]

The Edwardian Baroque style and its extension abroad can therefore
be seen as corollary to the "unionist" political agenda of the period that
envisaged the possibility of forming a British super state, or *zollverein*,
through imperial federation and systematic tariff reform.[16] This idea
was also driven by anxieties over the increasing competition Britain
faced from its major foreign and industrialized rivals, in particular
Germany, Russia, and the United States of America.[17] Thus, against this
wider backdrop of shifting spheres of influence, and beleaguered by
anxieties of its own, the colony of Hong Kong seemed like the perfect
location in which the bold and ebullient forms of the Edwardian
Baroque could find favor among those looking to stamp the majesty
of empire on the urban fabric of the city of Victoria and thereby the
authority of Britain on the wider region. But the colonial government
in Hong Kong had other ideas.

Between London and China: Tensions in Developing the New Supreme Court

By the time Aston Webb and E. Ingress Bell came to design the new
Hong Kong Supreme Court, they had already established a reputation
in Britain as an outstanding architectural partnership. They had not
only been appointed consulting architects to the Crown Agents for the
colonies,[18] but Webb had designed, among other buildings, the new law
courts in Birmingham (1887–91), the Royal United Services Institute
(1893–95) in London, and had won the competition for the Victoria &
Albert Museum (1891–1909). It was in their capacity as architects to
the Crown Agents that Webb and Bell first became involved with the
design of the Supreme Court in Hong Kong.

The project, however, did not run smoothly. The building's confident exterior belies the unease that characterized much of the planning
process. The tensions that developed between Whitehall and the local
legislature in Hong Kong over the building's design highlight the
difficulties inherent not only in managing an architectural project at

distance but also in attempting to negotiate issues of authority and identity in the wider British imperial world. Initially the committee appointed by the governing authority in Hong Kong (1894) to oversee the erection of a new supreme court had not anticipated employing an architect from Britain. The intention was to hold a limited competition open to architects from Hong Kong, Shanghai, and Singapore. Apart from a new courthouse, the committee had hoped that the competition would also provide the opportunity to develop the entire site, including a new complex of municipal buildings and a post office.[19] It was taken for granted that experience in designing buildings for the tropics, as well as knowledge of local building materials and practices, was essential for a satisfactory result.

However, in June 1896, after receiving knowledge of this proposal from the Hong Kong executive, the then Secretary of State for the Colonies, Joseph Chamberlain (1836–1914), swiftly rejected the idea. He was prepared neither to approve the competition in principle nor sanction the additional buildings. The question as to who would foot the bill for such a complex of buildings was of course central to his decision, especially now that Hong Kong's sanitary system required major redevelopment.[20] Moreover, Chamberlain believed that architectural competitions were a waste of time. In his reply to the Hong Kong executive, he remarked curtly that the consulting architects to the Crown Agents ought to have been engaged from the very beginning, insisting that they (Webb and Bell) possessed the requisite experience in designing buildings for the tropics.[21] As the Hong Kong government was unable to realize their vision without assistance from the Imperial Parliament in London, it was left with little option but to acquiesce. In February 1898 it officially dropped its plan for additional buildings and focused solely on a new Supreme Court.

Not having visited Hong Kong, Webb and Bell based their design on knowledge they gleaned from maps and photographs.[22] The site for the new building formed part of the Praya Reclamation Scheme (also referred to as the Central District Reclamation Scheme) completed in 1895. At first the Hong Kong Legislative Council wanted to place the new Supreme Court opposite the recently completed Hongkong Club, but the architects recommended that it be situated west of the cricket ground.[23] By September 1898, preliminary sketch plans had been prepared and sent to Hong Kong for consideration. Among the sketches sent was a perspective drawing that emphasized the building's key architectural features. In the letter that accompanied this drawing, the architects explained that if the new court was to convey the correct impression as a public institution, then it had to be composed of bold and imposing elements.[24]

The initial reaction to this proposal was relatively positive. However, it was not until a year later, when the final plans arrived in Hong Kong, that significant problems began to arise. After consultation with the colony's Director of Public Works (R. D. Ormsby), the Chief Justice, the Puisne Judge, the Acting Attorney General, and other officials, it became apparent that the final design was not what the government had expected. Despite their supposed experience in designing buildings for the tropics, Webb and Bell had failed to include even the most basic shading devices on the building's exterior. "The said Plans," complained Ormsby,

> are far from what they should be, in fact they may be said to be faulty. There are several portions of the building without any verandah and other portions with uncovered verandahs—in short wholly unsuitable for the climate here.[25]

It was also noted that the architects had "placed the main Entrance and Façade on the wrong side of the building, viz.—on the East side."[26]

These problems gave the Hong Kong Legislative Council further ammunition for demanding that the project be handed to a local firm. They reiterated their warning to Chamberlain that a local architect would have been "far more likely to produce a satisfactory and economical" design.[27] But if these problems had been identified at meetings in which the preliminary sketch designs were discussed, Ormsby had failed to communicate them to the architects. It seems that the committee had simply assumed the main entrance would face west across the public gardens. Ormsby also complained that the final design did not correspond with the preliminary sketches. "The appearance of the dome in particular is entirely different," he noted, "and the graceful proportions of the sketches do not seem to have been maintained in the finished drawings."[28]

In response to these objections, Webb and Bell cited issues of security (a discrete entrance for prisoners) and ease of access as the main reasons for orientating the building toward the east, adding "of course large scale elevations have a different appearance on paper than when put into perspective."[29] Not having visited Hong Kong, it seems that Webb and Bell had entirely misunderstood the geographical significance of the site, believing that the new court was best placed overlooking the cricket ground rather than the public gardens. Defending their decision, the architects argued that they were not told of the Hong Kong government's requirement to have the building face the public gardens and that it would be a major inconvenience to alter the design at this late stage.[30] The Colonial Office agreed, stipulating that the orientation of the building should remain as designed unless changing it was deemed absolutely necessary.

In June 1900, in response to further agitations from Hong Kong, the architects sent six new drawings for consideration. Although these drawings did not show a reorientation of the building, they did show a modification in the upper floor plan and a reversal of the main elevations so that the pediment now looked over the public gardens (the main entrance was to remain on the eastern side of the building).[31] But Webb and Bell were not content in making these changes, pointing out that such alterations would undoubtedly compromise the building's internal function.[32] Though acknowledging the architects' objections, the Hong Kong government insisted that the entire building be reversed, having the public entrance to the west and the judges' rooms to the east. Accordingly, Webb and Bell submitted a revised scheme in September 1900.[33]

Despite this squabbling, Webb and Bell's overall design managed to maintain favor with the Hong Kong authorities. Their decision to employ a "colossal order" and to cap the building with a monumental dome was a simple yet effective solution; one that the governing authorities were easily persuaded would lend novelty and distinction to the city's skyline. As the photographs of the site Webb and Bell received reveal, their proposed law court was surrounded by buildings of a rather formulaic nature. These included the north façade of the Hongkong and Shanghai Banking Corporation (HSBC), the town hall (known as City Hall), the Queen's Building, the Prince's Building, and the elite Hongkong Club (see Figures 8.5 and 8.6). Designed by local firms, these buildings were composed in a style that combined the architectural traditions of the colony and the "free classic" Italianate manner that had become popular in Britain and its colonies during the late nineteenth century. Since described as "compradoric,"[34] this style had reached Hong Kong via India as an adapted form of classicism suited to tropical conditions. It first appeared in southern China during the late eighteenth century, used predominantly by European merchants for their warehouse factories in the port city of Canton (Guangzhou). When the city of Victoria was established as a British colonial settlement in 1842, it quickly became a standard building style. Although striking, the buildings along the harbor front designed in this style conveyed a certain feebleness and monotony, especially when viewed at a distance. Webb and Bell's idea of strengthening the Supreme Court's visual effect with bold, sculptural elements—accentuated by the intense tropical light—was intended to give it a sense of scale and legibility far greater than any of the buildings nearby.

Figure 8.5

The Prince's Building (1899–1904) (left) and the Queen's Building (1890s) (right) were located opposite the new law courts across the public garden (Statue Square).

Figure 8.6

The harbor front in the early 1890s showing "compradoric" style merchant premises

Although adapted in various ways to the climate, it is clear that a deliberate effort was made to distinguish the new law courts and to associate them more specifically with emerging trends in modern British architecture. Whether this was the result of a lack of sympathy on the part of the architects for local practice, or simply the desire to pursue their own creative agenda, it nevertheless worked to suppress the local "compradoric" influence, stamping the design, as Herbert Baker might have said, with a clear and identifiable sense of metropolitan authority.

What the design and construction of the new Supreme Court in Hong Kong reveals is the difficulty that oftentimes accompanied such endeavors. It was neither a case of sending drawings from England nor of implementing them as planned. It is clear, initially at least, that the local authorities in Hong Kong felt both confident and justified in controlling the project, insisting not only on a local architect but also that the entire site be redeveloped. It is equally clear, however, that they were accountable to Whitehall and, when it came to the deployment of Exchequer funds, the Colonial Office did not shy away from making its opinion known.

This diplomatic spat reminds us that there were many different and oftentimes conflicting agencies bound up in the imperial
enterprise, even at the level of administration. Although the various
people involved had overlapping interests, they did not necessarily
view empire or colonization in the same way. As demonstrated here,
this could lead to misunderstanding and division within the imperial
power itself as lines of responsibility were challenged, broken down,
and then recalibrated. There was, no doubt, an air of authoritarian
posturing in the way the matter was handled by Chamberlain and the
Colonial Office, but this was to be expected. The colony of Hong Kong's
record with the Imperial Parliament in Britain was far from exemplary.
Tensions between Whitehall and the executive authorities in Hong
Kong dated back to the colony's foundation in 1842, and these were
only exacerbated with the design of the new Court. Understanding
these conflicts is important in assessing the degree to which a building
such as the Hong Kong Supreme Court may be seen to have embodied
and stood for notions of British national and imperial identity.

In Loco: The Law, Architecture, and the Significance of Place

The Hong Kong Supreme Court was more than just an image of
national genius; it was, as its function suggests, an important civic
institution. It existed to facilitate a more efficient and rigorous form
of legal administration in the colony, one that had suffered for years
owing to inadequate amenities.[35] It was therefore a structure that in
its day-to-day functioning was intended as a machine for upholding
English civilization and the rule of law.

Importantly, the building was located in a space that was already
politically charged and therefore culturally significant. Owned by
the Hongkong and Shanghai Banking Corporation, this space was
reclaimed from Victoria Harbor as part of the 1895 Reclamation
Scheme. It was initially envisaged as a public garden but was dubbed
"Royal Square" after a statue commemorating Queen Victoria's golden
jubilee was erected there in 1896.[36] It later became known simply as
"Statue Square" after memorials to other dignitaries such as Edward
VII, Queen Alexandra, George V, and the Duke of Connaught were
placed there during the early twentieth century. (see Figure 8.7)

Figure 8.7

Statue Square showing the new Supreme Court (upper right) and the Queen Victoria Memorial (upper left). The Hongkong Club can be seen in the background behind the law courts.

Directly to the east of this site were the grounds of the Hong Kong Cricket Club, while to the south was City Hall and the Hongkong and Shanghai Bank headquarters building. Across Queen's Road was the military parade ground (Murray Barracks), the southern edge of which ran adjacent to the Anglican cathedral (St. John's) and, further up the hill, Government House. In time, other socially eminent institutions such as the Hongkong Club relocated to this site. Thus, by the time the decision was taken to erect the new Supreme Court on this reclaimed piece of land, it had acquired a considerable degree of meaning for the European community in Hong Kong, becoming fundamental to their sense of colonial and imperial identity. (see Figure 8.8)

Evidence of this can be found, for example, in the ceremony that accompanied the unveiling of the statue of Queen Victoria in 1896. The master of ceremonies on that occasion, the influential American-born businessman Catchick P. Chater, wasted little time in reiterating the well-worn rhetoric of British imperial ascendancy. Addressing

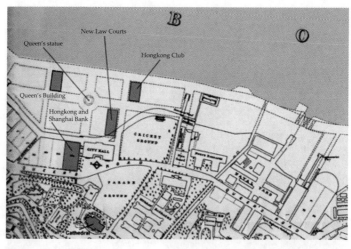

Figure 8.8

Site plan showing relative location of significant buildings and spaces in and around Statue Square

Sir William Robinson (the colony's Governor), Chater explained why there had been such a delay in erecting the statue:

> It was not because Hongkong was one whit behind other British Colonies in wishing to prove its dutiful regard for Her who reigns over us ... No, Sir. It was because we recognized that such a Statue as this should be placed in an appropriate and conspicuous spot, a spot worthy, ... here in this commanding position, in the best part of this City, named after our QUEEN.[37]

Even after the colony's most familiar names had "vanished and been forgotten," he added,

> this Statue remains, to impress upon those who follow us the rights and privileges which, under British laws, they will ever enjoy, the security which the British Constitution throws over those who live within the sphere of its protection, and above all, Sir, the freedom, the greatest benefit perhaps that mankind has ever known, which exists to-day, and always must exist, beneath the Royal Standard of Great Britain.[38]

The key sentiment underpinning Chater's speech was liberty. The way he drew instinctively on the eternal appeal of self-determination as constituted through the notion of British law, invested the site, indeed, the whole city, with a distinct aura of British liberal idealism. His entire speech was an unambiguous use of culturally emotive language that reflected in a rather credulous manner the apparent worth and universal appeal of metropolitan values.

Although this is but one example of the peculiar way in which space was culturally appropriated in nineteenth-century Hong Kong, it is significant for its explicit connection between colonial identity and concepts of liberty, justice, and the rule of law. Such values were considered especially worthy of evocation given that Hong Kong Island was understood to be surrounded by the illiberal and despotic forces of a culturally backward "Mandarindom" (China), and that somehow Britain's presence in the region was a beacon of modernity.[39]

These sentiments are important because they formed the basis of the ceremony for the laying of the new Supreme Court's foundation stone several years later. Attended by the elite of Hong Kong society, the stone itself was laid by the then-Governor, Sir Henry Arthur Blake, on the afternoon of November 12, 1903.[40] Like Chater before him, Blake sought to remind those present of the gravitas by which British colonial rule had maintained its authority in Hong Kong. Referring to the architecture of the new building, he emphasized its symbolic power. When Victoria had developed into a larger and more prosperous city, Blake observed, the Supreme Court "with its lofty dome" would remain "a fitting and proper temple for the pure, impartial and incorruptible administration" of British law. Although rather innocuous, the true significance of Blake's comments is revealed when considered alongside those of the colony's Chief Justice, Sir William Goodman (1847–1928). In his own speech, which immediately preceded Blake's, Goodman drew attention to Britain's responsibilities as a European power in Asia, professing that: "It is most important, *especially so in the Oriental countries*, that justice should be administered not only with firmness, impartiality and promptitude, but also with dignity."

Goodman's remarks approach what Rudyard Kipling had described only four years earlier as "the white man's burden." They are laden with the assumption that Asiatics were "inferior" to Europeans, and that it was somewhat incumbent upon the "white man" to guide such people towards "law and order" and to inculcate notions of Western civilization (for their own good). Such pronouncements, it must be said, were not uncommon in Hong Kong and were symptomatic of widely held opinions regarding the character of Asian peoples.[41]

Nevertheless, part of the professed function of the British legal system in the colonial world was transparency in the dispensation of practical justice: transparency in this case being the appearance that due process was an effective bulwark against corruption and personal injury—i.e., justice not only had to be done but had to be *seen* to be done. Although the colonial authorities in Hong Kong had implemented numerous racially partial laws since the colony's foundation in 1842, it was generally considered imperative that key administrative functions such as the judicial system lead by example, particularly if Britain's broader "civilizing mission" was to have any hope of affecting the colony's Chinese population.[42] In this sense, the notion of "dignity" to which Goodman referred in his speech was concerned as much with the aesthetics of British law as with its practice.

In fact, as the remainder of Goodman's speech made clear, it was the allusion to notions of British justice that Webb and Bell's new building would convey. Through its solid, classically inspired forms, the Hong Kong Supreme Court would reflect the long-established and well-recognized legal and administrative practices of Western civilization, dating back to Roman times.

Here the correlation between British law and architecture becomes historically contingent, for this rhetoric of liberal idealism was akin to that of the ascendant Whig oligarchy in eighteenth-century Britain—a class of people who understood architecture's ability to represent the essential nature of English, indeed, British national life. Through its reference to the antique sobriety of the Anglo-Palladian tradition, Webb and Bell's design deliberately recalled this idealism. It embodied a clarity of form that emphasized those principles of liberty, justice, and "civilization" that were still considered to be the basis of British government everywhere. Thus, despite the wrangling that characterized the Supreme Court's design, the resultant image was a powerful one, reflecting the like-minded spirit of Hong Kong's merchant and administrative elite, articulated in a series of forms with which many of these elite would have been familiar from their connection with Britain and British culture.[43]

At the opening of the Supreme Court in 1912, the then-governor of Hong Kong, Sir Frederick Lugard (1858–1945), initiated proceedings by observing:

> It is a little over eight years ago since my predecessor, Sir Henry Blake, laid the foundation stone of these Courts of Justice ... They have taken long to build, and have cost much money, but in their massive granite walls and pillars they stand unrivalled in the Far East, ... [I]t seems to be a thoroughly British sentiment that our Courts of Justice shall always surpass all other structures in durability, firm set on their foundations and built four-square to all the winds that blow, as an outward symbol perhaps of the Justice which shall stand firm though the skies fall, and which we take pride in associating with the British flag. ... Constitutions of Empires may change, the map of the world may change, but day by day through the long vista of the years to come the statue of Justice, with shrouded vision holding impartial scales, which surmounts the portals of these Courts, shall stand impervious to all changes and all storms; ... It is a grand conception—it is the conception on which the British Empire has been built.[44]

Sir Francis Piggott (1852–1925), the colony's Chief Justice, whose speech immediately followed Lugard's, acknowledged the structure in a similar way. "The progress has been so slow and the time of observation has been so long," Piggott conceded,

> that even the least of us with very little knowledge of architecture have come to criticize with a vein of sarcasm. ... But, sir, to-day on behalf of the King you have pronounced the inaugural benison, and I think we must be blind to the blemishes of the building and remember only its many virtues.
>
> In the first place there is the stability of the building. I think the Colony may be justly proud of the famous masonry which through all these years has been gradually put together, and if I may prophesy that when Victoria has ceased to be a city, when the harbor has silted up, when even the Hongkong Club has crumbled away, this building will remain like a pyramid to commemorate the genius of the Far East.[45]

In a strange and coincidental parallel to Gustave Doré's image of forty years previous (*The New Zealander*), Piggott evokes a powerful vision of architecture as the marker of cultural identity. More than this, his suggestion posits architecture as the manifestation of an apparent and universal truth, as if the classical and enduring monumentality of the new Supreme Court was corollary to the indissoluble tenets of British law and liberty. With the capacity to bear meaning across time and space, Webb and Bell's building would remain as testament, believed Piggott, to the achievement of the British Empire in Asia. (see Figure 8.9)

Figure 8.9
Detail from Gustave Doré's *The New Zealander* (1872)

Compliance or Collaboration? The Hong Kong Chinese and the Supreme Court

Although work on the foundations of the Supreme Court was able to commence as early as 1899, problems in obtaining a reasonable tender for the building's superstructure delayed construction for a number of months. It was not until November 1903 that a suitable contractor was finally found and the foundation stone officially laid, at which point the walls were already four feet high.[46] The erection of the building was very slow. This was partly because a suitable supply of granite could not be found, and partly because the colony lacked masons capable of dressing it to the required standard. Owing to the building's importance, great attention was paid to the quality and color of the stone used. Much of the local granite contained minute particles of iron and was therefore prone to discoloration after a relatively short period of exposure. Eventually a suitable, low-iron supply was found at a quarry in the New Territories, but its inconsistent operation caused further delays.

Webb and Bell were naturally frustrated with proceedings. Just prior to the commencement of work they sent an engineer from London to supervise the project; however, he was forced to return to England owing to serious illness in 1904. The contractor, Chan A. Tong, was an experienced local builder who had successfully executed a number of major government projects. But he too fell ill and died in 1904, leaving the completion of the building in the hands of his son. These problems, in conjunction with the limited supply of skilled labor (due to other major construction projects), meant that work was not completed until 1912.[47]

But behind the "famous masonry" composing the Supreme Court's sturdy walls lurked less liberal, even malevolent intentions. Typically, the Chinese experience of British justice in Hong Kong was much worse than that of their European counterparts. Despite assurances by the British government that the Chinese would be treated according to their own laws and customs (First Proclamation, 1842), once on the Island, they were often subject to indiscriminate treatment and summary justice. One example of this was the requirement for all Chinese to register with the colonial authorities, obtain a night pass, and carry a lamp whenever out of doors after 10 p.m. (Ordinance No. 16, 1844; No. 17, 1844; No. 6, 1857). This law was not repealed until 1897. As Christopher Munn has shown, the trial of Chinese immigrants under the colonial legal system was open to widespread abuse and corruption.

> The language, procedures and assumptions of the English courts systematically disabled Chinese defendants. The belief that Chinese people had been brutalized by their own society gave rise to dual standards of sensibility that demanded heavy punishments and intrusive control for the Chinese but urged consideration and leniency towards Europeans.[48]

Thus, the Chinese community in Hong Kong had every reason to distrust British law—to them, it was anything but transparent or impartial. Unfortunately, the situation had changed very little by the time the new Supreme Court was opened.[49]

Discriminatory sentiments of this kind were also evident in public ceremonial. As we have seen, at one level these events were a celebration of larger and more distant imperial associations, but at another they were infused with pointed devices pertaining to cultural superiority and racial discrimination. For example, the spectacle of the military parade—often on display at such occasions—was designed to reinforce notions of order and control, suggesting an "object lesson to the Chinese," noted *The China Mail*, "of what it is possible to do with British troops under the discipline of British officers."[50] Moreover, both Goodman and Chater (key figures at such events) were signatories to the 1904 petition to extend the Hill District Reservation Ordinance in Hong Kong—a law that had excluded Chinese from living or owning property in the elevated and affluent parts of Victoria since 1877.[51] Although the necessity for this measure was claimed on grounds of public health, it had more to do with protecting the aesthetic "character" of these areas and excluding the growing number of wealthy Chinese who would, it was feared, inflate (or in some cases deflate) real estate prices and disintegrate European communal identity.[52]

In Hong Kong, as in many British colonial settlements, the use of architecture as an instrument for the control of urban space was a serious political endeavor.[53] For the colony's prevailing ethnic minority, architecture was a familiar and powerful means by which to give substance to ideas of cultural identity. The careful arrangement of signs and symbols was designed to establish a sense of cultural continuity between the center and periphery of the British colonial world. In many ways, the proud architecture of the Hong Kong Supreme Court merely added to this language of superiority and suppression, especially with regard to the way local concerns were projected onto the building. Although many of the Chinese in Hong Kong were immigrants who either came seeking employment or fleeing civil unrest elsewhere, they were automatically designated "subjects" of the British crown whether they liked it or not. This may have afforded them certain rights and privileges of which they might never have dreamt under imperial rule in China, but it also left them open to manipulation and abuse, a predicament that the law was not always able or even willing to recognize.[54] Therefore, the image of liberty, social order, and civilization the Hong Kong Supreme Court was supposed to signify in the minds of the colonial elite could easily have been (and was) construed by the subordinate majority as a gesture of domination.

But there is a further complication. Ironically, perhaps, this symbol of foreign rule and oppression was erected by Chinese hands. This reminds us, as John M. Carroll has observed, that many among the so-called Chinese bourgeoisie—contractors, compradors, and other businessmen—did not necessarily view the colonial regime as a conquest state. This class within the Chinese population of Hong Kong benefited greatly from the relationships it established with the government and the European merchant elite. Such relationships were of course mutually beneficial and demonstrate that a considerable degree of co-operation and collaboration was necessary in the construction and maintenance of new economic, social, and political infrastructures.[55] To complicate matters even further, these collaborators were considered by Chinese officialdom as *gan*, or "traitors." These people, many of whom assisted the British during the Opium Wars, included members of the building trade.[56] Their particular role in the development and prosperity of Hong Kong, especially in contracting for government projects, was writ large throughout the urban landscape.

But was Chan A. Tong a traitor, or, like so many others in Hong Kong (Chinese and European alike), was he merely looking to take advantage of the opportunities that an entrepôt such as the city of Victoria offered? He was certainly savvy in the way he cultivated his relationship with the Hong Kong government. At the laying of the Supreme Court's foundation stone, for instance, he presented an ornamental trowel as a gift to the governor, Sir Henry Blake.[57] It seems that such gestures were designed to strengthen his collaborative partnership with the colonial authorities. As noted, they paid off, as Tong was already a well-known and successful government contractor by the time he was awarded the job to build the Supreme Court. Moreover, the government understood fully that the physical development of Hong Kong was almost entirely reliant on such contractors and their ability to raise skilled labor. In this respect, the Supreme Court was no different from any other government building in Hong Kong. Although designed by architects from Britain in consultation with the colonial government, it was actually constructed by a Chinese labor force overseen by a Chinese contractor. Without each of these parties playing its respective role, the erection of such a building would not have been possible.

Conclusion

This essay has considered the design and construction of the Hong Kong Supreme Court against the backcloth of the wider cultural, political, and artistic concerns that were fundamental to its form and interpretation. Particular attention was given to issues of identity residing at the heart of the Edwardian Baroque style and its articulation in the context of late nineteenth- and early twentieth-century Hong Kong. Yet, this style of architecture, with its self-conscious sense of patriotic exuberance, was predicated in part on a general feeling of insecurity that pervaded Britain and its colonial empire during this period. Thus, behind the apparently self-confident façade of the Hong Kong Supreme Court lurked anxieties and frustrations that ran contrary to the full extent of its intended mission.

This reveals that the processes by which the Hong Kong Supreme Court was brought to fruition were more complex than what might initially have been suspected. The final design was only made possible by the friction that characterized the relationship between the executive authorities in Hong Kong and the Colonial Office back in London. Therefore, the building may appear prima facie to project an image of confidence and authority, but its history presents a somewhat more mixed and confused reality. As we have seen, it began life as a design that was neither wanted nor appreciated but ended up as a building considered the very embodiment of everything valuable in British colonial rule.

This less than straightforward history posits the building in many ways as a monument to the often strained and somewhat fragile interchange between metropolitan authority and the realities of life at the colonial frontier. Moreover, the way in which notions of liberty and justice were associated with the building also tended to suppress, even conceal, the reality of the way "British law" operated in colonial contexts, especially with regard to its treatment of the indigenous underclass. Again, it was the disparity between the rhetoric that surrounded the building—shorn of all its inconsistencies and contradictions—and the tensions inherent in its realization and function that belie its projected image of transparency, equality, and justice.

The involvement of the Hong Kong Chinese in the building's fabrication further (and necessarily) complicates our understanding of it. There is, perhaps, no small irony in this but, as John M. Carroll has argued, it forces us to consider more carefully the exact role that colonialism played in an entrepôt state such as Hong Kong. Moreover, as Nicholas Dirks has suggested, colonialism was maintained in part upon the ill-coordinated nature of power, and colonial regimes both exploited and co-operated with their subjects.[58] We see these factors in evidence in the design, construction, and operation of the Hong Kong Supreme Court. In so many ways the building represents a microcosm of the colonial condition in Hong Kong at the turn of the twentieth century.

Notes

1. For example, see Anthony D. King, *Colonial Urban Development* (London: Routledge, 1976); Robert Irving, *Indian Summer: Lutyens, Baker and Imperial Delhi* (New Haven and London: Yale University Press, 1981); and Thomas R. Metcalf, *An Imperial Vision: Indian Architecture and Britain's Raj* (London: Faber & Faber, 1989). For the relationship between architecture and empire in Britain, see G. A. Bremner, "Nation and Empire in the Government Architecture of Mid-Victorian London: The Foreign and India Office Reconsidered," *Historical Journal* 48, no. 3 (2005): 703–42.

2. Alastair Service, *Edwardian Architecture* (London: Thames and Hudson, 1977), 140.

3. Andrew Saint, "The Reputation of St. Paul's," in *St Paul's: The Cathedral Church of London 604–2004*, eds. Derek Keene, Arthur Burns, and Andrew Saint (New Haven and London: Yale University Press, 2004), 459–60.

4. British architects still gleaned freely from the work of other "Renaissance" architects, such as Nicholas Hawksmoor, John Vanbrugh, and James Gibbs, but it was Wren and St. Paul's that retained a special place in the British architectural imagination. For recent scholarship on the so-called "Wrenaissance" and its national associations, see Andrew Saint, "The Cult of Wren," in *Architecture & Englishness 1880–1914*, eds. D. Crellin and I.

Dungavell (London: Society of Architectural Historians of Great Britain, 2006), 37–58.

5. Other well-known buildings in this style include the Mersey Docks Building (1903–07), Liverpool, by Arnold Thornely; Belfast City Hall (1897–1906) and Stockport Town Hall (1904–08) by Arthur Brumwell Thomas; Portsmouth Town Hall by William Hill; and Colchester Town Hall (1897–1902) and the Ashton Memorial, Lancashire, both by John Belcher. In London itself there were, among others, the Central Criminal Courts (1900–06) by Edward Mountford; Admiralty Arch (1900–12) by Aston Webb; and along Whitehall and Parliament Square, the War Office by William Young and the Government Offices by John Brydon. As Colin Cunningham has observed, the emergence of the style in a conscious manner can be traced back to William Young's 1881 design for the City Chambers in Glasgow. See Colin Cunningham, *Victorian and Edwardian Town Halls* (London: Routledge, 1981), 138, 154.

6. These architects had not only championed the Edwardian Baroque style at various stages in their careers but also believed in the idea of empire. For example, see Herbert Baker, *Architecture and Personalities* (London: Country Life, 1944).

7. As Baker himself would later observe, buildings such as these were clearly distinguished by "the stamp of British sovereignty." Herbert Baker, "The New Delhi: Eastern and Western Architecture—A Problem of Style," *The Times*, October 3, 1912, p. 8.

8. The National Archive (NA), London: Colonial Office series 129, Hong Kong/302: 141 (hereafter CO 129/–).

9. In elevation, at least, the Hong Kong Supreme Court echoes many of the designs for houses found in Colen Campbell's *Vitruvius Britannicus* (1715–25). It was also noted in the introduction to John Belcher and Mervyn Macartney's *Later Renaissance Architecture in England* (1898–1901) that if "there is to be a fresh development in our national architecture, it is only reasonable to suppose that the point of departure should be from the period in which it reached its greatest excellence. The increasing study of the 'Later Renaissance' is a hopeful sign ... Such study will conduce to an increased regard for proportion, and to a greater simplicity and refinement the extravagant and excessive use of ornament which has vitiated the public taste will no longer be tolerated in our buildings ... There are an infinite combination and unexhaustible [sic] changes within the reach of the artist, such will insure ever increasing novelty and originality" (p. 12). Webb was a subscriber to Belcher and Macartney's publication.

10. The final design received media coverage in England and was displayed at the Royal Academy exhibition of 1908. See *The Builder* (May 2, 1908).

11. *The Builder* (March 2, 1889): 169.

12. Indeed, a move in this direction had already been made by the time of Brydon's appeal. It was evident, for example, in at least two of the six designs submitted for the Imperial Institute competition held in 1887, and it would appear again later in Brydon's own design for the new Government Offices project on Parliament Square (1898–1912). See G. A. Bremner, "'Some Imperial Institute': Architecture, Symbolism, and the Ideal of Empire in Late Victorian Britain, 1887–93," *Journal of the Society of Architectural Historians* 62, no. 1 (2003): 50–73.

13. Duncan Bell, *The Idea of Greater Britain: Empire and the Future of World Order, 1860–1900* (Princeton: Princeton University Press, 2007).

14. Webb quoted in Ian Dungavell, "The Architectural Career of Sir Aston Webb (1849–1930)" (PhD diss., University of London, 1999), vol. 1, 169.

15. For more on this project, see G. A. Bremner, "'Imperial Peace Memorial': The Second Anglo-Boer War and the Origins of the Admiralty Arch, 1900–05," *British Art Journal* 5, no. 5 (2004): 62–66.

16. For a concise discussion of the ideas and debates surrounding the concept of "imperial federation" in late nineteenth-century Britain, see E. H. H. Green, "The Political Economy of Empire, 1880–1914," in *Oxford History of the British Empire*, vol. 3, ed. A. Porter (Oxford: Oxford University Press, 1999), 345–68; and A. S. Thompson, *Imperial Britain: The Empire in British Politics c.1880–1932* (Harlow: Longman, 2000).

17. Metcalf, *An Imperial Vision*, 177. See also Bremner, "'Some Imperial Institute'," 52.

18. See Dungavell, "The Architectural Career," vol. 1, 85–87. See also Hong Kong University Library, Special Collections: *Hong Kong Blue Book* (1912), 36. Referring to the *Colonial Office List* for 1888, Dungavell notes that Webb and Bell were consulting architects for no less than forty-nine British colonies and protectorates.

19. Hong Kong Public Records Office: PRO/REF/81: A. I. Diamond, "The Courts of Justice," 3–4. See also letter from William Robinson to Joseph Chamberlain, April 28, 1896, CO 129/271: 690–95. The building of a new Supreme Court in Hong Kong had been first mooted as far back as 1861. See J. W. Norton-Kyshe, *The History of the Laws and Courts of Hongkong*, vol. 2 (Hong Kong, 1898), 19, 525.

20. *The Builder* (October 13, 1883): 474–75.

21. "New Government Offices," CO 129/271: 687–89. Although Webb and Bell may have consulted on many projects in tropical colonies, up until this point they had only designed two buildings in such a climate: a prison at Bathurst in Gambia (1892–93), and a church at Accra, Ghana (1893–94). Dungavell, "The Architectural Career," vol. 2, 367f.

22. These photographs were sent to the architects by the committee. See Webb and Bell to Hong Kong Crown Agents, September 8, 1898: CO 129/286: 471.

23. *Hong Kong Blue Book* (1912), 36.
24. By employing what they described as a "colossal order," and "crowning" the whole structure with a dome, the architects noted that the building would not have to be as high as its neighbors in order to compete with them in terms of scale and grandeur. See unpublished letter, Webb and Bell to Hong Kong Crown Agents, September 8, 1889: CO 129/286: 471.
25. "Expenditure on Public Works Extraordinary," December 1, 1899: CO 129/296: 486.
26. Ibid.
27. Ibid., 487. T. H. Whitehead, a member of the Legislative Council, sent the Colonial Office photographs of the Hongkong Club, the Queen's Building, and the Prince's Building (then under construction) to show them what local architects could achieve.
28. Enclosure 1—"Memorandum," in letter from Governor of Hong Kong to Joseph Chamberlain, December 29, 1899: CO 129/294: 636–37.
29. Ibid., 141.
30. Unpublished letter, Webb and Bell to Hong Kong Crown Agents, February 5, 1900: CO 129/302: 134.
31. Ibid., 204.
32. Ibid. Writing to the Crown Agents, the architects protested that: "In the original plans the routes for the Judges and the Bar, the Solicitors and the Witnesses, and those for the public were carefully kept quite distinct. In the modified plans these routes necessarily cross at several points to the inconvenience and discomfort of all." The building committee's rejection of their suggestions is rather curious, given that one of the main reasons that a new court was considered necessary in the first place was precisely because of this "inconvenient" coalescence. See Norton-Kyshe, *The History of the Laws and Courts*, vol. 1, 398.
33. Unpublished letter, Webb and Bell to Hong Kong Crown Agents, September 21, 1900: CO 129/302: 231.
34. C. L. Yip, "Four Major Buildings in the Architectural History of the Hongkong and Shanghai Banking Corporation," in *Eastern Banking: Essays in the History of the Hongkong and Shanghai Banking Corporation*, ed. F. H. H. King (London: Athlone, 1983), 113. See also F. H. H. King et al., *The Hongkong Bank in Late Imperial China, 1864–1902* (Cambridge: Cambridge University Press, 1987), 355–60.
35. Norton-Kyshe, *The History of the Laws and Courts*, vol. 1, 237.
36. Z. Zhang, S. S. Y. Lau, and H. Y. Lee, "The Central District of Hong Kong: Architecture and Urbanism of a Laissez-Faire City," *Architecture + Urbanism* 322 (1997): 15.
37. Speech delivered by Catchick P. Chater on the occasion of the unveiling of Queen Victoria's statue, unpublished letter (Enclosure 1) from Governor W. Robinson to Joseph Chamberlain (June 3, 1896): CO 129/272: 156.

38. Ibid., 157.
39. Christopher Munn, "The Criminal Trial under Early Colonial Rule," in *Hong Kong's History: State and Society under Colonial Rule*, ed. Tak-wing Ngo (London: Routledge, 1999), 46. The perceived "utilitarian universalism" of English law and its application in Asia dated back to Macaulay and Mill. See S. den Otter, "'A Legislating Empire': Victorian Political Theorists, Codes of Law, and Empire," in *Victorian Visions of Global Order: Empire and International Relations in Nineteenth-Century Political Thought*, ed. D. Bell (Cambridge: Cambridge University Press, 2007), 89–112.
40. *Hongkong Telegraph* (November 12, 1903).
41. For instance, see P. Wesley-Smith, "Anti-Chinese Legislation in Hong Kong," in *Precarious Balance: Hong Kong between China and Britain, 1842–1992*, ed. M. K. Chan (London: M. E. Sharpe, 1992), 91–105. See also G. A. Bremner and D. P. Y. Lung, "Spaces of Exclusion, the Significance of Cultural Identity in the Formation of European Residential Districts in British Hong Kong, 1877–1904," *Environment and Planning D: Society and Space* 21, no. 2 (2003): 224ff.
42. John M. Carroll, "Chinese Collaboration in the Making of British Hong Kong," in Ngo, *Hong Kong's History*, 14.
43. On this point, Goodman further observed that a building such as the Hong Kong Supreme Court would provide surroundings "thoroughly worthy of the position of this Colony" and reflect "the traditions of the administration of British justice." These sentiments had also been foreshadowed moments earlier by the Director of Public Works, William Chatham. See *China Mail* (November 13, 1903).
44. *Hongkong Telegraph* (January 15, 1912).
45. *Hongkong Telegraph* (January 16, 1912).
46. *Hong Kong Blue Book* (1904), 178.
47. *Hong Kong Blue Book* (1912), 36–38.
48. Munn, "Criminal Trial," 66. Munn goes on to note that "for the great majority of the Chinese population … English justice in Hong Kong meant intrusive policing, racial and class discrimination, and periodic campaigns of repression."
49. Jung-Fang Tsai, *Hong Kong in Chinese History: Community and Social Unrest in the British Colony, 1842–1913* (New York: Columbia University Press, 1993), 114–16; Wesley-Smith, "Anti-Chinese Legislation."
50. *The China Mail* (May 29, 1896).
51. See "Humble Petition of the Undersigned," CO 129/332: 639. The petition was signed by over eighty other influential members of Hong Kong's European community, including C. W. Dickson, G. Stewart, H. E. Pollock, Edbert A. Hewett, Marcus W. Slade, H. J. Gompertz, J. W. Jones, and J. H. Kemp, all of whom attended either or both the opening and stone-laying ceremonies.

52. Minutes of Legislative Council meeting, April 19, 1904, CO 129/443: 392ff. See also Bremner and Lung, "Spaces of Exclusion," 235–45.

53. For a study of the Hongkong and Shanghai Banking Corporation in this light, see S. Wong, "Colonialism, Power, and the Hongkong and Shanghai Bank," in *The Unknown City: Contesting Architecture and Social Space*, eds. I. Borden, Joe Kerr, Jane Rendell, and A. Pivaro (Cambridge, Mass.: MIT Press, 2002), 160–75.

54. This was certainly the case in the mid- to late nineteenth century. See Munn, "Criminal Trial," 46–73.

55. Carroll, "Chinese Collaboration," 14.

56. Ibid., 16–17.

57. *The China Mail* (November 13, 1903).

58. Dirks cited in Carroll, "Chinese Collaboration," 25.

9
Making Space for Higher Education in Colonial Hong Kong, 1887–1913

Peter Cunich

Despite all the evidence to the contrary, people still like to imagine the British Empire as a monolithic structure, which exerted from its center in London a high level of control over the scattered colonial possessions and other spheres of influence in which the British nation had interests. This is, of course, anything but an accurate depiction of how the empire really functioned. The mandarins in Whitehall were seldom able to supervise Britain's far-flung colonies to the extent that they would have liked, and much imperial policy, although decided in London, was left to those on the periphery to implement. This more nuanced interpretation of colonial governance certainly helps us to account for the variety of ways in which British imperialism expressed itself around the world during the Victorian period, but there is still something rather unsatisfactory in the notion that the greatest empire of the modern period had so little control over the peripheral entities that contributed so much to the delineation of British imperial culture. This is not to deny that British domestic policies had an important impact on the colonies and dominions, but there can be no mistaking the fact that there were many areas in which clear "imperial" policies simply did not exist and where the colonial state was therefore able to exercise independence in implementing policies dealing with subject peoples.

Education was one area of development in which metropolitan policies have long been recognized as having played a central role in influencing colonial culture. A large literature already exists which demonstrates the impact of domestic British educational policy on the individual colonies in the late nineteenth century, manifested in projects which ranged from state-supported elementary instruction all the way through to higher education. Like much else in the sphere

of education, British higher education was undergoing a rapid transformation during the second half of the nineteenth century and much
has already been written about colonial appropriations of metropolitan
institutional models in terms of both governance structures and undergraduate curriculums. Some colonial universities naturally chose to ape
the old Oxbridge collegiate model in their organization and governance, while others preferred the federal model of London University
and the "godless" colleges of Ireland. In some parts of the empire,
these typologies were mixed to create new structural models, and in
the early twentieth century the civic universities of England's industrial cities became an attractive alternative as emblems of modernity.
A significant feature of this transference and hybridization in higher
education was the variety of outcomes that may be observed across the
empire. This strongly suggests that the British Empire lacked a formal
"policy" for higher education in the late nineteenth and early twentieth centuries and that developments in higher education within the
colonies were driven by "colonial" rather than "imperial" concerns.[1]

The Spatial Dimension of Higher Education in the British Colonies

Although the university is at heart nothing more than a corporate body
of scholars who organize themselves in a variety of different ways
in order to provide opportunities for teaching and research, to most
people a "university" is most clearly identified as a physical space or
a collection of built structures in which the processes of teaching and
research take place. These physical embodiments of the university's
existence have long been recognized as potent symbols that impart
"intangible meanings" through "tangible materials."[2] For this reason,
considerable sums of money have always been spent on providing
meaningful physical settings in which the intellectual work of the university can take place. The provision of space for university campuses
and the construction of buildings fit for the purposes of higher education were therefore matters of great importance for colonial admin-
istrators and educational planners in the late nineteenth and early
twentieth centuries. Surprisingly, however, very little research exists
on the transfer of ideas about the built form and urban context of these

institutions. While it is clear that many of the buildings erected for new universities in nineteenth-century Australia, Africa, and Canada displayed an eclectic reliance on established metropolitan forms in their architectural design, their placement within the built colonial environment was often very different from the British norms because of virtually unlimited space available in areas where colonial universities were planted. In India and East Asia, there was a similar reliance on European architectural grammars but, unlike the wide open spaces of the settler colonies, the physical settings in Asia also tended to present similar site constraints to those existing in British urban landscapes.

British universities were generally found in cities where academic buildings stood cheek-by-jowl with residential, commercial, and public facilities, whereas colonial institutions were usually able to take advantage of more abundant supplies of land on the outskirts of new cities. They were also able to exploit the great wealth generated by non-industrial colonial economies to establish university campuses designed to display a heightened sense of cultural status. In Australia in the 1850s, for example, the universities of Sydney (1850) and Melbourne (1853) were both laid out on a grand scale in elevated positions within botanic garden-like campuses that provided ample space for future development well into the late twentieth century.[3] Such campuses were protected from the more unsavory features of nineteenth-century urban life by their liminality and the invisible intellectual *cordon sanitaire* that tended to separate them and their inhabitants from the adjacent cityscape. There was no metropolitan precedent for such a lavish outlay of land for university campuses; in fact the whole idea of a dedicated "campus" within which all of a university's buildings could be constructed, although popular in Canada and the United States, was unheard of in Britain until the foundation of the University of Birmingham in 1900. The buildings erected at both Sydney and Melbourne universities were unashamed displays of colonial wealth which nevertheless sought to accentuate the strong intellectual bonds between the old world and the new, using the popular Gothic revival style to link the new institutions stylistically with Oxford and Cambridge. (see Figure 9.1)

The fact that these new universities emphasized so overtly the cultural bonds between the older metropolitan and the younger colonial

Figure 9.1

The University of Sydney's splendid Gothic revival Main Quad was set within a large "park" on the edge of the city, a significant departure from the cramped urban sites of most universities in Britain. (University of Sydney Archives, G3/224/0943)

educational systems could perhaps be interpreted as an attempt to use these institutions as instruments of intellectual control over emergent colonial societies. Indeed, the colonial governments granted large parcels of land so that the new institutions would be a credit to the colonies and even provided lavish capital grants for construction of buildings and generous recurrent subventions to pay the salaries of academic staff. What is surprising, however, is that in both cases these building programs, although generously sponsored by the state, were essentially private initiatives over which the two colonial governments exercised relatively little input or control, and which were initiated and implemented without any interference from the Colonial Office in London. Moreover, the colonial state played only a supporting role at best in the development of the two universities because their governance was vested in autonomous governing bodies composed of independent-minded colonial grandees. While certainly being symbolic of incipient "national" pride, therefore, neither of the institutions established in Sydney or Melbourne ought to be interpreted as expressing "imperial" initiatives. There was no apparent policy in London during the mid-nineteenth century controlling the establishment of colonial institutions of higher education, nor would there be one until after the Asquith Report in 1945.

A greater level of government control was exercised in India over the core institutions of the universities of Calcutta, Bombay, and Madras, founded in 1857. These universities were all federal institutions. Not only were governance styles and curriculums incredibly varied in their affiliated colleges, but architectural expressions of the higher education offered within their walls also demonstrated an enormous diversity. The construction of central buildings for the three Indian universities was a relatively low priority in the early years, nor did the crowded cities of India offer the large tracts of land for higher education developments that were available in Australia's colonial capitals. Most of Calcutta University's early administration was therefore transacted in private residences scattered around the city, and the governing body met at the old Presidency College, one of the new university's constituent colleges, until a new classically-inspired Senate Hall and library complex was opened on a cramped urban site in 1873.[4] Likewise, in Madras, the new university functioned as a guest in the Presidency College until its own Senate House was completed in 1873 but, unlike Calcutta, the new building in Madras was constructed on a large open site, which was later extended to provide space for a sprawling complex of buildings.[5] The government architect employed the vernacular Deccan style for the building rather than borrowing patterns from Europe, so the building had a very Moorish appearance. This was an early example of the type of "associative" or "adaptive" architecture about which Gwendolyn Wright and Jeffrey Cody have written: one that was still an exercise of authority by the colonizing power but that was thinly cloaked with a condescending respect for indigenous cultural norms.[6]

In East Asia, the problem of providing physical space for new institutions of higher education tended to be regulated by the same urban norms as existed in the overcrowded and industrializing cities of Britain, although in Singapore, land supply was less of a problem than in Hong Kong. From its first settlement by the British in 1841, the crown colony of Hong Kong was a city with two very different faces: the airy Mid-Levels and Peak districts reserved for the expensive classically-styled European habitations of the colonial elite, while the cramped and fetid Chinese quarter nearer the harbor represented all that was worst in nineteenth-century urban design and city planning. Land was always in short supply and the city of Victoria was constantly bursting at the seams as its boundaries moved further east and west to encompass more and more of the northern shore of the island. Physical space for higher education in Hong Kong therefore had to be carved out of a limited supply of urban land that was in much demand for other purposes. In the earliest years, all attempts at higher education were carried out in borrowed spaces and, as was the case with all other urban space in the colony, these physically undifferentiated sites of intellectual endeavor were subject to the same threats of disease caused by overcrowding and the unregulated disposal of untreated human waste.

Educational Space in Early Colonial Hong Kong

Hong Kong's three early theological colleges (one Anglican and two Catholic) were each forced to share space with secondary schools or other church institutions on confined urban sites. In the case of the first Catholic seminary, a separate building was initially provided but the institution was eventually forced to move away from the insalubrious neighborhood of the Wanchai cemetery after many of its students succumbed to sickness. It then had to share the crowded mission compound in Wellington Street for the next fifty years. Likewise, when Sir John Pope-Hennessy suggested a medical school for Chinese surgical dressers in 1878, its teaching was to take place in the government's Central School and the recently-opened Tung Wah Hospital. This scheme failed, but when Patrick Manson and a group of local medical practitioners successfully launched the Hong Kong College of Medicine in 1887, its teaching activities were for many years based in the London Missionary Society's Alice Memorial Hospital and the government's Victoria (later Queen's) College. Queen's College was again used as a borrowed space for evening classes when the Hong Kong Technical Institute was launched in 1907. The Technical Institute continued to use these facilities until its eventual demise in 1937, and unlike the municipal authorities in many British industrial cities, the colonial government in Hong Kong never saw its way to providing a separate building in which the Institute's highly successful activities in adult education could grow and prosper. Apart from a small annual subvention, the government paid little attention to the Institute, and by 1931, technical education in the colony lagged well behind most other parts of the empire where large buildings for technical colleges had sprung up in every major city. Colonial government policy in Hong Kong before 1905 was thus woefully inadequate in the areas of vocational, technical, and higher education, and its commitment to finding adequate space and buildings for these activities was poor.

Attempts by the College of Medicine to secure a permanent home initially met with little success. The Alice Memorial Hospital (see Figure 9.2) proved too limited in terms of space and facilities for establishing a modern medical school and the government turned a deaf ear to requests for a site on which to erect a dedicated college building. In 1891, a wealthy donor, Emanuel Belilios, was found. He was willing to provide funds for a building, but negotiations with the government for the site of the old Central School were unsuccessful.[7] A renewed offer by Belilios in 1892 would have seen his house in Sai Ying Pun altered for the College of Medicine, or else he was prepared to construct an entirely new building on an adjacent block of land. This was a good site, situated conveniently close to the Government Civil Hospital with room for expansion, but once again the government failed to

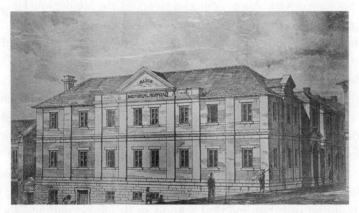

Figure 9.2

The Alice Memorial Hospital (1887), in which the Hong Kong College of Medicine operated until its closure in 1915. (Council for World Mission/SOAS Archives, LMS/South China/Incoming Correspondence/Box 10)

provide an endowment fund for the College, Belilios' only condition.[8]
A further attempt in 1896 to donate his property to the College on the
same terms was similarly unsuccessful, owing perhaps to the political
fallout from James Cantlie's report on the 1894 bubonic plague which
caused so much embarrassment for the colonial government. This
time, the government tried to take control of the College and turn it
into a state-funded and government-controlled institution but Belilios
was outraged at official duplicity and withdrew his offer.[9] Another
opportunity to acquire a site and building in 1897 was lost when the
Diamond Jubilee Committee gave preference to three other projects to
improve the health and welfare of the colony's residents.[10]

It was not until 1905, nearly twenty years after the College's
founding, that the government finally offered a site at the eastern end
of Blake Garden in the Tai Ping Shan resumed area. By this time, the
College's enrollments had grown significantly and buildings for lecture
rooms, offices, a library, and laboratories were desperately needed. The
site chosen for the College buildings was at the very epicenter of the
bubonic plague outbreak of 1894 and its geographical setting perhaps
reinforced the idea that the College's primary mission was to serve the
Chinese community and somehow sanitize an urban space that was
best known for death and suffering.[11] Two plots of land were reserved in
very close proximity to the government's new Bacteriological Institute
and not far from the Alice Memorial Hospital, the Nethersole Hospital,
and the Tung Wah Hospital. Plans were drawn up for two buildings
costing $50,000, but it took some time to secure a wealthy Chinese
donor who would be prepared to pay for the buildings.[12] By early 1908,
tenders had been accepted for the first stage of building works when
then-governor Sir Frederick Lugard announced his university scheme
and effectively brought further preparatory work on the College site to
a halt.[13] In the case of the College of Medicine, therefore, the colonial
government was slow to act in providing an adequate site and then
only after much pressure was exerted by members of the local medical
profession. The site eventually chosen was very much in keeping with
the tradition of urban medical schools in Britain—small and located
in the middle of the city, close to hospitals and the consulting rooms
of the local medical practitioners who acted as part-time lecturers at
the College. It was these medical practitioners who determined the
location and layout of the proposed college buildings, not the colonial

government. Nor did the Colonial Office in London show much enthusiasm for the proposal or try to influence the scheme in any way once
the grant of land had been approved.[14]

Finding a Site for the University of Hong Kong

Sir Frederick Lugard's university project, suggested to the public for
the first time in February 1908, was a far more ambitious undertaking than either the College of Medicine or the Technical Institute, and
although he enthusiastically supported the idea as governor, Lugard
was at pains to point out to the scheme's backers that this was a project
that the government could not be expected to finance. It was clear from
the start, however, that land would have to be found somewhere in
the colony for a university building. Within days, Lugard received an
offer from Hormusjee Mody, a Parsee opium dealer turned real estate
developer, to donate a university building to the colony valued at the
enormous sum of $150,000. Mody was celebrating his fiftieth year as a
resident of the colony and, having already been involved in a number
of large urban development projects, including the central reclamation
scheme and the laying out of Statue Square as a civic space, he was
looking to make a very grand statement about his hopes for the future
of Hong Kong. He was no doubt also aware that such a gift for educational purposes had the power to neutralize any residual embarrassment arising from the uncomfortable origins of his vast fortune. The
gift of such a splendid building needed a suitable setting, however, and
Mody was not prepared to settle for anything but the best site available.

The College of Medicine had slightly different ideas about the site of
Lugard's planned university. Presuming that the colony's new university would be organized along the same lines as the Indian universities,
the College agreed that their institution would be affiliated with the
university and suggested that the main building should be constructed
adjacent to its own new buildings in Tai Ping Shan.[15] The two areas of
land suggested by the College were unassigned plots of crown land
in a steeply sloping corner to the east of Blake Garden.[16] These were
plots which had proven unattractive to other buyers when the area was
resumed by the government after the 1894 plague, and while perhaps
suitable from the College's point of view, would have resulted in a
hopelessly cramped set of buildings wedged uncomfortably between

the YMCA and American Board of Missions' properties with no space for future extension. Moreover, the place was considered by Mody to be "a hot-bed of plague and shunned by the Chinese who would not send their sons there"[17] (see Figure 9.3). Mody's anxiety about the unhealthiness of the proposed site therefore reflected wider Chinese concerns, which may have been partially based on *fengshui* considerations, always a factor in the siting of major public buildings. Mody was perhaps also aware that new universities were being established throughout the British Empire on large greenfield "campus" sites, and that the older notion of university buildings being squeezed haphazardly into urban spaces as at Oxford, Cambridge, and London was no longer the norm. Lugard realised that Mody's financial support for the university project might be lost if a solution were not found to the site issue. He therefore immediately suggested an alternative plot of land in the Mid-Levels which he hoped would meet with Mody's approval and this magnificent site was readily accepted by Mody as a fitting position for the university building.[18]

Figure 9.3

The Tai Ping Shan Cleared Area after the demolitions following the bubonic plague of 1894. Sir Frederick Lugard's new university was offered a site at the east end of this new urban open space, as shown in this photograph. (The National Archives, Kew)

The College of Medicine's governing body did not agree. They decided that the new site would be inconvenient for both the medical students working at the Alice and Nethersole hospitals and their lecturers, who would be forced to travel all the way from their consulting rooms in town in order to give lectures. They now counter-suggested another site, the "No. 2 Tank" on Caine Road to the southwest of the Bacteriological Institute (originally part of the city's water-supply system), and issued an ultimatum to Lugard threatening that if the Caine Road site was not to the donor's liking, they would proceed to complete their own College buildings in Tai Ping Shan. If this were allowed to happen, the College would always remain physically separate from the university.[19] One last effort was made to find a compromise between the College of Medicine and Mody. The larger West End Park on Seymour Road was suggested by the College as an alternative site, but this was judged unsuitable by Mody's agent because, being "buried between 3 hills, it is one of the very hottest spots in Hong Kong … its position is very noisy, and the area is inadequate for a group of fine buildings to be erected upon."[20] At this point in the negotiations, the leader of the Chinese community, Dr. Ho Kai, entered as an intermediary, holding a meeting of past and present students of the College of Medicine at which they unanimously agreed to Lugard's proposed site at the junction of Bonham and Pokfulam roads. It is notable that until this timely intervention, the Chinese community had played no role in the initial negotiations which resulted in the establishment of the university.

The site selected for the university was a large plot of land encompassing approximately nine and a half acres on a magnificent open knoll facing the harbor above West Point (Sai Ying Pun), with expansive views and plenty of fresh air. It was one of the first points viewed from the sea upon entering Victoria Harbor from the west and for many decades had marked the limit of Hong Kong's urban sprawl along the western Mid-Levels.[21] In this sense, it was a liminal urban space similar to those on which the universities in Sydney, Melbourne, and Madras were established, but the hilly geography of this part of Hong Kong Island and the steady advance of the city meant that the site was already quite circumscribed in terms of future development. Despite this drawback, it appeared to be a perfect site on which to erect the "fine buildings" that Mody desired, but perhaps even more symbolic was the fact that the land selected was just within the area of the Mid-Levels reserved for European residents only. Rather than building on a hemmed-in and unhealthy site in the traditionally Chinese part of town, therefore, the choice to locate the university within the boundaries of the European reservation said much about the purpose and ambitions of the new institution. This imperial educational establishment would be firmly rooted in the colony's "British" residential zone and would teach modern Western science and letters as an aid to China's modernization process. Moreover, the university would help to create an elite class of graduates drawn from Hong Kong, the Mainland, and nearby British territories who could be relied upon as missionaries for British scientific, industrial, and economic expansion within the foreign spheres of influence in China.[22] Both the university's curriculum and its very location within the urban environment therefore had the potential to raise its Chinese students to a new status in the strictly hierarchical colonial society, one that manifested itself to no small degree according to an individual's place of residence.

The future site of the university (Inland Lot No. 832) had originally been proposed in 1882 for a new prison, but forty years before that it had been one of the locations of a severe outbreak of the deadly "Hong Kong Fever." Unlike the rejected Tai Ping Shan site, however, the earlier visitations of death and disease in the area during the 1840s were well outside of living memory and the location seemed to provide exactly the sort of garden environment that was becoming favored for institutions of higher education. By 1908, the land was still more or less undeveloped even though it had now been reserved for the construction of a new government civil hospital. Lugard felt it was "eminently well adapted" for the university scheme and, as there was "practically no other" site in the colony to which Mody would agree, the Colonial Office eventually acceded to a grant of the land in fee simple rather than the usual leasehold.[23] Despite the seemingly perfect geographical setting for the university, the local Chinese elite nevertheless became concerned about a different type of contagion emanating from the nearby red-light district of Shek Tong Tsui. The moral threat posed by the brothels and "houses of public entertainment" located so close to the university was of real concern to prudish Chinese parents and continued to be a worry for years to come.[24] It was difficult to erect an effective *cordon sanitaire* around the university to protect the moral health of the young men studying there when it lay in such close proximity to one of the colony's most notorious red-light districts.

Valued at $115,102, the university site represented a significant contribution to the scheme by the cash-strapped colonial government, but it did not take long for Lugard and his committee to realize that the university project required much more space, and further grants would be made out of crown lands in the vicinity over the next ten years.[25] The site was close to the teaching hospitals and the public mortuary in Sai Ying Pun and its position was declared "central" enough to enable the local medical lecturers "to attend with no inconvenience or loss of time."[26] Alfred Bryer's original "block plan" submitted to the Colonial Office in 1908 had presumed that all the university's teaching and residential facilities would be located within a single building, but after "protracted discussions and revisions," it was concluded that this scheme was "altogether inadequate" for a university in which three faculties would require teaching space. Consequently, a new plan was adopted in late 1909 in which the main building would be devoted entirely to educational purposes while the professors and students would be accommodated in entirely detached residences. This represented a significant departure from the original idea of having the whole university in one building and required a renegotiation of Mody's donation, but it allowed for the expansion of student enrollments expected once the university had established itself as "an educational centre for South China, and for the Chinese in the neighboring countries."[27]

These new plans required an additional four acres of land to accommodate the student residences, and as compulsory residence was a key feature of Lugard's vision for the university, the Colonial Office had little choice but to approve an additional appropriation of crown land, noting that, "It is not for us to approve the plans. When passed by the committee they will be proceeded with forthwith."[28] This was, therefore, a project with clearly stated "imperial" objectives, but one which the Colonial Office recognized it had little power to influence. Nor did the mandarins in Whitehall seem to have had any real desire to interfere with either the goals or the physical planning of the new institution. In the meantime, further changes to the site layout had been agreed in Hong Kong, bringing the total land grant by the beginning of January 1910 to 15 acres (6 hectares) valued at $174,788.[29] Still more land was required in December 1910 when it was decided to move the vice-chancellor's residence to a more elevated position on a spur immediately above the playing field.[30] The additional plot of land was chosen for its "central, commanding and cool position," but its juxta-position with the planned government filter beds was considered prob-lematic. By the middle of 1913, a year after the university had opened, it was realized that the university's future development needs would be far greater than initially anticipated by Lugard and his committee, so his successor Sir Henry May proposed that immediate measures be taken to "prevent prejudice to the future extension of the institution." This involved moving the planned water treatment facilities to another site on the western border of the university campus, the reservation of additional plots of crown land along Bonham Road to prevent the construction of non-university dwellings, and the appropriation of the land originally intended for filtration beds. This added approximately 13.5 acres (5.5 hectares) of land to the earlier grants and created a truly contiguous "campus" over which the University had full ownership.[31]

The completed university campus thus encompassed approximately 31 acres (12.5 hectares) of land valued at more than $240,000. This was a handsome contribution to the university scheme by the Hong Kong government, but this largesse was frowned upon by the officials in the Colonial Office. They did not approve of the colonial government making a free gift of such a large area of land to a private institution and the Secretary of State for the Colonies insisted on reserving his right to charge a "reasonable rent" for the additional parcels of land when the time came to erect buildings on them.[32] The final arrangements for the site represented a trade-off between the needs of the university on the one hand and the requirements of the colony's water supply system on the other, a relationship which would continue to be problematic throughout the university's history.

Figure 9.4

The University of Hong Kong's Main Building near completion in early 1912. The University looked across Victoria Harbour to the Chinese mainland and the nation it sought to "modernize." (HKU, Communications and Public Affairs Office)

The University Buildings

Hormusjee Mody was determined from the start to provide for Hong Kong a suite of university buildings which would be a credit to the prosperous and increasingly important colony, and he was prepared to pay whatever was necessary to see his dream become reality. Mody had already decided that Alfred Bryer of Leigh and Orange would be his architect for the project. Leigh and Orange was a reputable Hong Kong firm, but their work was principally in the areas of domestic and commercial architecture. They had designed a lavish new house on Conduit Road for Mody's business partner, Sir Paul Chater, and also Mody and Chater's splendid new office buildings in Central, the Prince's and Queen's buildings. Alfred Bryer was the new senior partner in the firm, but he appears to have had no previous experience of educational, let alone university, commissions. Despite this lack of experience, he was undoubtedly influenced by the current thinking on the design of British university buildings, and his initial idea was to provide all academic and residential accommodation in one building.

While he proved flexible in amending his designs to the changing requirements of the University Committee, the impracticability of a single grand building on such a restricted site to cater for a three-faculty university would have been obvious to a more experienced university architect. His client perhaps had a very clear idea of the type of building he wanted to donate to the colony, and Bryer was able to provide a final plan which was consistent with Mody's wishes.

Bryer had a magnificent but difficult site to work with and he attempted to make the best use of the limited amount of level land with minimal resort to back-cutting and heavy retaining walls. His original plan shows a two-storied main building arranged around two courtyards, including a central hall with libraries on either side of the entrance, a dining room, six spacious lecture rooms, science and engineering laboratories, and dormitory accommodation for 150 students.[33] It was designed in such a way that it could be extended in future by the addition of three ranges of buildings around a back courtyard. This was a feature that was incorporated into the revised plans, which provided for more teaching space while staff accommodation and student dormitories were moved out into separate buildings. The amended scheme was estimated to cost closer to $235,000 and Mody immediately agreed to pay for the larger building no matter how much it would eventually cost.[34] Further enlargements to the plan were made during 1909 in response to comments from the Indian educational experts Sir Herbert Risley and Sir Gerald Bomford, who advised that the university would have to be established "on a sufficiently large scale" allowing adequate space for "the inevitable expansion," especially for engineering machinery and laboratories.[35] Bryer appears to have taken all this advice on board, and his final set of plans approved at the end of 1909 were on a very grand scale. Ultimately, the building costs rose to $365,000—more than double Mody's original offer—but Mody honored his promise and paid for everything except fittings and furnishings.

The Main Building is a highly distinctive structure, combining a heavy reliance on neoclassical design features but tastefully using local materials, giving it an originality that is immediately apparent.[36] Unlike the architectural schemes for educational buildings in some British and French colonies and at the American missionary colleges in China, Bryer made no attempt at assimilative, associative, or adaptive approaches in his architectural designs.[37] The Main Building was an exercise in colonial domination, and the monumental symmetry of the building and its overpoweringly Western architectural features speak clearly of an attempt to impose something new on the indigenous culture. There is no hint that Chinese culture was being appealed to in any of the principal design features or the decorative scheme. The massive granite foundation courses and the classically inspired columns of the principal façade are nevertheless typical of Hong Kong buildings from this period. Indeed, the use of the Ionic order for the pillars and in many of the other design elements of the building immediately locates the structure within a well-attested "Hong Kong style" for public buildings. Delicately colored pink granite hewn from Hong Kong Island's rocky spine anchors the building into its physical surroundings and is used architecturally to accentuate both the vertical and horizontal lines of the structure. The same stone is used in the massively proportioned entrance foyer and the grand staircase, which rises gracefully to the high-ceilinged *piano nobile*. This use of Hong Kong's distinctive local granite gives the structure an unmistakable masculinity, which is so much in keeping with Sir Frederick Lugard's idea of what a good university should be, but there is also a more subtle Beaux-Arts femininity about the building which helps to give it balance.

The Main Building's two principal floors were placed over a monumental basement level along the northern façade, giving the building a strongly symmetrical appearance. The main features of the ground floor were the Great Hall with its apse-shaped stage area, decorated with Corinthian pilasters and ornate plasterwork rising through two stories to a barrel-vaulted ceiling. This was a space designed to celebrate the power and dignity of Western higher education, and the classical style is used throughout, a significant contrast with other British colonial universities where the Oxbridge Gothic Revival style was favored. On either side of the stairs were two large rooms for the library, while the teaching rooms, laboratories, and professors' offices were ranged around the eastern and western wings. Perhaps the most impressive feature of the Main Building was the graceful central tower with its four attendant cupolas along the front elevation serving to accentuate the strict symmetry of the overall design. It is clear from the original plans that Mody intended to lavish a great deal of expense on the central tower which could be clearly seen from both the harbor and virtually every corner of the western district of the city. A clock was envisaged from the first and at least two recumbent statues are shown flanking the tower pediment, with another standing statue atop the main pediment. These decorations were never executed, probably owing to the ballooning costs of the project and Mody's untimely death shortly before the building was completed, but the tower nevertheless became an iconic landmark and symbol of the university from the time of its completion. It was to be the beacon from which the light of learning would be radiated across Victoria Harbour and into China, and formed the central axis that would later be used in all future planning exercises. When completed, the Main Building was, in Edmund Blunden's words, a "noble landmark" set "amid scenes of especial beauty," an edifice which spoke eloquently of the university's purpose and mission, but it was also a loud statement about the power of British cultural institutions in a colony whose denizens were fixated with money-making and the conspicuous display of personal wealth and status.[38] (Plate 24)

A Beacon of Western Modernity for China

The University of Hong Kong's "imperial" mission as a beacon of Western modernity for the rest of China sits uncomfortably against the background of how the institution came to be founded and located within the sprawling built environment of Britain's principal trade entrepôt in China. Both the Colonial Office in London and the local colonial government initially refused to play any major role in the scheme, and it was largely through Sir Frederick Lugard's tireless pushing of his "pet lamb" project that the Main Building was completed and the university was finally opened in 1912. It is deeply ironic that the Main Building, which so quickly came to symbolize the only British university in East Asia, was paid for and designed under the direction of a Parsee merchant from Bombay who had made his fortune dealing in opium. His architect had never designed a university building before and the geography of Hong Kong Island was not conducive to modern university "campus" planning. Although enthusiastically supported by Lugard as an "imperial" project for the benefit of China, the symbolic heart of the university was a contested space where the pragmatic desires of the Chinese elite and the informal imperial ideals of the governor were imposed on a structure that served mainly as a memorial to one of the colony's most successful non-British merchants. It is significant that the local Chinese "gentry" played no role in the design and construction of the university buildings. Their contribution to the university project was limited primarily to the not unimportant endowment fund-raising campaign, and agitation by Chinese members of the University Council for the foundation of an arts faculty that would provide a liberal education alongside Lugard's more technically orientated medical and engineering faculties.[39] Neither Lugard nor the Chinese therefore had much of a say in the physical embodiment of the governor's university project.

In this sense, the Main Building does not perhaps represent what it seems to be saying to us as historians and scholars of the built environment. It hints, rather, at the relative powerlessness of the great British Empire in areas such as higher education, when politically and economically it seemed to be at the height of its dominion. Such a view is helpful in explaining why British higher education made such a faltering start in East Asia in the early twentieth century. Apart from the University of Hong Kong, the only other British institution of any note in this region until 1928 was the King Edward VII College of Medicine in Singapore. This was a medical school which, unlike the Hong Kong College of Medicine and the University of Hong Kong, was placed firmly under the control of the colonial government of the Straits Settlements, but for the first twenty years of its existence it was housed in a rather mean collection of buildings clustered around an old lunatic asylum. It was not until 1926 that a splendid new classical building was erected to add some gravitas to the noble aims of British higher education, which the College represented.[40]

This failure to develop and enforce a British imperial policy in the realm of higher education in East Asia during the early twentieth century may be contrasted with the extraordinary successes of American missionary bodies in establishing throughout China during the same period a series of Christian colleges which appeared to be expressing

Figure 9.5

The Main Building as completed in 1912 (Mrs. Shelagh Meade)

a unified set of educational ideals. As Jeffrey Cody has demonstrated, the different American missionary organizations used the "tangible built form" in China to impart "intangible educational ideals" to their target audience, the Chinese.[41] This was undoubtedly a form of cultural imperialism, but one which was achieved not through the policies of a powerful imperial state like Britain, but largely through the professional efforts of architects such as Henry Murphy, who had long experience in designing American university buildings, working for clients who were more open to the benefits of adapting their Western message to the indigenous culture. Assimilation, association, and adaptation were the name of the game for these missionary bodies in their attempts to win the hearts, minds, and souls of the Chinese intellectual elite during the republican period. Cody has demonstrated that a clear progression can be delineated in the translation of an essentially Western grammar of architectural design to meet local needs in campus and building design in the first thirty years of the twentieth century.[42]

The influence of the so-called "Chinese Revival" or "Chinese Renaissance" style was paramount in these attempts to blend Western higher educational institutions into the ancient Chinese urban land-scape. American missionary societies usually relied on established firms of architects with experience in China to plan and build their colleges. In the planning of their new campus at Changsha, the Yale-in-China Committee decided that "every possible step should be taken to conserve the architectural heritage of old China, blending it with the structural requirements that the modern world makes" in order to make the intrusive work of foreigners seem more palatable to the local population.[43] Hybrid buildings and campus landscapes that combined the best modern American planning ideals with historical models based on Chinese courtyard design were therefore widely employed both in Changsha and elsewhere in China.[44] This style can be seen in the work of Stoughton and Stoughton at the Canton Christian College in the first decade of the twentieth century; Perkins, Fellows and Hamilton at Nanking University in the second decade; Murphy and Dana at Yale-in-China, Changsha (1913–18), Ginling College (1918–23) and Yenching University (1919–29); and William Henry (Harry) Hussey at the Peking Union Medical College (1916–19). These campuses are unmistakably "Chinese" in their style, and therefore exuded a completely differ-ent atmosphere when compared with the "British" buildings of the University of Hong Kong.

If buildings are "silent teachers,"[45] the lesson we can learn from the University of Hong Kong's Main Building and the earlier attempts to find space for higher education in the colony of Hong Kong is that the British Empire did not have a formal imperial policy for higher edu-cation in the early years of the twentieth century. Nor did the British see the need to adapt to vernacular Chinese building styles in the way that American missionary societies attempted to hybridize their educational buildings on the Mainland at that time.[46] The British goal was not to adapt Western learning to meet the needs of a modernizing China, but rather to impose an established canon of improving Western knowledge on what they perceived to be a backward and degenerate empire. These factors perhaps help to explain why the British were largely unsuccessful in bringing any consistent scheme of Western higher education to China in the first half of the twentieth century while the American missionary establishments enjoyed a much greater level of success.

Figure 9.6

The University of Hong Kong's Main Building soon after completion in 1912, which dominated the West Point area and the waterfront district of Sai Ying Pun. (Ko Tim-keung)

Notes

1. This point has already been suggested in the case of Hong Kong by Alfred Lin, "The Founding of the University of Hong Kong: British Imperial Ideals and Chinese Practical Common Sense," in *An Impossible Dream: Hong Kong University from Foundation to Re-establishment, 1910–1950*, eds. Chan Lau Lit-ching and Peter Cunich (Hong Kong: Oxford University Press, 2002), 1–22; and "Imperialism and Practicality: The Founding of the University of Hong Kong," in *A Sense of Place: Hong Kong West of Pottinger Street*, eds. Veronica Pearson and Ko Tim keung (Hong Kong: Joint Publishing, 2008), 284–86, 292–95.

2. Jeffrey W. Cody, "American Geometries and the Architecture of Christian Campuses in China," in *China's Christian Colleges: Cross-Cultural Connections, 1900–1950*, eds. Daniel H. Bays and Ellen Widmer (Stanford: Stanford University Press, 2009), 27–28.

3. For Sydney University, see Clifford Turney, Ursula Bygott, and Peter Chippendale, *Australia's First: A History of the University of Sydney*, vol. 1, *1850–1939* (Sydney: Hale and Iremonger, 1991), 87, 95–98. Sydney's campus contained 126 acres. For Melbourne University, see R. J. W. Sellick, *The Shop: The University of Melbourne, 1850–1939* (Melbourne: Melbourne University Press, 2003), 5. Melbourne's campus contained 100 acres, considerably more than the 25 acres originally requested.

4. Pratulchandra Gupta, "Foundation of the University," in *Hundred Years of the University of Calcutta*, ed. Pramathanath Banerjee (Calcutta: University of Calcutta, 1957), 66; and Niharranjan Ray, "The Formative Years, 1857–82," in *Hundred Years of the University of Calcutta*, ed. Pramathanath Banerjee (Calcutta: University of Calcutta, 1957), 74, 76, 79.

5. K. K. Pillai, *University of Madras, 1857–1957*, vol. 1, *History of Higher Education in South India* (Madras: University of Madras, 1957), 21, 136.

6. Ibid., 139. For "assimilation," "association," and "adaptation" in colonial architecture, see Gwendolyn Wright, *The Politics of Design in French Colonial Urbanism* (Chicago: University of Chicago Press, 1991), 73–74.

7. University of Hong Kong archives [hereafter HKUA], Hong Kong College of Medicine [HKCM] Court Minutes, vol. 1, 37–39 (January 28, 1891), 43 (February 9, 1891), 49 (June 3, 1891); HKCM Senate Minutes, 69 (May 22, 1891). The old Central School building on Gough Street had been vacated in July 1889 with the opening of the new Victoria College in Staunton Street. Belilios later paid for the construction of a public school for girls on this site (1893).

8. HKUA, HKCM Court Minutes, vol. 1, 51 (January 15, 1892).

9. Ibid., 83 (January 17, 1896) and 87 (September 29, 1896); "Report of Committee Appointed by His Excellency the Governor to Enquire into and Report on the Best Organization for a College of Medicine for Hongkong" (July 15, 1896), *Hong Kong Government Gazette* (1896), 479–81, and letter from Belilios to Robinson (August 4, 1896), 485.

10. This idea originated from Dr. Francis Clark in a Senate meeting on December 30, 1896 (see HKCM Senate Minutes, vol. 1, 143). See also HKCM Court Minutes, vol. 1, 89 (March 16, 1897). *The Daily Press* (April 27, 1897) reported the meeting of April 26 in which General Black was quoted as saying in support of the Victoria Road scheme to cut a coastal road around the southwestern side of Hong Kong Island that "roads are the precursors of progress and civilization: they distinguish a rising from a barbarous state." The report of the committee dated April 15, 1897 is in The National Archives, Kew [hereafter TNA], CO129/275/96, fols. 466r–469r.

11. HKUA, HKCM Court Minutes, vol. 2, 61–63 (March 3, 1905), 69 (August 25, 1905).

12. HKUA, HKCM Court Minutes, vol. 2, 93–97, 99, 119–21 (June 1 & August 31, 1906; June 14, 1907). The donor was Ng Li Hing.

13. Ibid., 139–41 (January 17, 1908).

14. TNA, CO129/328/135, fols. 493–97, Sir Matthew Nathan to Alfred Lyttelton, May 19, 1905; CO129/340/166, fols. 600–04, Henry May to Lord Elgin, June 22, 1907.

15. HKUA, HKCM Court Minutes, vol. 2, 147 (February 14, 1908).

16. University of Hong Kong Libraries, Ms 378.5125 U58 zc, "The Conception and Foundation of the University of Hong Kong: Miscellaneous

Documents" [hereafter *Miscellaneous Documents*], 5b, plan of proposed sites dated February 14, 1908.

17. *Miscellaneous Documents*, 4, Minute by Lugard to F. H. May, n.d.; 3, H. N. Mody to A. H. Rennie, February 19, 1908.

18. *Miscellaneous Documents*, 4, A. H. Rennie to Lugard, February 24, 1908.

19. *Miscellaneous Documents*, 7b, Minute from F. H. May to Lugard, February 27, 1908.

20. *Miscellaneous Documents*, 8, Rennie to Lugard, March 4, 1908. This site was granted to the Church Missionary Society in the 1920s for St. Stephen's Girls' College.

21. Edmund Blunden would later use Byronic terms to describe the site as an idyllic modern-day setting for a temple of learning; see Blunden, "The Setting," in *University of Hong Kong: The First 50 Years, 1911–1961*, ed. Brian Harrison (Hong Kong: Hong Kong University Press, 1962), 1.

22. For Lugard's "imperial" policy for the university, see Elaine Y. L. Ho, "Imperial Globalization and Colonial Transactions: 'African Lugard' and the University of Hong Kong," in *Critical Zone 2: A Forum of Chinese and Western Knowledge*, eds. Q. S. Tong, Wang Shouren, and Douglas Kerr (Hong Kong: Hong Kong University Press, and Nanjing: Nanjing University Press, 2006), 107–45; and Peter Cunich, "Godliness and Good Learning," in *An Impossible Dream: Hong Kong University from Foundation to Re-establishment, 1910–1950*, eds. Chan Lau Lit-ching and Peter Cunich (Hong Kong: Oxford University Press, 2002), 39–40, 54.

23. TNA, CO129/355/12, fols. 26–27, Lugard to Lord Crewe (January 12, 1909); and fol. 35v, Crewe to Lugard (April 27, 1909).

24. School of Oriental and African Studies, Archives and Special Collections [hereafter SOAS], John Swire & Sons, JSSI 4/3, Box 1171, HK University 1909, *Report on the Seventh Meeting of the University Committee*, December 13, 1909. There were more concerted efforts by the Chinese elite to move the university to more salubrious surroundings in the early 1920s, for which see "The University and West Point," *The China Mail*, October 20, 1923, p. 5; and "Shift the University: Suggestion Not Well Received," *The China Mail*, October 30, 1923, p. 4.

25. *Miscellaneous Documents*, Appendix A, fol. viii (verso), William Chatham to Lugard (January 19, 1909).

26. SOAS, John Swire & Sons, JSSI 4/3, Box 1171, HK University 1909, *Report on the Seventh Meeting of the University Committee*, December 13, 1909.

27. Ibid.; TNA, CO129/359/380, fols. 56–61, Lugard to Crewe, December 9, 1909.

28. CO129/359/377, fols. 20–21, Lugard to Crewe, December 6, 1909; CO129/359/380, fol. 55r, file note of January 26, 1910.

29. TNA, CO129/365/22, fol. 81, Lugard to Crewe, January 19, 1910.

30. SOAS, John Swire & Sons, JSSI 4/3, Box 1171, Minutes of the 16th Meeting of the University Committee, December 28, 1910.

31. TNA, CO129/403/297, fols. 96–97, Henry May to Lewis Harcourt, August 18, 1913.
32. Ibid., fols. 95r–95v, 99r–99v.
33. *Miscellaneous Documents*, 36 & 38; also printed in Frederick Lugard, *Papers Relative to the Proposed Hongkong University* (Hong Kong: Noronha, 1909), 9.
34. Mody to Chater, May 21, 1908, in Lugard, *Papers Relative*, 11; Mody to Chater, August 25, 1908, and "Memo by His Excellency the Governor," August 3, 1908, in Lugard, *Papers Relative*, 19.
35. *Miscellaneous Documents*, 127, Risley to Lugard, March 3, 1909.
36. Lugard's splendid set of architectural drawings for the university buildings, presented together with a silver model of the building by Hormusjee Mody's son at the opening ceremony in 1912 are to be found in the University of Hong Kong Archives, the gift of Mrs. Shelagh Meade.
37. Cody, "American Geometries," 27–28, 55–56.
38. Blunden, "The Setting," 1–2.
39. Lin, "The Founding of the University of Hong Kong," 7–10, 17–21; Cunich, "Godliness and Good Learning," 54–57.
40. Edwin Lee and Tan Tai Yong, *Beyond Degrees: The Making of the National University of Singapore* (Singapore: Singapore University Press, 1996), 26–30.
41. Cody, "American Geometries," 54.
42. For Murphy's campus architecture in China, see Jeffrey W. Cody, *Building in China: Henry K. Murphy's "Adaptive Architecture," 1914–1935* (Hong Kong: Chinese University Press, 2001), 108–25, 151–64. Examples of these buildings and those of other architects with their hybrid architecture may be seen in Deke Erh and Tess Johnston, eds., *Hallowed Halls: Protestant Colleges in Old China* (Hong Kong: Old China Hand Press and The United Board of Christian Higher Education in China, 1998). The lasting influence of this style of architecture is surveyed in Jeffrey W. Cody, Nancy S. Steinhardt, and Tony Atkin, eds., *Chinese Architecture and the Beaux-Arts* (Honolulu: University of Hawai'i Press, and Hong Kong: Hong Kong University Press, 2011).
43. Quoted in Cody, *Building in China*, 35.
44. Ibid., 37.
45. Brian Edwards, *University Architecture* (London: Spon Press, 2000), vii.
46. It should however be noted that the British missionary societies involved in the union schemes with American missionary societies at Cheeloo University in Shandong and the West China Union University in Chengdu used "adaptive" architecture in their buildings.

[illegible] ... Lugard, August 1911.

Endacott, [illegible] 1962 [illegible] Hong Kong University Press, [illegible]

Kowloon [illegible] Hong Kong [illegible] 1900 [illegible]

Meade to Colonial [illegible]

[illegible] Bowring [illegible] 1911.

Meeting [illegible] Colonial Office, [illegible] 1909.

Lugard [illegible] for the [illegible] Hong Kong [illegible] University of Hong Kong Archives, the gift of Mrs. [illegible] Meade.

[illegible]

[illegible] and Good Fortune [illegible]

[illegible] Hong Kong University Press, 1994.

[illegible] American Cemetery [illegible]

[illegible] Chinese [illegible] Hong Kong [illegible]

[illegible] Hong Kong University Press, [illegible]

[illegible]

[illegible] Hong Kong [illegible] the British [illegible] American [illegible] Hong Kong [illegible] China [illegible]

10
Colonial Hanoi

Urban Space in Public Discourse

Lisa Drummond

A few short years after the conclusive French conquest and occupation of the imperial citadel in Hanoi, the urban development of this new, soon-to-be capital became a priority for the colonial administration and a key concern of the civil population. The self-designated spokesperson for that small but fast-expanding European community, the editor of the first French language newspaper, *l'Avenir du Tonkin*, made urban commentary an integral part of this new medium. Successive editors continued this role, using the paper and its *Chronique Locale*[1] column, as well as front page columns when the occasion demanded it, to voice criticism and confidence in the growing city and its rapidly developing landscape. In particular, the editorial voice of the paper served to reflect back on itself the preoccupations of the European community, to reprimand and criticize behavior unbecoming on the part of the French and the Vietnamese, to laud the administration and the community on their successes, and to negotiate this strange new landscape which was to be, and so evidently was not, a French city. *L'Avenir*'s editors attempted to explore and explain, often to deplore and disdain, the ways in which Vietnamese Hanoians occupied the city, shaping a landscape both exotic and repulsive.

Many early editorial descriptions of the city, reflecting, perhaps, the young and pioneering spirit of the founder of the paper, tended to boosterism, emphasizing progress and development, praising new public works and buildings. Despite such editorial enthusiasm, it quickly becomes apparent, in the pages of *l'Avenir*, that on a daily basis, Hanoi was for the French a space to be endured more than enjoyed: dangerous, smelly, and backwards. The *Chronique Locale*, in addition to charting the European community's social calendar, praising and critiquing the administration, and commenting extensively on new urban developments of the expanding city, also emphasized the everyday inconveniences and outright dangers of the new colonial city. Sudden deaths of Europeans were chronicled at length, attempting to pinpoint the dangerous phenomena in this new tropical environment; sightings of stray dogs were reported, fires, their causes and their damages were recounted in great detail, along with frequent and often scornful accounts of the dirty and smelly Vietnamese quarters of the city. Over time, and as the editorship changed, the tone of urban commentary darkened significantly from its initial youthful enthusiasm to emphasizing the dangers and inconveniences of life in Hanoi. The streets and the Vietnamese areas were clearly spaces in which the Europeans felt insecure and at risk. But this unpromising base was also the platform from which a grandiose colonial city would be constructed. So the streets, the landscape, Hanoi itself, simultaneously held both problem and promise, were both incomprehensible in the present and integral to the future.

The discourse of public space in the colonial period is thus bifurcated between danger and desire—the dangers lurking in the city, which had to be avoided and eradicated, and the desires for grandeur and modernity, which must be embodied in the urban landscape.[2] This chapter, based on research from a larger project on attitudes towards public space in Hanoi from the colonial era to the present, explores this dichotomous discourse, as evident and as evolving during the early colonial period in Hanoi. The news media, while reflecting individual opinion, also reflects as well as forms common ideas about the character of public space and specific sites, and everyday conversations and actions. As part of that larger project,[3] I read these editorial columns for insight into public opinion (as the authors attempted both to convey and to form it), for a sense of the daily experience of Hanoi as it became a colonized and colonial city, and for a sense of how resident subscribers to the French paper might find their experiences reflected through these commentaries on the minutiae of urban colonial life.[4] Here, I examine the discourses circulated in *l'Avenir* on the urban landscape of Hanoi, analyzing the editorial commentaries on urban development, the state of the city, Vietnamese behavior, and the use of public space by both communities. I also briefly discuss some of the initiatives undertaken by the French authorities to respond to the city they encountered and its urban practices, and remake it into the city they desired.

Dangerous Streets

Several phenomena show themselves clearly as near-obsessions or constant concerns when reading the daily snippets of local news in *l'Avenir du Tonkin*, contributing to a picture of the streets as spaces in which vigilance was ever-required. The colonial city was already dangerous enough—hot, humid, with threat of known and unknown disease, exotic, in the early years often under threat from the rebels whom the French always termed "pirates," and a space dominated by a strange language most *colons* never learned. These additional near-daily indications of specific threats added to the immediacy of the dangerous colonial city and gave a specific form to things to fear and avoid. These included a wide range of the concrete and the intangible, from mad dogs and corpses found on the streets to disappearing children and nauseating smells. Moreover, these dangers were given a specific and thus avoidable location—the public spaces of the city.

Mad Dogs

In the January 14, 1906 issue of *l'Avenir*, due notice was given that eight dogs ("of which four were of the French race") had been captured and taken to the pound the previous day.[5] These reports were a near-daily feature of the paper, along with news of how many mobile vendors, how many homeless, and how many beggars had been arrested or removed from the city.[6] On March 7, 1913, *l'Avenir* reported that in the previous month and a half during which the ban on dogs in the streets had been in effect, the police had rounded up 150 strays. Alongside such articles, short items recounted each case in which someone was bitten by a dog, with follow-up details in subsequent editions of the results of the rabies test on the dog, if it had been killed or captured (few seemed to escape completely), and whether or not the victim had taken rabies treatments. A fairly exact location of the incident was usually reported—at least the name of the street (which in many cases was short enough to be a reasonably precise locator). Particularly in the older, pre-1900 issues, a degree of grisly detail was offered, perhaps with some intention of sensationalizing, but likely also to underscore the unpleasantness of the treatment and the desirability of remaining always on one's guard while out in the city:

> This Sunday the 12th, the *boy* [term used to denote a house servant] of M Escande, under-inspector of posts and telegraphs, took his sister, at around two-thirty, to the home of M le Doctor V. Le Lan, doctor in the municipal services. Le-thi-Tam had just been bitten by a dog presumed rabid. The doctor had to immediately take the precautions in use, and, with the aid of a thermo-cauterizer heated until red, cauterized the wound, which was, afterwards, bandaged in the antiseptic method.[7]

Decrees banning unleashed, unmuzzled dogs from the street were frequently enacted in two-month installments, in some years for much of the year.[8] Lapses in official vigilance prompted media scorn, particularly from the sharp-penned editor of *l'Avenir*:

> A rabid dog, having bitten an *indigène*, took refuge in the house of a European who [then] killed it.
>
> No agent appeared and M. X … found himself having to go himself to alert the police superintendent and ask him to complete the necessary [formalities].
>
> For our part, we would like to signal the following points to the municipality:
>
> The day before yesterday, around 5:30 p.m., in the rue du Coton, a dog belonging to a European threw itself at an old *femme indigène*.
>
> Very luckily, the latter drew back in fright.
>
> Almost at the same moment, a few steps away, a Vietnamese dog was biting a *coolie pousse-pousse*. Naturally, there was no agent there, either.
>
> Many cases of hydrophobia have occurred recently. Many of these cases were followed by serious complications and even death.
>
> Despite that, one still encounters at every step dogs which are skinny, dirty, mangy, coming from who knows where, running around under the benevolent eye of the agents who seem to attach no importance to them.
>
> We heartily wish that the municipality would take vigorous measures and especially that the civil servants whose job it is keep strict watch over their execution.[9]

The sarcastic headline "The Police Keep Watch!" [*La Police Veille!*] decorated a January 11, 1906 report that the police had picked up in one
morning five dogs (all of which were of the "*race annamite*"), as well
as three cows and three calves which had been strolling on a central
boulevard.[10] Such was the frequency of rabid dog encounters that
l'Avenir lamented their regularity: "There is not a week which passes
when neither a suspect dog nor some *indigènes* or Europeans who have
been bitten is sent to the relevant authorities."[11] The occasional news
item concerned the actions of those who had contracted rabies:

> Yesterday around 3 in the afternoon, a Vietnamese of a certain age,
> who found himself not far from the square Paul Bert chased, foaming
> at the mouth, [other] locals [*indigènes*] and endeavored to chase the
> Europeans who came there *en pousse* on their own business.
>
> A police officer from the Mayor's service managed, not without
> trouble, to get him tied up and taken away.
>
> In all probability, this local was infected with rabies; he would
> have, if one hadn't been able to secure him, bitten another local.[12]

These frequent reports of dog encounters and captures continued well
into the 1930s, although they were most intense in the period up to 1920.

The threat of these rabid dogs was ever-present and clearly a constant
concern—rabies was and is certainly a terrifying disease and the treatment extremely unpleasant, even if administered in time. These almost
daily reminders and the large numbers of dogs captured would no
doubt have had a most sobering and fear-inducing effect on many as
they moved about the city. As so many of the attacks seemed to occur
in the Old Quarter and other predominantly Vietnamese quarters of
the city, this would have added to the sense of danger of those areas—
already strange and smelly, if often also exotic.

Corpses and Disappearing Children

Equally carefully, *l'Avenir* reported every incident of corpses found on
the streets of the city. These were numerous, and were, in later years
and under later editors, often indicated by the subheading "lugubrious
discovery" [*découverte lugubre*] or "lugubrious find" [*lugubre trouvaille*]:

> Yesterday morning, at 7:30 a.m., the corpse of a young indigenous
> girl, aged about 4 months, was discovered at the side of the School

of Medicine Street. The body, which could not be identified and showed no traces of violence, has been deposited at the morgue.[13]

Tuesday morning, the corpse of a baby of the masculine sex aged around 6 months was discovered near the Cemetery. The corpse, which bore no trace of injury and of which it has not been possible to establish the identity, has been placed in the Morgue. An inquiry has been opened.[14]

In addition to the near daily reports of mad dogs and their constant reminders of the threat of rabies, these frequent reports of corpses found abandoned in the city—many, if not most, the bodies of children—would have contributed heavily to a sense of the city as a dangerous and frightening place. In some periods, corpses were reported found almost every other day. In January 1911, for example, reports of abandoned corpses in the streets were published in *l'Avenir* on the 4th, 11th, 18th, 19th, 26th, 27th, and 28th. The locations of these *lugubre trouvailles* were, respectively, under an arcade in the rue du Papier (newborn baby girl); on the verge of the School of Medicine Street (four-month-old girl, noted in full above); at Voie 71 and boulevard Rollandes (two boys, a six-month-old and a one-year-old); in Van Ho cemetery (five-month-old girl); on the sidewalk of Voie 59 (thirty-five-year-old woman holding a newborn in her arms); and near the railway access ramp (child aged three months). For these items, unlike those involving potentially rabid dogs, there was rarely, if ever, any follow-up reporting on these "inquiries."

Why bodies were left as they were is an interesting question, given how important proper burial is in Vietnamese culture. This point was never raised in the *l'Avenir* reports. Brenda Yeoh argues in her study of colonial Singapore that the Chinese often failed to report deaths in order to avoid paying death taxes or burial fees.[15] Deaths had to be registered with the civil authority and a death certificate was needed which would have required a fee (a 1905 news item noted that as of January 1 of that year, burials in the city cemeteries for Vietnamese would cost two *piastres*, a considerable expense, presumably, for many[16]). It is possible that poor Vietnamese families were simply unable to pay the fees, or had to make the difficult decision not to spare the fees for children who died. At the least, there might well have been considerable reluctance to become entangled in the bureaucracy. The bodies reported found were boys as well as girls, so it was not, or not simply, a case of female infanticide in a strongly patriarchal culture. In the case of older persons found dead, they may have been homeless living on the streets of the city; perhaps some of the children may also have been living rough. At certain periods, many such deaths were likely linked to conditions in the countryside (food shortages and famines, such as *la Grande Famine* of 1906 or the subsistence crisis of 1915–17 as well as increasing land-lessness),[17] which prompted many to attempt to find refuge in the city.

Frequent reports of missing children would have lent an additional chill to the sense of public space in the city. As none of the reports of bodies found ever seemed to be linked to the reports of *enfants disparus*, it would seem that the latter were mainly runaways or kid-napped. To give an example of frequency, in one week in March 1913, five Vietnamese children aged eight to thirteen were reported missing in the city. This phenomenon may have been even more frightening to members of the French community, as something that could con-ceivably endanger a European child. While finding a corpse on the street would be unpleasant, certainly, the Europeans were unlikely to be allowed to fall into such destitution as to be left to die in public space (in fact, the civil administration was called upon from time to time to fund a "return passage" to France for indigent *colons*, these occasional grants appearing as municipal council items of business in the *Bulletin Municipal de la ville de Hanoi*). *L'Avenir* reported one or two cases of European children going missing, but they were found very quickly and seemed to have wandered away rather than having been kidnapped; these reassuring results were always published. Many of the missing Vietnamese children were very young—babies and toddlers—so kidnapping seems the most likely explanation, though there were few indications to that effect in the reports themselves. By the turn of the century, however, there was more acknowledgement of the problem of human trafficking (e.g. in an editorial on September 6, 1907, complaining that the relevant laws were too lax). In 1910, several arrests were reported of people caught with stolen children, and a 1914 report noted that two Vietnamese women had been stopped in Lao Cai on the Chinese border, having taken two girls to sell into prostitution (presumably in China).[18] In general, however, it seems to be assumed that the paper's readers would already understand that the missing children had been kidnapped and trafficked, just as explanation was considered unnecessary for the frequent appearance of corpses in the streets and other public spaces.

Repulsive Landscapes

Much of the early French commentary on the city of Hanoi, as the French encountered and attempted to remold it, focused on how it needed to be improved and made modern. Part of a more general colonial concern with hygiene, the French were particularly afraid of the threat of fire from the thatched roof housing which the Vietnamese used widely [*paillottes*], of death from illnesses of which they knew and understood little, and of the strange and often unpleasant odors produced in this damp and swampy landscape.

The risk of fire was ever-present and particularly acute in areas where *paillottes* were the primary constructions. Fires were reported in excruciating detail in the *Chronique Locale*, likely both as a way of encouraging demands that the *paillottes* be removed and made illegal, and as an event of some sensation in a small town with few diversions. The banning of construction in *paillotte* was one of the first steps in modernizing the streets of Hanoi thereby reducing the threat of fire, which, as more Europeans moved into the town, became a direct threat to European goods, households, and interests.

Also reported, sometimes in equally extensive detail, particularly in the first decade or so of publication, were the deaths of Europeans from tropical fevers. It is not exactly an exaggeration to say that for the French, the climate of Hanoi was indeed as "dangerous" as Vietnamese often today still caution foreigners. Governor General Paul Bert himself died of dysentery in November 1886. One particularly memorable though not atypical news report was of a civil servant in the late 1880s who experienced roughly the following summer day: he woke up, breakfasted at his usual time, and presented himself at the office by 7:30 a.m. At the lunch break he had a full meal and then went back to the office. In the afternoon he had a headache and after work decided to ride his bicycle around West Lake. He went home sweaty from the exercise and heat, showered, had dinner, and went to bed. He awoke about 2 a.m. with a fever, and by morning was dead. A twenty-first-century reader is left wondering: what were the contemporary, nineteenth-century readers of *l'Avenir* intended to take away from this detailed report? That one should not shower after exercise? That a headache may turn fatal? Very possibly, the editor had no particular moral to impart—these reports were a sharing of what little information was available so that each might draw his or her own conclusions in this foreign, unknown, and seemingly unknowable environment, and act accordingly.

One tool the French did have to both diagnose and cure the foreign environment in which they found themselves was the notion of hygiene. There is already an extensive literature on colonial concerns about this new science of the nineteenth century, with its novel ideas about the spreading of germs, and the infectiousness of miasmas and bad air; the latter led, for example, to the development of hill stations to which the Europeans repaired from their delta cities during the hot seasons.[19] In Europe, too, the science of hygiene was beginning to take widespread hold. At the 1878 meeting of the International Congress of Hygiene and Demography, a new institution of the nineteenth century, topics included everything from "The Art of Raising Infants" to "Workers' Housing in Le Havre," "Feeding Troops in the Field," "The Contagion of Rabies, Methods of Avoidance," and "Minutes of the Meetings of the Central Commission of Local Public Health Committees of the Greater Bruxelles Area."[20] In the Paris of the 1880s, public health, and in particular waste disposal's impact on public health, was a topic of great concern and innovation.[21] Many of the problems of public health were understood as specifically urban problems, resulting from industrialization, as well as urbanization through rural-to-urban migration of the working classes (and especially the working poor), both of which put pressure on already stretched and insufficient urban infrastructure.[22]

It is not surprising, then, in light of this new knowledge and its scientific orientation, that the Vietnamese parts of the city, or "the indigenous city," often drew criticism from the paper for their odors, which were offensive and "dangerous" to the French. These comments were geographically specific, both to alert the municipal authorities—to recall them to their duty—and to advise the French to avoid these areas wherever possible. Hanoi, a city built on swamps, was particularly damp and dotted with pools of often-stagnant water. These were slowly being filled in to create new land to incorporate into the expanding city,

but this process was a slow one and the swamps persisted for decades
(Hanoi still is plagued by drainage problems). Hoan Kiem Lake—the
city's centerpiece—was also often singled out for complaints about the
foul odors emanating from the dirty water, as were the many places in
the city where the Vietnamese dumped garbage (with specific locations
always identified). Thus news items such as these:

> The legendary stream [*ruisseau*] of the Street of the Mandarin
> Camp [*Camp des Lettrés*], which has been poisoning the whole
> neighborhood for years, has been exuding for some days an odor
> so infectious that the administration is moved.
> [...] Why in this part of the city, do we let the residents empty
> their gutters, household wastewater and their manure [*purin*]? The
> infection begins at number 6 where, from the sidewalk, one can
> see a latrine bucket [*tinette*] separated from the public by a bamboo
> cover [*natte*] from which the overflow trickles into the stream.[23]

> In Rice Street between the Water Tower and the market exude
> strong foul odors. One would think them the emissions of putrefy-
> ing animals; this is disagreeable and perhaps dangerous.[24]

> **Urban dumps**—We have said and re-said often, Hanoi is a dirty
> city. All over the place thanks to a general let-it-be attitude [*lais-
> ser-aller*] one sees so much garbage accumulated and dumps get
> created. Who is it who has thus accumulated in this or that place
> in the city these piles of refuse and rubbish? It is everyone and it
> is no one. It is the *indigenes* and the Europeans and as the Public
> Roads Department [*Voirie*] has never bothered whoever it is, any
> more than it has ever worried about removing this filth it follows
> that now we have formed the habit of finding these rubbish dumps
> natural. [. . .] It is thus to this colonial nonchalance, this admin-
> istrative carelessness that the state of dirtiness in which our city
> wallows should be attributed, this state of dirtiness which sprawls
> everywhere in every street.[25]

The Vietnamese and their urban practices were often the target of
pointed and negative commentary in *l'Avenir*. Some of this emphasized the apparent inability of the Vietnamese to organize space,
and conduct themselves rationally, for example, in traffic. Many critiques of the Vietnamese use of space extended even into the home,
deriding the poor arrangement of Vietnamese living spaces, the lack
of sunlight, and the poor air circulation within the small, dark rooms.
To the Europeans, the Vietnamese were unsanitary, unable to properly

arrange the disposal of waste, and uncooperative with the new French systems of waste disposal. The reluctance of the Vietnamese to use the *tinettes* (latrine buckets collected daily, for which fees were payable), or to put them out at the proper time for collection was a source of repeated complaints in the paper. In this comment on a proposed garbage and sewage service, the editor expands on the lack of hygiene inherent in Vietnamese urban life:

> This contract, if given to the right people, will be a real benefit to the population, because a number of quarters have become, due to Vietnamese carelessness and the dirtiness, hotbeds of infection presenting grave dangers in a time of epidemics. [The large area between the *route du Hue*, the *Camp des Lettrés*, and the palace of the *kinh luoc*] serves as a depository for coolies paid to empty the boxes which serve as *tinettes*; when the deposits are full enough, swarms of women come from the countryside to take them away in the small pails and baskets that we know. People often bury their dead [there]. As there is no decree forbidding inhumations in the very heart of the city, the police can do nothing.[26]

This "improper" form or lack of waste disposal, combined with the stagnant swampy pools found across the landscape outside the core central area, and with the heavy unfamiliar odors of Vietnamese cooking, led to a characterization of the Vietnamese urban landscape as "smelly." The local practice of keeping the bodies of the dead at home was also criticized by one editor who complained that the Vietnamese kept their dead so long that one could smell the funeral processions in the street, which was particularly distressing when these wound through "European" streets.

Also criticized (indeed ridiculed) was the intermingling in domestic space of people and animals:

> **Complaints**—The residents of the 8th Quarter complain, and one of them writes to us to point out the dirtiness, which reigns supreme in certain streets neighboring the Hue Road.
>
> In this quarter, which is very populous, public hygiene is considered something of little importance.
>
> The raising of pigs is conducted here on a large scale, despite municipal by-laws, and the co-residence of locals and the *habillés* of silk are most intimate. Beasts and people live under the same roof, one above, the others under the family bed, and the most perfect harmony reigns between them.

This family life, so touching, presents a serious inconvenience: the laws of public cleanliness are violated. In this quarter, filth [*immondices*] abounds and pestilential odors are let loose just about everywhere. It is a real foyer of infection, a place propitious for the hatching and the development of all kinds of illness, those which only spread rapidly, given the dirtiness which reigns a little everywhere.

What is the Hygiene Commission doing? It is in this quarter that we point out that it could operate and make evident its practical utility. The expenses for activities which have been allocated in the municipal budget: what do these amounts serve if the Commission does not meet and does not visit these quarters which have been pointed out to it as particularly unhealthy and unclean?[27]

Altogether, the presence of potentially rabid dogs, the appearance of corpses, and the disappearance of children are particularly striking examples of the ways in which the streets and public spaces of colonial Hanoi were depicted as frightening, dangerous spaces. Through repeated commentary on Vietnamese urban practices and lack of "proper" planning, the landscape of the city itself was further represented as unpredictable, unhealthy, and often repulsive. The early newspapers, in particular, reported obsessively on the occurrence of fires, the smells emanating from the Vietnamese and their quarters, and the deleteriousness of the swamp-filled terrain. In addition, commentary was frequent and extensive on cases of sudden deaths among the European population, highlighting the seemingly inexplicable dangerousness of the landscape itself.

Yet, at the same time, this very unstable, unpredictable, and unhealthy landscape was the object of urban desires.

Desired Landscapes

In 1885, at the end of *l'Avenir*'s first month of publication, its founder and editor Jules Cousin wrote of Hanoi:

The spirit of the populations is satisfactory. The *indigène* is getting used to us, bit by bit, commerce is going very well, all the profits in it go to him, and he will not be slow in becoming attached to us through [his own] interests.

The streets of Hanoi are more and more animated and there take place a multitude of small transactions.

As a result of the ever-increasing population, the ancient city, entirely rebuilt, is already too small, neither Europeans nor *indigènes* can any longer find accommodation there and every day one or two [new] Vietnamese houses are built.

The repairs and widening of the streets have begun. The work of cleaning the city's canals continues.[28]

Running parallel to the discourse of Hanoi as a site of danger—dangers of various kinds—was this simultaneous discourse of Hanoi as a site for the materialization of urban desires. For the French colonial authorities (and later for the leaders of the newly independent socialist state, and for Hanoi's current leadership), the capital city's landscape reflected the state's idea of itself and visions of its future. For the colonial state, Hanoi was to be its grand statement of French urbanity and civilization in the tropics of Asia. The construction and development of a magnificent European landscape in Hanoi was of enormous importance to the prestige of the colonial state and its French supporters. This city-building project has already been well covered by other scholars[29] and cannot be ignored; in the context of this chapter, the interesting point is the way in which these grandiose plans were reflected in, supported by, and demanded by the public discourse circulating in the newspapers. The editors of *l'Avenir* in turns lauded and lambasted the municipal government and the larger French enterprise in Indochina, according to the state of the urban landscape.

The French community, as far as its premier paper exemplifies it, was very much concerned with the appropriate development of the city. At the end of 1885, for example, Cousin gave over the front page of *l'Avenir* to a lengthy, two-and-a-half page description praising the building of a grand encircling boulevard providing a circumferential promenade around the city:

The city of Hanoi is day by day taking on a bearing more and more European, one sees on all side the raising of brick houses belonging to the French, and many Vietnamese have already built houses in the European style, they know that they will do well in renting them out to new arrivals. An excellent measure that has just been taken is the demolition of certain interior gates, which separated different parts of the city.

[…] But that which will more than anything stamp Hanoi as a European city, is the building of the grand exterior boulevard

[...] Thus, the capital of Tonkin will possess 45 km of promenades, across a charming countryside offering splendid landscapes and superb viewing points.[30]

The *Chronique Locale* concerned itself with all manner of developments in the city of Hanoi, from a note in July 1885 that two new houses had been built in brick and eleven building construction proposals had been registered,[31] and a 1900 recommendation that the timing of the street-sweeping service be changed so as not to raise dust while people were going to work in the morning—

the clouds of dust descend upon them as much in their eyes as in their mouths which is contrary to the most elementary rules of hygiene. Certainly the Parisien counterparts of these knights of the broom are earlier risers [*sont autrement matineux*][32]

—to a 1913 suggestion on the appropriate height at which the trees lining the streets should be pruned: a very important matter because "on some streets in Hanoi one has one's hat knocked off by falling branches."[33]

Pride in the development of Hanoi was not just limited to the grand developments and major construction projects, but also often as much invested in the small increments in the normality of everyday life for the French, giving an additional sense of just how thoroughly uncomfortable they were on a daily basis. The growing French community articulated (or had articulated on its behalf) needs for facilities that would make daily life more tolerable and familiar. An item in the August 5, 1885 edition noted that, "The French residents of Hanoi demand: a butcher's shop, a French laundry, a tailor, a shoemaker, billiards in the cafes." In 1887, the Chamber of Commerce listed the enterprises which were "necessary to Hanoi's prosperity: the construction of markets, abattoirs, a waste disposal system, and a water tower."[34] As they materialized, one by one, each installation of an ice-making machine, of an abattoir, of new games, and any other such small accoutrements of daily life and recreation was greeted with great fanfare.

One of the more entertaining, and also rather touching, examples of a small innovation which seemed to make a great impact on colonial daily life, comes from an editorial on January 13, 1911, noting the opening of the "Grand Antiseptic Laundry of the Far East" by M. Paul Pierre on the Paper Village Road. M. Pierre had not only installed the latest laundry machinery in Tonkin, "a factory which was entirely lacking and of which the establishment was urgent," but he also merited congratulations for

> being in conformity with all the laws of hygiene to produce for his clients laundry washed with *clean water*, constantly renewed; [... and] finally laundry mechanically ironed, which does away with this horrible practice the Vietnamese have of dampening their shirts, intimate garments, handkerchiefs with saliva and water.

The inauguration was apparently a major event, attended by Dr. Le Roy des Barres who was Director of the Municipal Bureau of Hygiene, Dr. Gouzien, M. Babillot, the chief of roadworks, and a M. Vola, with lunch and champagne toasts. In addition, the news report noted,

> Several women attended this interesting visit, doubling as a small party, and they were in ecstasy over the way in which the Vietnamese, instructed by Mme Pierre, ironed, by means of the latest model iron, new garments, fine garments, all the delicate and [illegible] treasures which our elegant [ladies] guard with a jealous care.

On the other hand, countering these instances of improvement in the urban facilities of everyday colonial life, lapses of municipal management were roundly criticized, often in scorching terms. Poorly swept streets, uncut grass in the parks, lack of streetlights, and all manner of urban neglect or mismanagement were sharply pointed out in the paper. Thus an early 1911 editorial rant about the state of Hoan Kiem, the central lake, begins:

> **Sad sight**—It's a very sad and lamentable sight, which offers itself right now to those walking around the little lake. On the banks, so much garbage, the bare lawns [*gazons pelés*], the poorly kept walkways, on the water disintegrating leaves, dead animals, all kinds of garbage, everywhere a sense of abandonment, dirt, lack of maintenance, which is painful to see.[35]

And the editor then goes on at some length to castigate the Municipal Services (Public Works) for demonstrating an "I-can't-be-bothered attitude" [*m'enfichisme*]. Such terms were not unusual in editorial commentary on the ways in which the municipality was not living up to its duty to make and keep Hanoi modern and pristine, right down to details such as the improper placement of street signs, which the paper demanded be rectified.[36]

All of this effort, large-scale and small, encouraging and criticizing, marked progress towards creating a city that was modern, a colonial city of which France could be proud.

Urban Responses

The colonial municipal authorities responded to the urban landscape they encountered and subsequently developed—the dangers posed in the alarming nature of everyday life and of the city itself, as well as the desire that the city reflect the importance of the French colonial enterprise—with attempts to change local practices and to change the landscape. The latter involved transformation of the city's built environment, a project that lasted as long as the colonial endeavor, and consisted mainly of attempts to open up and order the city. In the Old Quarter, for example, the colonial government famously tore down the gates that had separated one guild street from the other, and widened the streets to make them better suited to surveillance and the passing of troops.[37] Streets were then to be aligned more rationally (to allow vehicular use, particularly); this project continued right up to at least the Second World War, with decisions being passed in the municipal council to buy or exchange small, often very small, parcels of land which were blocking street alignment plans. Key sites of the feudal city were demolished, including the citadel and a number of pagodas, large and small, wherever they impeded or impinged on French plans for the city.

Equally wide-reaching, perhaps more fundamental, was the project to transform Hanoi from a settlement around swamps into a stable and relatively dry city by having the swamps filled in. Perhaps not quite on the scale of contemporary Singaporean land reclamation projects, Hanoi's reclamations still brought a considerable amount of urban and potentially valuable land into existence.

At the same time, a Europeanization program of new urban practices and the spaces and systems they required was implemented. The French colonial urban authorities used the term "*assainissement*" (cleaning or sanitary reform, as La Berge translates this term) to describe many of their urban development projects—including swamp-filling, covering canals and ditches, as well as getting rid of *paillottes*—as if the city needed to be thoroughly cleaned before the real work of building a modern city could begin. Thus as each neighborhood or quarter was developed, it was first "sanitized" then "aligned." Alignment was a long-term goal, towards which much time and effort was invested, in order to bring the physical city into correspondence with the mapped imagined city of straight lines and logical street layouts. Well into the 1930s, as noted earlier, this project of *alignement* following *assainissement* was assiduously pursued.

A map could be drawn of the year-by-year induction of formerly Vietnamese streets into Europeanness, first as the decrees banning the building of *paillottes* then ordering the demolition of existing *paillottes* extended out from the French Concession to the new French boulevards to the rest of the city. Sidewalks followed soon after the *paillottes* were banned. In each case, as a formerly Vietnamese street became increasingly inhabited by Europeans, it eventually became (informally) deemed European; once so, it had to be fitted out with the accoutrements of European urban modernity—drainage canals, paved roadways, sewage and garbage services, and sidewalks.

At the same time, the city was undergoing a massive construction boom. The colonial government was undertaking an ambitious program of building, including government offices and official residences, police stations (such as the ornate central station at the southwest corner of Hoan Kiem Lake, still today a police station), jails, schools, and public health facilities.[38] Significant investment was made in creating urban public spaces and monuments, though *l'Avenir*'s editors and no doubt many in the community complained that more were needed (and, as noted above, better maintenance of those that existed). These included the promenade around Hoan Kiem Lake, which first required the expropriation of the private residences and enterprises which bordered it, the botanical gardens and the zoo, the Square Paul Bert with its statue of the former Governor-General, the *fontain Chavassieux* in a square beside the Metropole, and numerous other small parks and gardens. Urban investment was made, in other words, in both the grandiose spaces of the city—such as the Governor's Residence—and the sometimes mundane spaces of everyday use, such as sidewalks, markets, and parks.

The private sector was no less active, and indeed in many respects preceded official developments. The 1885 Bastille Day report in *l'Avenir* recorded in detail the many company offices and other prominent buildings already dotting the new colonial city's landscape:

> The most beautiful place in the city is certainly the little lake, it is there also that are found the most beautiful illuminations. [...] On the two banks must be noted: the *general glow* [italics sic] of the *Cercle Français*, of which it is impossible to count the lanterns entangled in the flags and banners; the lakeside rotunda is surmounted by a magnificent star; we compliment the proprietors of this establishment, it would be impossible to do better. On the edge opposite the rue du Lac, the lakeside proprietors, the houses of MM Saillard and Guiomar, formed a pretty corridor of light happily extended by the multicolored lights of the *Poste* and the *Villa* of *l'Avenir*.
>
> We ran all over the city during the day and the evening and we would like to praise the houses which stood out for the good taste of their decorations and illuminations: the *Résidence de France, la Direction des postes et des télégraphes, l'Imprimerie du Gouvernement, les Travaux publics* [...] Rue des Incrusteurs [Inlayers Street, later *rue Paul Bert*] we must cite the cafés *du Commerce, de Beire, de la Paix, Lamblé, Block,* and *l'hôtel Albin,* whose illuminations made up for the lack of decoration. [...] Finally, Embroiderers Street, one French house is dressed only in a flag, and in the evening in this intersection it contrasts poorly [*détonne mal*] beside the illuminations of the neighboring house, the police station, and the café de France.
>
> Jean-Dupuis Street or New Street, the Path of Hanoi [*Sentier de Hanoi*] Quarter, deceived us; we hoped for better, much better. Three houses to commend: the *Compagnie française du Tonkin et de l'Indochine, Ulysse Pila et Cie, Pottier et Wibaux*.[39]

Important buildings, some of which still exist and many of which existed until very recently, such as the Hanoi Opera House (still standing), hotels including the Metropole (substantially renovated) and the Hanoi Hotel (recently torn down), clubs, cinemas, the offices of *l'Avenir* itself, and the shops lining the stylish *rue Paul Bert* (Hanoi's Champs Elysées), and of course the many villas of the European Quarter, were constructed by private companies and individuals.

To change urban practices to fit this new and longingly modern landscape, the French municipal authorities introduced a number of new services which residents were required to use. These included systems such as the *tinettes*, then the installation and connection of sewers,[40] and garbage collection. The municipal government also regulated the use of urban space at all scales, starting with the family and individual, assigning households the responsibility for keeping swept and clean the sidewalk outside their residence, and the insistence on "proper" use of sidewalks enforced through policing. The French also used various measures to change the meanings of urban spaces and their arrangement, from performing the *Retrait des Flambeaux* — a military parading through the streets to demonstrate strength, pomp and French mastery of the streets (the itinerary, published in *l'Avenir*, showed that it varied from time to time but always passed through the Old Quarter, proceeding from the French Concession on the riverside, and moving westward to the barracks on the site of the citadel) — to the construction of French sites of authority over formerly Vietnamese sites (e.g. the Governor-General's palace on the razed citadel)[41] and the implementation of public health and building codes which regulated how domestic (and retail, industrial, etc.) space should be arranged in quite precise ways, effectively insisting on French ideas about the arrangement and management of space. Later urban plans, such as those by Pineau and Hébrard, some of which were implemented, others not,[42] indicate the far-reaching French intentions for changing the ways in which space should be thought and used (e.g. through zoning).

Conclusion

French colonial Hanoi's discourse of public space revolved around, or swung between, a sense of danger lurking in the strangeness and unpredictability of the city and its indigenous population, and the desire to make Hanoi a grand city attesting to France's superiority and successful colonial enterprise in Asia. Daily life for the French, especially in the early years of the colony, involved a variety of menacing urban phenomena. As reported in the French community's newspaper, a number of threats emanating mainly from Vietnamese customs and urban practices confronted the French as they moved (no doubt warily) around the city. The exotic attractions of the Vietnamese quarters had to be weighed against their smelliness and dirtiness; mad dogs had to be avoided; or one might stumble across a corpse. The city recorded in the colonial newspaper was one where death, debilitating illness, or disappearance occurred daily, where the modern city of the future was ever out of reach, thwarted by the backward customs of the locals and their consequent lack of hygiene, by municipal inattention, and by individual irresponsibility. And yet, that future city of glorious modernity was a passionate motivation for urging its citizens and its leaders to a constant striving.

On a daily basis, Hanoi was a city to be endured, or braved, rather than enjoyed. But at the same time, the desire for a future city of order and cleanliness and impressive buildings was strong. These two circulating discourses, of danger and desire, equally strongly present in the French community's media of longest standing, exposed a tension in the French attitude towards Hanoi, comprising both love and loathing.

Notes

1. The name of the column changed from time to time but its basic purpose and format remained quite stable from the paper's inception (1884) to its cessation in the early 1940s, with steadily diminishing editorial commentary and elaboration during and after World War I.
2. Both these concepts of desire and danger are well established in the literatures on colonialism and urban space, respectively and together.
3. The project *Tracing Modern Space: Public Space in Hanoi from the French Colonial Period to the Present* was funded by the Social Sciences and Humanities Research Council of Canada.
4. I read every available issue from 1884 to 1905 in the *Centre des archives d'Outre Mer* (CAOM), France. In the National Library of Vietnam, I read from 1906, the earliest year in the library's holdings, to 1940, the last year in the library's holdings (the years 1912, 1920, and 1941 were missing entirely; 1933 apparently exists but was perpetually unavailable, over three years, while "being rebound."). For these years, I read daily editions for at least three consecutive months per year of each year for which any editions were available (the newspapers had been bound in quarterly segments). I attempted to read different quarters of the years, again, according to availability. All translations and the mistakes therein are my own.
5. *L'Avenir du Tonkin* (hereinafter abbreviated as *AT*), January 14, 1906. The "race" of every dog captured — "Annamite," "French," and sometimes "European" were the options — was always scrupulously noted in these items.

6. See also Lisa B. Welch Drummond, "The Ground Beneath Their Feet: Scuffling over Sidewalks in Hanoi, Vietnam" (paper presented at the Association of American Geographers annual meeting, Chicago, 2006).

7. *AT*, May 15, 1895.

8. In 1934, for example, unleashed, unmuzzled dogs were banned from the streets for two-month periods by *Arrêtés* Nos 18 (January 6, 1934), 88 (March 6, 1934), 174 (May 5, 1934), 281 (July 6, 1934), 368 (September 6, 1934), and 496 (November 6, 1934), *Bulletin Municipal de la Ville de Hanoi*, 1934.

9. *AT*, April 28, 1899.

10. "La Police veille!—The Hanoi police, which Europe envies, captured yesterday morning 5 dogs, all Vietnamese exceptionally for this time. Three cows and three calves on a sentimental walk on the boulevard Henri d'Orléans met the same fate. 26 mobile vendors all mothers of families trying to make a few *sapèques* to feed their children [*bécons*] were taken in military fashion [*sic* "manu milliari"] to the police station. Citizens, sleep peacefully, the police keep watch!" *AT*, January 11, 1906.

11. *AT*, May 17, 1899.

12. *AT*, September 27, 1900.

13. *AT*, January 11, 1911.

14. *AT*, January 4, 1906.

15. Brenda S. A. Yeoh, *Contesting Space: Power Relations and the Urban Built Environment in Colonial Singapore* (Kuala Lumpur: Oxford University Press, 1996).

16. *AT*, January 18, 1905.

17. See Van Nguyen-Marshall, *In Search of Moral Authority: The Discourse on Poverty, Poor Relief, and Charity in French Colonial Vietnam* (Peter Lang: New York, 2008).

18. A 1915 front page article, however, headlined "The Theft of Children," discussed the problem of human trafficking, specifically the trafficking of children many of whom were "stolen from the delta and taken to the upper regions, or China, and became as soon as their age permits domestics for life to those who purchased them." *AT*, September 22, 1915.

19. See, for example, Anthony D. King, *Colonial Urban Development: Culture, Social Power, and Development* (London and Boston: Routledge and Kegan Paul, 1976); Ann L. Stoler, "Making Empire Respectable: The Politics of Race and Sexual Morality in 20th-Century Colonial Cultures," *American Ethnologist*, 1989, 16, no. 4: 634–60; Alison Bashford, *Imperial Hygiene: A Critical History of Colonialism, Nationalism, and Public Health* (Basingstoke and New York: Palgrave MacMillan, 2004); Kerrie L. MacPherson, *A Wilderness of Marshes: The Origins of Public Health in Shanghai, 1843–1893* (Oxford: Oxford University Press, 1987), among many others.

20. Transactions of the 1878 International Congress of Hygiene and Demography, Internet Archive, accessed January 26, 2012, http://www. archive.org. These titles were taken from the table "Ouvrages Addressés au Congrès."

21. Ann F. La Berge, *Mission and Method: The Early Nineteenth-Century French Public Health Movement* (Cambridge: Cambridge University Press, 1992).

22. Ibid. See also Engels' graphic descriptions of the living conditions of the urban poor in F. Engels, *The Condition of the Working Class in England* (Oxford: Blackwell, 1958).

23. *AT*, March 7, 1891.

24. *AT*, December 28, 1900.

25. *AT*, February 19, 1910.

26. *AT*, June 30, 1888.

27. *AT*, September 6–7, 1909.

28. *AT*, January 15, 1885.

29. Cf. Gwendolyn Wright, "Indochina: The Folly of Grandeur," in *The Politics of Design in French Colonial Urbanism* (Chicago and London: University of Chicago Press, 1991), 85–160; W. S. Logan, *Hanoi: Biography of a City* (Sydney: University of New South Wales Press, 1999).

30. *AT*, November 22, 1885.

31. *AT*, July 23, 1885.

32. *AT*, October 20, 1900. Only two months later, however, the editor was complaining that the garbage collection was too early: "The vehicles which collect the household refuse and the road sweepers come a little early in the morning in some streets, Wooden Bridge Street, for example. In this season, the Europeans have a lot of trouble to make their local servants arrive before 6 am; very often it is more 7 am than 6. If the vehicle comes at the latter hour, it cannot take anything from the doors of most of the residences which are not yet swept ..." *AT*, December 3–4, 1900.

33. *AT*, February 13, 1913.

34. *AT*, March 19, 1887.

35. *AT*, January 5, 1911.

36. *AT*, May 29–30, 1899.

37. See Logan, *Hanoi*, and *AT*, November 22, 1885.

38. See Logan, *Hanoi*.

39. *AT*, July 15, 1885, pp. 1–2.

40. The manual collection of sewage and garbage continued, particularly in the Vietnamese quarters where many declined or could not afford to install more modern toilets, and the city was at pains to regulate the proper disposal of this waste. A series of news items in the summer of 1915 attests to a police crackdown on the women waste-pickers, whom the editor nicknamed "the perfume merchants," as in this short commentary: "The Hunt for the Merchants of Perfume [*La chasse aux marchandes du parfum*]—the

hunt for 'perfume merchants' continues methodically and without respite. During yesterday, the police of the first district arrested 56 waste-pickers [*vidangeuses*], and the police of the second district 46, who all, with their 'merchandise' were taken to the dump. This hunt has the goal of stopping, in the middle of the street, during the day[,] the transportation of waste which not only inconveniences everyone but constitutes a permanent danger[.] There are prescribed hours of the night for the practice of this trade, the merchants of this trade, the perfume merchants, have only to conform to the regulation." *AT*, July 25, 1915.

41. See Logan, *Hanoi*; and Wright, "Indochina."
42. See Wright, "Indochina"; and Hazel Hahn, "Ambiguous Modernism: Politics of the Municipal Council and the Urban Planning of Hanoi, 1935–1943" (unpublished paper presented at the Centre for Southeast Asia Research, University of British Columbia, Vancouver, Canada, March 12, 2007).

11
Hygienic Colonial Residences in Hanoi

Laura Victoir

> There is no such thing as good colonization without good hygiene
> ... If it is necessary to colonize in order to live, it is first necessary
> to live to colonize.[1]

Major shifts in the paradigm of Western medical thought and practice occurred in the late nineteenth century, during the high age of imperialism. The discoveries made by Louis Pasteur, Robert Koch, and a host of other bacteriologists from the 1860s onward had profound effects on medicine and empirical science. Germ theory underpinned the conception that diseases, through the knowledge of particular pathogens, could be prevented and cured. The understanding of the basis of infection and contagion led to the implementation of preventive measures that greatly reduced disease-related mortality, and touched everyday life through courses of vaccinations, water purification, sanitation, and so forth.[2] These advances in medicine, such as the use of quinine as a prophylactic against malaria, had such a profound impact on the enterprise of colonization that they have been described as a "tool of empire."[3] Most European colonial powers had, by this point, reached their maximum territorial gains and were allocating resources away from conquest and towards maintenance and development.

With the tendency towards greater specialization within the field of medicine, an entire area of expertise of tropical medicine was established, focusing on maladies specific to the torrid zone. This field was given a boost with the opening of the world's first two schools of tropical medicine in Liverpool and London in 1899; similar schools were opened by other colonizing states in continental Europe shortly thereafter. A sub-field of tropical medicine was tropical hygiene, which dealt with the promotion of healthy living and the preservation of well-being of Europe's colonial émigrés. The conservation of health in tropical climates was considered more elusive than in more temperate zones, so the stakes for medicine and hygiene there were, in a sense, even greater than at home. As one author of a book on tropical hygiene wrote:

> The hygienist must think about the elements of the tropical climate, study their influence on the European being and create prescriptions he judges to strengthen their physiological resistance. The goal of hygiene is to make the individual last longer.[4]

Although manuals about tropical hygiene had been published for the better part of the nineteenth century, they usually were aimed at an audience of military personnel or medical professionals. It was not until the turn of that century that a multitude of books written for the individual colonist came out on the market. This chapter will explore French tropical hygiene manuals from this period to analyze in what ways the transformation of medical thought influenced tropical and subtropical residential architecture.[5] It also attempts to shed light onto the medicalization of life in the tropics, as well as look at how medical thought was applied to colonial housing and house maintenance, with reference to Hanoi, which was made the capital of French Indochina in 1902. Hanoi is a particularly interesting case, as it was undergoing rapid urban development during this period of heady medical discourse. This chapter does not claim to be exhaustive; there were, of course, many other factors influencing the formation of European residences in Hanoi.[6] The interest here is to examine how the burgeoning field of tropical hygiene entered the dialogue on tropical construction.

In France, the role of the doctor-hygienist was established between 1880 and 1902, when this profession, together with engineers, civil servants, and lawyers, created the first sanitary laws for French citizens (the laws of 1892 and 1902).[7] The authority of medicine and hygiene had grown greatly from the last quarter of the nineteenth century as it became more empirical, the concept that diseases were caused by specific micro-organisms became more widespread, and doctors were receiving better education and were increasingly applying clinical diagnoses. One author pays homage in his manual on hygiene to the "considerable role hygiene plays in colonization, thanks to techniques based on solid scientific methods, which are further perfected each day."[8] Another author, Georges Treille, wrote, "Here, the role of hygiene—general science, science for everyone—must be placed in an eminent position. Because, without it, nothing durable could be established in the colonies."[9] "Scientific medicine," as the underpinning for the recommendations made by the authors, was given more importance than experience or practical know-how.

Everything in the colonial life came under the close scrutiny of the hygienists. Boundaries were continuously being blurred as doctors had increasing access—both intimate and expansive—to the colonial domestic space. As Alison Bashford noted,

> Imperial Hygiene traces all kinds of public health spaces, and explores their intersection and oftentimes neat dovetailing with other governmental 'lines,' other real boundaries of rule: national borders, immigration restriction lines, quarantine lines, racial *cordons sanitaires* and the segregative ambitions of a grafted eugenics and public health.[10]

The rules of living set forth by the tropical hygienists involved a moral paradigm as well: the middle-class benefits of moderation, abstinence, progress, modernity, and rationality were extolled. As the historian David Arnold explained,

> The medicine of the late nineteenth and early twentieth century was thus of a peculiarly confident and determined kind, believing that it was acting in the best interest of the people. It was confidently assumed that there could be self-contained technical solutions to what were in reality complex social, economic and environmental problems.[11]

For example, one author, who was not a medical doctor but a missionary, assured the reader that he "has been able to observe and treat most tropical illnesses."[12] Similarly, while there is no evidence that the authors had any architectural training, each manual discussed in detail the correct construction of a healthful tropical abode.

These French guides on hygiene attempted to systematize and rationalize architecture through the lens of science and preventative medicine; architecture was intended to serve the colonist as a tool that could combat the incidence and spreading of disease and reduce the discomfort of living in tropical climates. It was believed that the house itself could have an enormous effect on the occupant—a well-planned and built house promoted health, while the opposite was true of a poorly designed and constructed one. In fact, the authors shared many similar concerns of modern architects, with great attention paid to natural light, comfort, and ventilation. Yet, it was implied that hygienic architecture in the tropics, particularly buildings that were both healthy and economical to build, was elusive. Pitfalls to constructing such a house abounded, and one needed an expert to guide the planning, erection, and maintenance of a healthful private residence. These manuals attempted to normalize the colonial living environment; readers were informed that a hygienic life could be achieved simply by following a certain number of prescribed formulas. The agency of the individual colonist was primary, however, for even with the guidance provided by the authors, his health was ultimately in his own hands.

Most of these guides specifically refer to certain regions located between the tropics of Cancer and Capricorn, with primary focus on Africa and Indochina, but they were written with the goal to be useful anywhere in the French empire. They are universal; they gloss over almost all differentiation between regions and cultures, and use the terms "colonial" and "tropical" to refer to large swaths of the globe. Particular references to the geography and climates of the Indochinese Union (the area which today is comprised of Vietnam, Laos, and Cambodia) were also pigeonholed and simplified. The colonial world, as viewed by these authors, appeared to be quite small and was collectively exotic. The subtropical climate of Hanoi, with hot, humid summers and dryer, milder winters, did not fit well into the descriptive paradigm.

The Changing Field of Tropical Hygiene

People leaving for the tropical colonies knew that they were subjecting themselves and their health to great risk. These guides were a form of reassurance, giving the impression that many aspects of this perilous environment could be controlled. The tone that most of these manuals put forth is one of certitude: even if not all the intricacies of medical science were fully understood at that time, the forward march of knowledge would eventually reveal the solution.

These books offered systematic rules to tropical living, and the authors warned that if these rules were not followed, dire consequences would result. As Treille starkly put it,

> If we had to formulate a summary of the moral preoccupation of
> the immigrant to hot countries, we would say: do not fight nature
> but rather go around the obstacles it produces—that must be the
> motto of the European living in the tropics. He should not defy
> the heat of the sun, he must listen to his physiological needs, he
> should not lose sight of the hygienic necessities he must obey to
> choose the location of his habitation, the construction of his house,
> and his way of life—if he does not, he will die. If he respects these
> rules, the European will quickly adapt to the climate, despite the
> great heat. He will therefore only have to worry about the sanita-
> tion improvement that has to be introduced to countries that have
> malaria, which is only a question of money and time.[13]

The rules were both intricate and complex: one was advised to eat
only certain foods in certain quantities at certain times. Bathing and
personal hygiene were regimented, such as dictating the temperature
of the bathwater. Napping was deemed necessary, as was exercise, if
done at a leisurely pace. The abdomen was to always be wrapped in
cloth, flannel preferably, underneath one's clothing, even in the swel-
tering heat.

These guides also prepared the reader for the variety of diseases
encountered in Indochina: malaria, cholera, dysentery, diarrhea,
dengue, hepatitis, typhoid, typhus, and plague.[14] Yet, it is clear that
these books were written during a period of flux in the field of tropical
medicine and hygiene. In addition to this list of Indochina's endemic
diseases, authors described archaic ailments, such as bilious fevers,
hemoglobinous fevers, congestion of the liver, tropical anemia, and
fevers of acclimatization. The authors blamed the climate and meteorological environment on the European's poor health in the tropics.
R. Wurtz described the physiological changes experienced by an
European when arriving in the tropics, such as increased body temperature, increased respiration and pulse, decreased digestive functions (which necessitated the ingestion of spices to ensure good liver
function), increase in feelings of depression or malaise, etc.[15]

As seen from above, these guides trace the tenacity of former
ways of thinking in this age of advances in tropical and preventive
medicine. One especially prevalent and erroneous theory was that
noxious gases emanating from soil and stone were pathological. Even
the names "malaria" (derived from *mala aria* or "bad air" in Italian)

and *"paludisme"* in French (derived from *palus* or "swamp" in Latin) result from the conviction in the harmfulness of miasmas. Belief in this miasmatic theory still proliferated even after the general acceptance of germ theory and the discovery of the Anopheles mosquito's role in the transmission of the Plasmodium pathogen that causes malaria.

In an effort to explain the source of infection, miasmatists held that infectious disease was the result of bad air, which was created by unhealthy surroundings, such as decomposing soil and refuse. This conviction gave rise to the belief that certain locations or environmental conditions could be healthy or unhealthy; in general, the tropical world was considered to be incredibly unhealthy. For example, according to the hygienist and author of several books on the subject, Gustave Reynaud, the most important link between diseases such as malaria, beriberi, dysentery, plague, and leprosy was "the nature of the ground, to its richness of organic matter, constitution and the degree of humidity." He continued, "The development of these micro-organic or parasitic diseases is greatly aided by tropical atmospheric conditions."[16] Reynaud found no discrepancy in quoting Pasteur and discussing the role of germs and *"microbiennes"* while still insisting that tropical disease were spread via *"agents telluriques."* He wrote,

> It has been known for a long time that the sanitary influences of the earth depend on what goes into it and what comes out of it. After the discoveries made by Pasteur, the study of gaseous dis-seminations from the earth have lost much of the great importance that was once attributed to them during the time it was thought that diseases were caused by miasmas, but it would nevertheless be excessive to neglect this theory completely, because if the earth is porous and permeable there is an exchange of gas between it and the atmosphere.[17]

Even after the acceptance of germ theory, the world could be still viewed in a dichotomic light; places were naturally healthy or unhealthy. Tonkin, the region in which Hanoi is located, was not in nature considered to be the latter, but that categorization was not immutable. The agricultural use of land, primarily rice paddies, in Tonkin had "made malaria disappear." But this salubrious state of being was likewise not absolute as it was determined that any great shifting of the earth could cause it to reappear.[18] Particularly to those authors who held residual miasmatic beliefs, a well-designed and well-positioned house could protect the occupant from the worst of the dangers posed by the tropical atmosphere.[19] Not only do these guides shed light on the gap between medical knowledge and practice at this period, they also demonstrate how medical discourse was disseminated to laypeople, the readers of these books. They were told to construct and maintain their tropical houses according to advice based on inherently contradictory medical theories.

Hygienic Tropical Architecture

As the historian Annmarie Adams explained, during this era "doctors attempted to analyze the house in section—as they saw the body—separating and categorizing the various systems as a way of understanding the whole."[20] This is precisely what the tropical hygienists do; their books almost read as an architectural pattern book, breaking down the details of a hygienic house into roughly five fundamental elements. The rules that applied to hygienic colonial residences did sometimes slightly vary from author to author, but were overall homogenous, and were sometimes repeated verbatim from one text to another.

The first aspect addressed was the placement of the house, for which it was recommended to be located far from forests, swamps, lagoons, and valleys. It was best to build upon an elevation, on ground with proper drainage. Land near the house was to be cleared, even up to one kilometer around the house, according to some. Yet, it was also confirmed that trees planted in a row could be an effective barrier against unhealthy winds. It was advised that European conglomerations or houses be segregated from indigenous villages, which were invariably described as sources of noise, filth, and disease. Moreover, indigenous villages housed indigenous children, who were thought, in particular, to harbor malaria.

The second aspect dealt with the orientation of house, primarily with regards to the sun and wind. Most authors suggested it is best to orientate the main façade of the house in the direction of the principal winds, unless they were too violent or humid or "unhealthy." How one was to judge if the prevailing wind was too humid or unhealthy was not explained in any of the guides.

The third feature was the choice of materials used to build the house. Of primary importance was the conductibility and specific heat (the amount of heat per unit mass required to raise the temperature by one degree Celsius) of the materials. Stone was deemed best; bricks, second best and more economic. Wood, while being inexpensive and having the benefit of being a poor conductor, was not advised for it did not last long in tropical climates. Ideally, floors were made of varnished brick joined by cement, so they could easily be cleaned. Using materials that were not conducive to the growth of mold was important, as mold could "serve as a repository for numerous species of pathogens (the bacillus of diphtheria and tuberculosis)."[21] Therefore, the interior of the house was supposed to be kept bare and clean; there was no use for wallpaper, rugs, or curtains in the hygienic colonial home. Furniture was to be sparse and made of bamboo or cane. It was advised that walls, of whatever material, be doubled. The ideal thickness of the walls and the distance between them, however, varied according to the different authors.

The forth dictate regarding the circulation of air was considered even more important in the colonies, where Wurtz estimated that the volume of air that needed to be renewed had to be quadrupled when compared to what was needed in France.[22] Treille had a similar view:

> The dilation of air due to elevated temperature, its concentration of water vapor, the absolute necessity for the heat to escape from a European's body, and the absolute necessity of exhaling water vapor from the lungs, means that a considerable volume of air is necessary. In hot countries, human breath … is deadly. One should not share a room [for sleeping] except in absolute cases of necessity. I had estimated a few years ago that one hundred cubic meters was the minimum size of a bedroom for one person, assuming that the doors and windows are closed; I have not changed this estimation.[23]

Ceilings, therefore, could not be less than four meters (over thirteen feet) high. Moreover, large windows were considered necessary in a hygienic residence. The general rule of thumb was that all rooms had to open to the exterior by two faces. Interior walls were not supposed to reach the ceiling, in order to facilitate the movement of air, and any interior structures that prevent ventilation were to be avoided. One doctor wrote that it was preferable that the large rooms span the entire width of the building,[24] but this suggestion become less implementable as houses in Hanoi became more elaborate.

Colonial houses were supposed to be outfitted with specific ventilation systems, which were sometimes outlined in these books. General Joffre's system, for example, was described as being used in barracks in Tonkin with good results. It was based on the high conductibility of metal roofs, which created currents of air when the roof heated during the day and cooled during the night (the main complaint about this system was that the metal roofs deteriorated rapidly in tropical climates).[25] Likewise, it was advised that chimneys be located at the center of buildings, connecting to all rooms, so that they could suck up hot air and allow cool air to enter through the windows or doorways. Attics were also used as a ventilation system. As the sun heated the roof, the lighter hot air was pulled upwards through hermetically sealed passages in each room giving onto the attic, and would be replaced by cooler air. Most authors agreed that a large attic was needed between the upper floor's ceiling and the roof, and that this should be opened to the exterior on opposite sides so that air could circulate.

The fifth facet was the importance of blocking sunlight from entering the house, primarily through the inclusion of a verandah. The verandah protected the house by blocking direct sunlight from entering and setting back the openings to the house and by providing a protective layer of air that impeded the penetration of hot air into the house. In Indochina, verandahs were a part of even the earliest French houses and were created by extending the roof over the four exterior walls of the house. Even though they were commonly part of the colonial house in Indochina, the verandah was later deemed to be a hygienic prerequisite: "the necessity to establish large openings giving onto the exterior, which conforms with the prescriptions of modern hygiene necessitates the need to protect them with a verandah."[26]

The verandah not only protected the house from sunlight, but also served as the barrier between the house and the outside world. As one author wrote, the verandah "conceals the occupants from indiscrete glances."[27] It provided a primary setting to colonial life; Wurtz and Navarre both describe the verandah as the place where one principally lived.[28] It proved to be a flexible architectural component, as in Hanoi where it was often partially or fully enclosed and appropriated as

interior living space. The enclosed verandah on the ground floor could
house an office or storage room, or serve as bathrooms on the first
floor. If the verandah was incorporated into the interior of the house,
the buffer between the domestic sphere and the outside world was
shifted outward, to the tall garden walls. Lush gardens surrounded by
high walls were ubiquitous in colonial Hanoi, even if they were not
an endorsed feature of a hygienic house; authors, as noted previously,
warned against any vegetation within the immediate vicinity of the
house. So while the garden and its walls were effective at shutting out
danger and noise posed by the colonial city, even these barriers could
be a source of disease if the yards were not properly maintained, as
they could serve as a breeding ground for mosquitoes; it was emphasized that any fallen leaves had to be cleared daily.[29] Danger in the
tropical world was everywhere, and vigilance was a constant necessity.

As a rule, the main house was separated from other unpleasantries
as well. The colonial residence had a number of outbuildings; it was
often recommended that they be located at a great distance from the
house. Places for personal hygiene, the *cabinets d'aisances* (toilets) and
salle de bains with *tinettes mobiles* (bathrooms with latrine buckets), could
be located within the house, but outside latrines were also to be maintained. Grall discussed the benefits to having the kitchen located within
the house, in that the housewife (*la maîtresse de la maison*) could, at any
time and without warning, keep an eye on the happenings therein. Yet,
according to him, the drawbacks—including odors, heat, and dirtying
of the floor—made him conclude it was best that the kitchen be located
outside.[30] The non-European servants' quarters were also to be situated
at a distance from the main house, due to the noises and odors (and
possibly diseases) that were supposed to emanate thence.

All books advocated for the use of a mosquito net on the bed, for
even authors who adhered to the belief in miasmas and meteorological
effects also understood that insects were not conducive to health. Yet,
interestingly, the use of metallic screens on windows as a prophylactic
to insect-borne diseases was only recommended later. Beginning with
the chapter written by Wurtz in 1907, authors progressively agreed that
protecting the openings of the house with screens or specially made
cloth, while interfering with ventilation, was worthwhile. [31]

These French authors borrowed from the work of other European scientists, citing not only their countrymen, but also British, Dutch, and German writers. Architectural preferences exhibited by colonists of different nations were noted, often in a comparative way. For instance, according to Reynaud, the English generally situated their colonial towns better than the French had, as they had learned from the experiences of their Spanish, Portuguese, and Dutch antecedents; even if they worked in town, they still resided at higher altitudes.[32] Likewise, Navarre noted,

> ... the English have a grasp of hygiene much superior to the French or other Latin races, and they know how to fight against their natural taste for alcohol, and they draw from the comfort of their habits, their houses, the choice of their residences, their winter homes, their sanatoria, their family life, a singular force to resist the unwholesome influence of Indian soil.[33]

There were evidently "national" techniques, as the British, it was written, favored constructing verandahs with a width of two and a half meters,[34] while the French preferred to make theirs three meters wide.

National pride sometimes took precedence over hygienic concerns. While several authors stated that the *paillotte* hut was a hygienic and comfortable form of shelter, as thatch roofing and thick mud walls insulated the house well from sun and heat, others could not recommend Europeans occupying them: "The miserable huts in *paillotte*, in *pisé* (rammed earth), or in wooden frame mounted on stone, which we find in too great a number in the colonies, are the shame of colonization."[35] The hut smacked too much of native housing. Likewise, Grall wrote, "The worst service that can be done to our race is to place one of its representatives in conditions inferior to those of the natives; it is necessary at all places and at all times that he dominates them or that he at least upholds that appearance."[36] Again, the readers of these guides were presented with eventuality: if one's house was substandard, "over time, if some kind of epidemic arrives in the region, those who live in such [inferior] interiors will become victims of choice."[37] Critiques of native methods of housing sometimes led authors to contradict themselves. For instance, Reynaud discussed why native houses were unhealthy, one reason being that they did not let in adequate light.[38] Yet, he strictly warned against letting direct sunlight enter

European houses. Likewise, some advice seemed too impractical to be implemented. For instance, Wurtz suggested that, whenever possible, each inhabitant of the house have two bedrooms: one in the north of the house for mornings, and one situated in the east of the house for the afternoons.[39]

Colonial Houses in Hanoi

Hanoi was a city that had only recently been conquered, and did not take on the appearance of a colonial city until the late 1880s; the period that these hygienic manuals were being published coincided very closely with the development of Hanoi. Until that point, it was described as a filthy place. During most of the year, wastewater from the city simply ran into the interconnecting swamps and spread across the southern outskirts in a series of marshes and ponds. Georges Dumoutier painted the scene around a lake in 1883:

> ... native huts crowded its shores; to go down to the water it was necessary to weave through narrow alleys, leaving the city's passable roads ... to run into a thousand detours [formed by a jumble of] straw huts where a destitute population swarmed, to hop among stinking puddles and piles of garbage; and often at the end of an hour after patient detours as in a labyrinth, the bold explorer found himself yet again at his starting point without having reached the shore. And even if he caught a glimpse of a little bit of the lake ..., he was not tempted to approach ... [because one commonly] encounters an unhealthy lagoon at a street corner or behind gloomy huts in old Hanoi.[40]

It was not until the end of the century that the city underwent serious attempts at modernization. Yet, the urban improvements done by the French were "much more a reflection of the ideas current in metropolitan France or adopted in other French colonies than a reflection of Hanoi's specific characteristics."[41] Some features the hygienists recommended were implemented to some extent in Hanoi. For instance, a visitor in 1907 described:

> Immediately after the street has bent, in the shade of gardens filled with trees, flowers and perfumes, are hidden away small private houses, buried in greenery. Some, the latest, built according to the

requirements of the climate which have finally been recognized, push their superposed stories as high as possible up to the sky, above the swamp ...

The same visitor remarked about the older residences,

... the pretty small houses must be rather poorly equipped against the tropical heat, the constant humidity, the winter drizzle, the typhoons, in short against the conditions of Tonkin. For this, one wishes them not less luck but more real charm that is due to the lucky adaptation of the local style or French taste to practical needs.[42]

Still, the architecture best suited for Hanoi did not neatly fit into the paradigm of tropical architecture as espoused by the manuals. Paul Doumer, Governor-General of Indochina from 1897 to 1902, wrote,

The buildings [in Saigon] that are light and airy and are perfectly suited for the climate of Cochinchina, would not work well [in Hanoi] where it is cold for several months of the year. In Tonkin, one can neither build tropical constructions nor European ones. In the summer, it is too hot for living in these; in the winter, it is too cold to live in the others. It is thus a mixed construction that must be found, where one is protected from the sun and the air can circulate during the hot season; where one can close it up and heat the house during the winter. The question was not resolved in 1897, and I do not think it has yet been, despite the research conducted, the numerous constructions and interesting enterprises since that time.[43]

Grall, likewise, described how for several years, houses in Hanoi had been built in a style that resembled those in the suburbs of big French cities, lacking such tropical necessities as verandahs. He condemned them as "houses of cards," poorly built, with thin walls that overheated in the sun; these residences, he deemed, were only habitable from September to mid-April.[44]

There is a lack of an inventory of the buildings of Hanoi built around the turn of the century, but there exist descriptions of what some residences looked like. The architectural historian Christian Pédelahore portrayed a typical colonial residence in Hanoi: the house was surrounded by a garden and wall, which was compulsory under early French rule. Behind the main house were located the outbuildings. The main house had two levels: the ground floor featured the rooms for entertainment and dining; the upper floor housed the bedrooms and bathrooms. The house was organized around one or two axes of symmetry. The main house "in the foreground, [provided the] the wide, light, functional and hygienic living space of the French colonist" whereas the indigenous servants worked and were housed in the dim background.[45]

Another description of turn-of-the-century residences in Hanoi is found in Grall's book, in which he described and critiqued three different houses he had inspected there. All three had common points in that they were not placed directly on the road and thus the orientation of the house was not completely determined by the direction of the street. They were all elevated. They were built with similar materials: stone for the foundations, bricks from a certain height, beams and ceiling in iron, and roofs in slate. The floors were made of local hardwood. The verandahs were enclosed almost completely, and had become usable interior space. The houses were almost perfect cubes, instead of being long and narrow, like the houses constructed at the beginning of the occupation of Indochina.[46]

The Family House

Not only did the hygienists address house construction, but also how the houses had to be maintained. Here, although the books do not explicitly state it, their discourses enter the domestic, feminine sphere of influence. Yet, the subject of women was peripheral, with only a few guides making more than the briefest assessment of women's lives in the tropical colonies: it was clear that the intended readership was men, apparently between the ages of twenty-five and thirty-five, deemed the ideal age for colonists.[47] Authors warned that European women in the tropics suffered from particular physiological problems, such as severely troubled menstruation, which could result in anemia. Menstruation of white girls born in the colonies was said to come on earlier than their European-born counterparts, even before the onset of puberty. There was a greater risk of miscarriages and complications with pregnancy, and even labor was rendered more difficult. A decrease in the supply of breast milk was almost always the rule, so that women incapable of exclusively feeding their children had the distasteful necessity of relying on an indigenous wet-nurse. According to the majority of these books, the filthy nature of the native would give any European woman pause before handing her newborn child to one for nourishment. And while there is no mention of the preferred socioeconomic level of the male colonist, class was considered a factor for women. "Just as it is for children, the higher the woman is on the social scale, that is the better-off she is, the greater her chance to live in good health in hot climates."[48]

The woman's role in the hygienic colonial house was not clearly defined, probably as there were so few women in the colonies during this period: only two hundred French women lived in Hanoi in 1900.[49] One author in particular did take into account the living conditions of women and children in various styles of house found in Hanoi.[50] Indeed, the acceptability of the house depended on whether the inhabitant was a single man, several men living together, a couple without children or a large family; each required specific hygienic considerations. For instance, a house that would be suitable for a single man (a single-storied raised house with two rooms) would not be suitable for a family, as it was concluded that there was no place for the children to sleep than under the house. Likewise, a poorly designed house would be particularly unsuitable for a family or married couple. One family house described by Grall was insufficient due to the width of the walls:

> despite being thirty-three centimeters, they were not thick enough to keep the house from heating up in the daytime. For a single man who only comes to the house to eat and sleep late at night, this inconvenience was bearable, but a woman who had to live there the whole day would suffer, for in Indochina, the cooling of the night was only noticeable two to three hours after the sun sets.[51]

The woman's place was at home. As Grall explicitly noted, "The woman [in Indochina], as in Europe, must live almost constantly and continuously in the house." Besides maintaining the residence, it was advised that the woman had personal occupations such as sewing and cooking. It was also "useful for her to keep her spirit by reading" and she must keep up external relations, as "it is hygienic to do so" although excessive outings from the home could be "fatal."[52] The interior was supposed to serve as a safe haven from the dirty, dangerous environment of Hanoi, and was thus the appropriate place for the fairer sex. The stakes of not residing in a hygienic house were therefore higher for women and children, because other locations in the colonial city were not at their disposal, as they were for men.

Conclusion

"Tropical architecture" as a generic term is not helpful, as each location had particular environmental characteristics, materials available for building, indigenous and colonial cultures, etc. Perhaps more useful than the advice written for the soon-to-be colonist was the confidence these books imparted upon them: although the colonial world was dangerous, it was tamable.

It was implied in these books that empirical science had determined such things as healthy and unhealthy building materials, orientations, constructions, locations, proximities, sizes, and so forth. But, as Arnold wrote and as is evidenced by these hygienic guidebooks, "[b] eneath the language of medical objectivity and the talk of 'sanitary science,' European medical attitudes often remained highly subjective, embodying the social and cultural prejudices of the age."[53] Moreover, the relationship between medicine and colonization was in flux: this was evidenced by several authors' beliefs in outdated theories while simultaneously drawing on references to new medical discoveries. A review of Chantemesse and Mosny's "Hygiène Coloniale" in the *British Medical Journal* opined that

> What is really wanted now in tropical sanitation is not so much new books, of which there are plenty, as practical application of well-known truths. This application, unfortunately, is very tardy, in its appearance, but it has been begun in some places, and it is really only a question of time till it spreads and becomes universal.[54]

These guides were very consciously tools of colonization. Some, more than others, particularly the earlier works, committed many pages to the importance and historical suitability of European colonization. For example, the manual published by the *Union Coloniale* in 1894 stated,

> Today, colonial hygiene is presenting itself in a new way. We are going to briefly lay out the rules of the hygiene of *colonization*, and not simply the hygiene of colonies .... Hence colonial hygiene is not only the hygiene of the European in the tropics; if we were

to restrict ourselves to this framework, we would be missing a lot of points as colonial hygiene is well *studied and understood* [my italics].[55]

The central idea of these guides of colonial hygiene was that with practical application of proper hygiene, Europeans could live anywhere in the world. As Reynaud stressed in his book of 1903, colonization and the *mise en valeur* of French possessions was, certainly, for the good of the metropole in a time of intense competition amongst European states. This important job fell to the colonist. Protecting the health of the individual colonist was not only a medical concern, but a national one as well.

Notes

1. Gustave Reynaud, *Hygiène des établissements coloniaux* (Paris: J.-B. Baillières et fils, 1903), 3.
2. Philip D. Curtin's work quantitatively illustrates the "mortality revolution" in the tropical world in the nineteenth century. Philip D. Curtin, *Death by Migration: Europe's Encounter with the Tropical World in the Nineteenth Century* (Cambridge: Cambridge University Press, 1989); Philip D. Curtin, *Disease and Empire: The Health of European Troops in the Conquest of Africa* (Cambridge: Cambridge University Press, 1998). See as well, Douglas Melvin Haynes, *Imperial Medicine: Patrick Manson and the Conquest of Tropical Disease* (Philidelphia: University of Pennsylvania Press, 2001); David Arnold, *Colonizing the Body: State Medicine and Epidemic Disease in Nineteenth-Century India* (Berkeley: University of California Press, 1993); David Arnold, ed. *Warm Climates and Western Medicine: The Emergence of Tropical Medicine, C. 1500–1900* (Atlanta, GA: Rodopi, 1996).
3. Daniel R. Headrick, *The Tools of Empire: Technology and European Imperialism in the Nineteenth Century* (New York: Oxford University Press, 1981).
4. G. Treille, *De l'acclimatation des Européens dans les pays chauds* (Paris: Octave Doin, 1888), 4.
5. I have attempted to consult the greatest number of these manuals as possible, including: *Publications de l'Union coloniale française: Manuel d'hygiène colonial* (Paris: Augustin Challamel, 1894); A. Chantemesse and E. Mosny, eds., *Traité d'hygiène: Hygiène coloniale*, vol. XI (Paris: J.-B. Baillière et fils,1907); Charles Grall, *Hygiène coloniale appliquée. Hygiène de l'Indo-Chine* (Paris: J.-B. Baillières et fils, 1908); Charles Joyeux, *Hygiène de l'Européen aux colonies* (Paris: Librarie Armand Colin, 1928); A. Levaré, *Le Confort aux colonies. La Vie dans la brousse. Le Jardin potager* (Paris: Editions

Larose, 1928); Henri Maurice, *Sous les tropiques; Notions d'hygiène et de médecine à l'usage des coloniaux* (Paris: Vigot frères, 1920); Georges Montel, *La Ville de Saïgon: Etude de démographie et d'hygiène coloniales* (Bordeaux: Imprimerie Moderne, 1911); P. Just Navarre, *Manuel d'hygiène Coloniale: guide de l'Européen dans les pays chauds* (Paris: Octave Doin, 1895); Reynaud, *Hygiène des établissements coloniaux*; Dr. Sadoul, *Guide Pratique D'hygiène et de médecine coloniale à l'usage des postes militaires dépourvus de médecin* (Paris: Augustie Challamel, 1895); Treille, *De L'acclimatation des Européens dans les pays chauds*.

6.   See, for example, Gwendolyn Wright, *The Politics of Design in French Colonial Urbanism* (Chicago: University of Chicago Press, 1991).

7.   Laurence Monnais, *Médecine et colonisation. L'aventure Indochinoise, 1860– 1939* (Paris: CNRS Editions, 1999), 30.

8.   Reynaud, *Hygiène des établissements coloniaux*, 3.

9.   Treille, *De l'acclimatation*, ii.

10. Alison Bashford, *Imperial Hygiene: A Critical History of Colonialism, Nationalism and Public Health* (Houndsmills [England] ; New York: Palgrave Macmillan, 2004), 1.

11. David Arnold, ed. *Imperial Medicine and Indigenous Societies* (Manchester: Manchester University Press,1988), 18.

12. Maurice, *Sous Les Tropiques*, vii. For more on missionary medicine, see David Hardiman, *Missionaries and Their Medicine: A Christian Modernity for Tribal India* (Manchester: Manchester University Press, 2008).

13. Treille, *De l'acclimatation*, 10–11.

14. Ibid., 77–8.

15. R. Wurtz, "Hygiène coloniale générale," in *Hygiène coloniale*, eds. A. Chantemesse and E. Mosny (Paris: J.-B. Baillière et fils, 1907), 26–29.

16. Reynaud, *Hygiène des établissements coloniaux*, 12–13.

17. Ibid., 177.

18. Ibid.; Sadoul, *Guide pratique d'hygiène*, 3.

19. Analogous to the residual belief in the dangers of miasmas, within these guides are also archaic references to the humoral practice of medicine. Perspiration was thought to be especially harmful, as it disrupted the balance of the body's chemistry (the equilibrium of the four humors— blood, phlegm, black bile, and yellow bile). Certain procedures were advised to protect the body from rapid heating or cooling by insulating the abdomen, such as by wearing a flannel wrap under one's clothing; not doing so put one at risk of diarrhea or dysentery. Water and other liquids were only to be consumed in moderation. This observation is also made in Curtin, *Death by Migration*, 42–43, where he notes that during the mid-nineteenth century, "all [medical authorities] drew from the prevalent humoral theory … [Whereby they] associated human health with human passions and habits of life. Heat was associated with fever; tropical heat

was associated with moisture as well. Heat and exercise brought on perspiration, and perspiration affected the humoral balance of the body. The
rules of hygiene therefore governed the intake and expulsion of liquids.
They also recommended or forbade particular kinds of exercise. They
recommended various kinds of temperature control … some recommendations called for light and looser fitting clothes, but others called for insulating materials like flannel."

20. Annmarie Adams, *Architecture in the Family Way: Doctors, Houses and Men,
1870–1900* (Montreal: McGill-Queen's University Press 1996), 6.

21. Alphonse Boucher, "Hygiène de l'habitation coloniale" (Université de
Montpellier, 1918), 48. Although this source is a published academic
thesis and not a guide, I have included it in this work as it uses published
hygienic guides as its primary, and almost exclusive, sources.

22. Wurtz, "Hygiène coloniale générale," 64.

23. Treille, *De l' acclimatation*, 141. Against what we would consider logical
today, while Treille insists it is of the utmost importance to have a well-
ventilated bedroom, he also insists that all windows giving into a bedroom
must be closed during the night.

24. Sadoul, *Guide pratique d'hygiène*, 7.

25. Boucher, "Hygiène de l'habitation coloniale," 40.

26. Ibid., 33.

27. Maurice, *Sous les tropiques*, 73.

28. Wurtz, "Hygiène coloniale générale," 62; Navarre, *Manuel d'hygiène coloniale*, 199.

29. Grall, *Hygiène coloniale appliquée*, 75–76.

30. Ibid., 74.

31. Wurtz, "Hygiène coloniale générale," 63–64.

32. Reynaud, *Hygiène des établissements coloniaux*, 171.

33. Navarre, *Manuel d'hygiène coloniale*, 65.

34. Boucher, "Hygiène de l'habitation coloniale," 34.

35. Treille, *De l'acclimatation*.

36. Grall, *Hygiène coloniale appliquée*, 53.

37. Treille, *De l'acclimatation*, 136.

38. Reynaud, *Hygiène des établissements coloniaux*, 210.

39. Wurtz, "Hygiène coloniale générale," 60

40. Quoted in William S. Logan, *Hanoi: Biography of a City* (Seattle: University
of Washington Press, 2000), 73.

41. Ibid., 70.

42. Gaston Cahan, "Hanoï. Les récentes transformations de la capital
Tonkinoise," in *Cities of Nineteenth Century Colonial Vietnam: Hanoi, Saigon,
Hue and the Champa Ruins,* ed. Walter E. J. Tips (Bangkok: White Lotus
Press, 1999), 212–13.

43. Paul Doumer, *L'Indo-Chine française* (*souvenirs*) (Paris: Vuibert et Nony, 1905), 115.
44. Grall, *Hygiène coloniale appliquée: Hygiène de l'Indo-Chine*, 73.
45. Christain Pédelahore, "Constituent Elements of Hanoi City," *Vietnamese Studies* 12, no. 82 (1986): 136–37.
46. Grall, *Hygiène coloniale appliquée*, 76–82.
47. Wurtz, "Hygiène coloniale générale," 31.
48. Ibid., 32.
49. Logan, *Hanoi*, 92–93.
50. Grall, *Hygiène coloniale appliquée*, 73–74.
51. Ibid., 76–77.
52. Ibid., 85–86.
53. David Arnold, "Introduction: Disease, Medicine and Empire," in *Imperial Medicine and Indigenous Societies*, ed. David Arnold (Manchester: Manchester University Press, 1988), 7.
54. "Handbooks of Tropical Medicine," *British Medical Journal* 2, no. 2440 (1907).
55. *Publications de l'Union coloniale française. Manuel d'hygiène colonial*, 11.

12
Domesticating the Suburbs

Architectural Production and Exchanges in Hanoi during the Late French Colonial Era

Danielle Labbé, Caroline Herbelin, and Quang-Vinh Dao

> Beware of saying to them that sometimes different cities follow one another on the same site and under the same name, born and dying without knowing one another, without communicating among themselves.
>
> Italo Calvino, Invisible Cities, 1972, p. 30

The urban built environment of Hanoi, Vietnam, has been the object of much writing in recent years. This scholarship focuses on the colonizers' attempts to assert their domination over the territory and people of Indochina through the transformation and expansion of Hanoi's urban space.[1] Writers insist on the intentional destruction of pre-colonial administrative and religious artifacts (citadel, pagodas, temples, etc.) and their replacement by pompous civic buildings symbolizing the dominance of the French tutelary power. Authors also typically highlight the vast urban planning operations that led to the construction of residential neighborhoods south and west of Hanoi's old merchant city. The broad avenues, flanked by luxurious villas, are presented as a device that entrenched the divide between the living space of the French and that of the indigenous populations. Altogether, these works tell the well-known story of spatial domination and division of colonial cities into visible and legible urban spaces under the firm control of the conquerors.[2]

What this scholarship tends to overlook is that by the late 1920s, architecture in Hanoi was no longer the sole purview of the colonizers. In the shadow of the colonial power, a group of native practitioners emerged out of the educational system set up by the French in Hanoi. Between 1926 and 1940, fifty or so Vietnamese professionals graduated from the *Section d'Architecture* at the *École des Beaux-Arts d'Indochine* (thereafter EBAI). Against the wish of the colonial administration, these young architects became increasingly active in shaping Hanoi's built form, their work coming forth through active exchanges with French architectural production in Hanoi and abroad. Yet, Vietnamese architects only selectively engaged with Western techniques and styles, rooting their work in traditional practices of urban space.

In this chapter, we recount the emergence of this group of young native professionals in the twilight of the French colonial era and explore their involvement in architectural developments in Hanoi.[3] First, this article discusses the important role played by the EBAI in shaping their practice and interactions with a variety of architectural doctrines and movements. Second, it analyzes the case of the first urban renewal project led by the French municipal authorities that was intended for the local Vietnamese. It demonstrates how this project created specific conditions for EBAI graduates to get involved in the redefinition of housing in Hanoi. The third and last part describes the unique buildings that were co-produced by French and Vietnamese architects during this period of intense cultural exchanges. It argues that the rise of this first generation of Vietnamese architects is deeply connected to a mix of repressive and generative processes of collaboration and contestation between colonial rules and indigenous forms, uses, and representations of urban space.

The EBAI: An Insurgent Vanguard of Cultural Exchanges

The Architecture Section at the EBAI was created in 1926 with a precise purpose: to fill the gap in subordinate draughtsmen in the Indochinese governmental architecture services.[4] After their graduation, the young men who entered the Architecture Section were expected to become technical assistants, working under the supervision of French professionals at the *Service Central d'Architecture et d'Urbanisme d'Indochine*, the *Service des Bâtiments Civils d'Indochine* or the *Service des Travaux Publics*, all of which employed a sizable number of French and Vietnamese civil servants.[5]

Despite these directives, the EBAI and its director, the painter Victor Tardieu, did not envisage the future of young Vietnamese architects as mere draughtsmen. Following the project elaborated by a group of French artists and intellectuals established in Hanoi since the late nineteenth century, Tardieu promoted the *métissage* of Western rationalist thinking with Eastern philosophy. He further encouraged the modernization of Vietnamese arts and its engagement with international artistic production. In taking the direction of the EBAI, Tardieu explained his intellectual and artistic vision:

> Would it not be necessary to establish an education that would be impregnated of the general principles that presided the construction of [vernacular] monuments, their ornamentation which result evidently of climatic necessities, their decorative elements which originate simultaneously from constructive imperatives, and their shape born out of the country's very nature? The general idea would not be to create a school replicating ancient forms without discernment or critical attitude. A school based on the servile imitation of the past would create art with no life, an eternal pastiche of vanished eras. Rather, we want to create a school, which, while respecting local traditions, will be adapted to modern needs.[6]

Tardieu's progressive vision was embodied in the curriculum of the Architecture Section, combining studies of Vietnamese traditions with that of the "learned" theories of Western architecture. Over the five years of their training, students were exposed to reinterpretations of their traditional built forms. This happened through teachings by French social scientists associated with the *École Française d'Extrême-Orient* (EFEO or French Far-East Studies Center), including renowned scholars such as Pierre Gourou, Paul Mus, and Henri Maspero.[7] The students further explored their own built environment through drawing classes, during which they surveyed and sketched hundreds of communal houses, pagodas, temples, and ordinary houses in and around Hanoi.[8] We can surmise that the countless hours that the future architects spent drawing traditional buildings provided them with an intimate understanding of their architectural heritage.

The students further attended classes on the doctrines of the European "avant-garde" in architecture. The period between the two world wars, during which the Architecture Section was active in Hanoi, was one of the most vibrant intellectual moments in the history of contemporary architectural and urban planning theory. It was the heyday of the German Bauhaus, which, under the leadership of such prominent figures as Walter Gropius and Mies Van der Rohe, tried to create a "total work of art" that would unify art, craft, and technology. These were also the years during which Le Corbusier and other members of the *Congrès International d'Architecture Moderne* (CIAM) formalized the principles of architectural modernism, fostering an understanding of the built environment as an economic and political tool to re-engineer human societies. The doctrines of these new architectural movements slowly percolated Vietnamese intellectual circles in Hanoi, notably through the teachings of the EBAI.

Beyond this training in vernacular and modernist architecture, the students of the EBAI were encouraged by their teachers to explore innovative avenues bridging local traditions of inhabiting space and Western universalist ambitions. Such a project was promoted by a group of French architects, including Ernest Hébrard, Arthur Kruze, and Louis-Georges Pineau, who spent part of their careers in Hanoi, both working for the colonial administration and teaching at the School of Fine Arts.

Ernest Hébrard stands as a key figure in this movement. Arriving in Hanoi in 1921, this architect and urban planner, already renowned for his work in Greece, embarked on a quest to develop a "localist" architecture. Hébrard ambitioned to design buildings which would simultaneously adopt modernist principles, translate the essence of the local culture, express a command of modern techniques of construction, and be adapted to the specific climatic conditions of Hanoi.[9] Although little is known about the teachings that Hébrard gave at the EBAI, we can surmise that he encouraged his students to participate in his architectural adventure to create what would retrospectively be labeled the "Indochinese Style." It is also likely that the EBAI students learnt as much from discussions with their architect-teachers in class as they did from looking at their prolific architectural production in Hanoi.

Nguyễn Cao Luyện (1907–87) is an emblematic product of this educational experiment.[10] Born in Nam Định in 1907 from a family of literati, Luyện graduated from the EBAI in 1933. He then briefly stayed in Paris, working as a trainee for August Perret and Le Corbusier. Upon his return to Hanoi, he established the first indigenous private architectural practice in Indochina with two of his former schoolmates: Hoàng Như Tiếp and Nguyễn Gia Đức.

Early on in his career, through his participation in the activities of different groups of Vietnamese intellectuals, Luyện expressed critical viewpoints on Western culture, techniques, and ways of life. He fought against insalubrious housing with the *Anh Sang* (The Light) Association, a group created in 1937 by the writer Nhật Linh with the aim of coordinating concrete interventions of intellectuals in social domains.[11] He was also affiliated to the *Tự lực văn đoàn* (Free Literary Group), an informal association of Vietnamese writers, poets, and progressive architects, which fostered the following objectives:

- the creation of endogenous work in opposition to the mere transfer or translation of foreign work;
- an intellectual production with a social character, participating in the modernization and development of society;
- artworks destined for the Vietnamese people, focusing on their popular practices, everyday manifestations, and simplicity;
- respect for individual freedom (at the expense of Confucian tradition);
- integration of Western scientific methods to Vietnamese material and intellectual productions.[12]

Yet, Hanoi offered young architects like Luyện very few opportunities to put these ideas into practice. In spite of the high level of education provided at the very selective EBAI, graduates were only granted the diploma of "Indochinese architects," a title understood to be subordinate to that of "French architects." Additionally, the French colonial administration was reluctant to commission Vietnamese professionals to design public buildings. Whenever this happened, it sparked heated debates among French professionals working in Hanoi.

Hence, Félix Godard, Léo Craste, and Jacques Lagisquet, architects working for the *Service des Bâtiments Civils* were highly critical of the Indochinese architects, going as far as calling their training in Hanoi a "flop." They accused Vietnamese architects of lacking competence, and resented instances where they got public commissions instead of French-educated architects, whom they believed to be more qualified.[13]

Despite these difficulties, ambitious native architects working for the *Service Municipal d'Architecture* or for their own private firms found a niche in Hanoi. Kept away from public commissions, these young professionals looked for work in the residential market and designed about a hundred private houses in the capital. Most of these buildings were located in the southern part of the colonial city, with a large concentration in the New Indigenous Quarter. In what follows, we describe the long struggle, which turned this neighborhood into a live urban laboratory where Vietnamese and French architects co-produced a new housing type in accordance with the principles taught at the EBAI.

The Tortuous Birth of the New Indigenous Quarter

The area later known as the "New Indigenous Quarter"[14] was annexed to Hanoi's municipal territory in 1890. A representative of the *Société Française des Allumettes*, then prospecting to establish a factory in this area, described its landscape as consisting of *"numerous, large and deep swampy ponds,"* covering over a third of the territory, the rest being used as *"farmland and paddy fields."* His report further indicated the presence of numerous tombs and ritual buildings, yet omitted to mention the four villages also located on the site.[15]

This rural area evolved rapidly. Located near the center of Hanoi, it attracted rural migrants seeking work in the city as well as Vietnamese populations evicted during the construction of the French administrative and residential neighborhoods. By the turn of the century, the municipal authorities expressed concerns about the urbanization process observed at the edge of the planned city. The French deplored the creation of dense neighborhoods, whose inhabitants lived in what they described as miserable, unhygienic, and unsightly *paillotes* (thatched houses). A census conducted by the colonial administration in 1889 indeed indicated that thatched houses formed 79 percent of all housing in Hanoi. In the area of the New Indigenous Quarter, 352 houses were surveyed, of which only three were not made of light materials.[16] The French deemed the *paillotes* an uncontrollable and dangerous built form responsible for urban disorder. Illustrating this view, the French novelist and journalist Jules Boissière, arriving in Hanoi writes:

> A few European buildings dominate [the city]: they become fewer and fewer as we move into the mostly indigenous neighborhoods; in seeing [these European buildings], don't you have the peculiar idea that they are necessary to keep the "shape" and hygienic alignment of a street, to prevent the overflow and crowding of this floating belt of poor *paillotes* persisting despite all regulations and municipal decrees?[17]

It is in large part to control the expansion of *"this floating belt of poor paillotes"* that the idea of creating a residential area called the "New Indigenous Quarter" was formulated by the French administration in 1902. The original project aimed to:

> ... group in the same place the Annamites[18] displaced by the opening of new roads ..., to allow workers, servants and diverse employees of the Europeans to build their houses near their place of work, [and] limit as much as possible the exaggerated expansion of the road network ... as well as the temptation of land speculation which, if not attended to, would lead to the collapse of the municipality's finances.[19]

A new residential neighborhood, planned by the French but exclusively devoted to Vietnamese households, was thus delimited. It was located between the old street (Phố Huế) to the west, the Bảy Màu Lake to the east, the French residential area to the north, and the concessions allocated a few years earlier to the *Société Française des Allumettes* to the south. (see Figure 12.1)

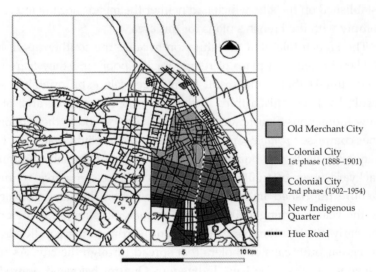

Figure 12.1

Delimitation of the New Indigenous Quarter (D. Labbé)

The street layout drawn by the municipal services was expected to wipe off the pre-existing rural landscape of paddy fields, ponds, and villages, replacing it with an orthogonal street grid defining regular, narrow blocks. The municipality first planned to divide these blocks into small plots and to allocate them to indigenous households through a leasehold system.[20] This scheme was rapidly brought to a halt by the chief of the Judiciary Service of Indochina, who reminded the mayor of Hanoi that the municipality did not legally own the land it intended to lease,[21] adding that the *Residence Supérieure du Tonkin* was not to allow this disguised sale of the Protectorate estate.

This property issue was partly settled by a governmental decree that allowed the municipality to appropriate vast areas of communal land at the edge of the colonial city.[22] This forced land acquisition allowed the privatization and subdivision of plots in the New Indigenous Quarter and their conditional transfer to indigenous households, in order to "sanitize the area." But this "land grab" did not suffice to tame the indigenous suburbs. The municipal authorities faced considerable resistance from the part of villagers and migrant populations already established on the site, which had neither the means nor the interest to comply with the French's plans for this area.

The French tolerated this situation because the southern periphery of Hanoi acted as a place of refuge for the poor, and they feared the social unrest that could result from large-scale expropriations. As a result, by 1928, only a third of the 527 built plots in the area of the New Indigenous Quarter accommodated a brick house; the remaining ones comprised *paillotes* and others constructed of light materials. Fires frequently destroyed hundreds of these highly inflammable buildings. Backyards were often filled with detritus and the commerce of human manure flourished in back alleys.[23] Population densities got higher by the year, reaching 1,500 to 2,000 persons per square kilometers in the early 1920s.[24] Rampant poverty and sordid living conditions led to regular outbreaks of cholera that spread through the city. As such, the zone to which the New Indigenous Quarter belonged figured on Hanoi's list of insalubrious neighborhoods for over twenty years,[25] standing as an obvious reminder of the colonizers' failure to create the "proper" indigenous suburb they had planned.

During the 1920s, the French started to upgrade the neighborhood. New roads were opened and paved, an electricity grid was installed, and water and sewage networks were built. Next to the New Indigenous Quarter, a tramway line soon after ran on Huê Street. Throughout this slow upgrade, the authorities enforced street alignments and encouraged a land readjustment process during which some *paillottes* were eliminated. But the colonial authorities' leniency towards the New Indigenous Quarter really ended in 1928. That year, the municipal council announced that, as was the case in the rest of the city, thatched houses and houses made of bamboo would no longer be tolerated in the southeastern part of the city.[26] The enforcement of these rules led those households who could afford it to begrudgingly rebuild their houses with solid materials. Yet, a large number of poorer inhabitants, unable to comply with the municipal regulations, were evacuated with so-called "clear-off indemnities" (*indemnisations de déguerpissement*). These households were relocated further out of the city, in areas where *paillotes* were still tolerated. The properties of poorer households who were expelled from the neighborhood were gradually acquired by a wealthier and more educated Vietnamese population moving out of the overcrowded merchant city to the new suburbs planned by the French.

Progressively, the colonizers came to the conclusion that private land ownership was the key to making their urban renewal plan come true. Up to the early 1930s, Vietnamese households could access residential plots in the New Indigenous Quarter under a lease agreement with the municipality but they could not legally own the land on which they lived. The French believed that this precarious ownership situation prevented households from investing in housing upgrades. So, starting in the 1930s, they began to sell serviced plots (with water and electricity) to Vietnamese households with or without a house built on it. Access was controlled though, as the French wanted to ensure the solvency of potential buyers. To be admissible, the future owners had to: (i) be citizens of Hanoi and have paid personal tax there for at least three years, (ii) be legitimately married, (iii) have a salaried job, and (iv) own no other property in Hanoi or in the provinces.

The above conditions and the cost of the plots (monthly installments of fifteen *piastres* for fifteen years) restricted access to land in the New

Indigenous Quarter to a small stratum of the urban population. It was mostly the emerging middle class, consisting of the new generation of traders from the old merchant city and of second-class civil servants of the colonial administration (mostly secretaries and interpreters), who bought serviced plots in the New Indigenous Quarter.[27] These new-comers now legally owned their property. They were also closely con-nected with the French and this perhaps explains why, as opposed to the poorer people who once occupied the site, they complied with the stricter regulatory framework imposed upon them by the administra-tion to ensure the "good development" of the area.

The municipality tried to ensure that all the residential plots that changed hands during the 1930s and 1940s covered one hundred square meters or more—an area considered ideal to accommodate a salubri-ous and hygienic house. The deeds of the properties further included clauses requiring the new owner to build a brick house with a tiled roof, in conformity with municipal regulations, within eighteen months of the land purchase. Old houses could not be repaired and new ones had to comply with a new construction code stipulated by the French administration. Applied to the New Indigenous Quarter in 1929, this code defined minimal volumes of rooms (one hundred cubic meters), the number (at least one) and minimal surfaces for courtyards (fifty square meters), human densities (one person per twenty-five cubic meters), and mandatory lateral setbacks between buildings (two meters on at least one side).[28]

The Co-Production of a New Indigenous House

Forced land acquisition, the "*paillote* hunt," expropriation of poor households with minimal compensation, and the stricter enforcement of municipal regulations amounted to an urban renewal operation. As a result, a large number of plots changed hands and the incoming gentri-fying population rebuilt many houses in the area. Although wealthier than the pre-existing population, the traders and civil servants moved to the suburbs of Hanoi with a limited budget. They also brought with them new housing aspirations, developed through contact with the French but also with other cultural areas of Asia such as Japan. The French and Vietnamese architects who designed houses for this emerging Vietnamese middle-class co-produced a housing type that reconciled pre-colonial traditions of inhabiting domestic space with the hygienic and aesthetic concerns of the colonizers.

The Mayor's Impulse

The reinvention of domestic space that followed was promoted by Henri Virgitti, the resident-mayor of Hanoi (1934–38). In an attempt to alleviate the enduring housing shortage in the city, Virgitti proposed a suburban housing scheme to the council: the municipality would acquire land formerly owned by the *Société Française des Allumettes* and redevelop it into individual dwellings of a new type.[29] "It is out of the question," the mayor insisted, "for the Municipality to build [vernacular urban housing] or to create workers' housing estates." The new suburban houses should rather "respond exactly to the tastes and needs of the Annamites."[30] The project was approved by the colonial government in 1937 with very little enthusiasm and under the condition that the affordable housing be concentrated in certain areas so as "not to spoil the rest of the city's aesthetic."[31]

The *Service d'Architecture de Hanoi* was put in charge of translating the mayor's vision into actual houses. At first sight, the buildings that these civil servants designed for the New Indigenous Quarter display Western traits. They are sober in appearance, with large openings and balconies as the only elements animating the facades. But as we move away from stylistic considerations to focus on spatial organization, we see that these houses are more than a mere transposition of working-class Western architecture. These buildings did, in fact, revisit Hanoi's most popular vernacular urban housing type and adapt it to suit French hygienic and aesthetic standards. (see Figure 12.2)

The model used by the architects of the *Service d'Architecture de Hanoi* is called the tube-house, a variation of the shophouses found throughout East and Southeast Asia.[32] At the neighborhood scale, this vernacular housing type creates an uninterrupted street front of very narrow facades, often less than five meters wide. This slenderness is accentuated by the depth of the plots, which can easily reach fifty meters. At the building level, the tube-house consists of a sequence of three or more independent constructions separated by exterior courtyards. The

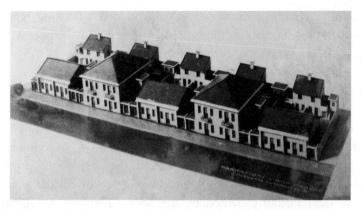

Figure 12.2

Model of affordable housings presented during the Municipal Council of Hanoi on November 30, 1936. Source: National Archive Center of Vietnam, *Fonds de la Résidence Supérieur du Tonkin* 4228, "*Projet de construction de logements à bon marché dans la ville de Hanoi 1936–38*"

first, opening on the street, shelters commercial and small-scale craft production activities, while those located further into the plot accommodate increasingly private domestic activities. With the exception of the latrines, located at the very back of the plot, both the exterior and interior spaces of the tube-house allow flexibility in terms of their use. (see Figure 12.3)

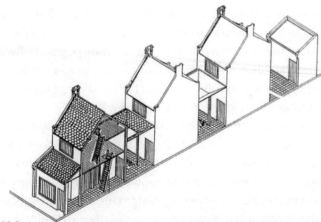

Figure 12.3

Axonometric representation of a typical tube-house from the old merchant city of Hanoi (D. Labbé)

Similar to assessments of the *paillotes*, the French officials thought the tube-houses to be a less than acceptable form of urban housing. Their main concern related to overcrowding and lack of ventilation and light, which, according to the modernist doctrine of the time were the key to salubrious residential areas. The colonizers also believed that the combination of craft production and retail with domestic activities was detrimental to the inhabitants of the old merchant city. In using this building type as an exemplar, the architects of the *Service d'Architecture de Hanoi* tried to remedy these perceived problems. They retained the organization of the house around courtyards, but also added front gardens and corridors to facilitate ventilation. They loosely structured the operations within the house by including large rooms of flexible use, corresponding to the tube-house's multifunctional interior spaces. In the New Indigenous house, these rooms were called "common rooms" to insist on their strictly residential purpose.

Vietnamese Designers Take over the Housing Experiment

The mayor's housing project was short-lived: Virgitti's successor abandoned it as soon as he took office in 1939. Yet, the organizing principles of the twenty or so prototypical houses built during the two years of this project inspired local professionals and builders who took over the renewal of the New Indigenous Quarter once Virgitti's scheme came to a close.

As increasing numbers of middle-class households moved to the southern part of the city, the demand for houses of the "new architectural style" increased, creating a new market for Vietnamese architects, developers, and builders. Although it remains difficult to this day to attribute the design of original houses built in the New Indigenous Quarter to specific architects or firms, available information indicates that it involved many EBAI graduates.[33]

These designers not only picked up the ongoing housing experiment where their colleagues from the *Service d'Architecture de Hanoi* had left it, but they took it one step further. The houses that they designed during the 1940s persisted in using the tube-house as a starting point. They retained the one-room-wide buildings arranged in order to create a courtyard. They also used exterior spaces as transitions between the main building, which gathered most living functions, and a secondary building, with the toilet and kitchen located at the very back of the plot. This spatial arrangement perpetuated the traditional segregation of living and service spaces found in the tube-house, and also the vernacular, public-to-private progression in functions as one moved from the street to the back of the house.

Yet, morphological and distributional characteristics from the French colonial villa were also brought into the design of these houses. As its name suggests, the colonial villa is a foreign built form introduced in Hanoi by the French. This building type contrasts sharply with that of the tube-house. The villa sits in the middle of a huge, square-shaped plot. The house itself consists of one large, detached volume on two floors rather than a series of small constructions. In contrast to the tube-house, rooms in the villa are accessible through an internal circulation system and are specific to each domestic activity: eating, sleeping, cooking, etc. The outdoor space that surrounds the main building is not used for economic production, as is the case in the tube-house. Fenced, landscaped gardens are rather hygienic buffers between the street and domestic spaces. Like the house itself, this exterior space is a symbol of wealth, comfort, hygiene, and intimacy.

Vietnamese architects who designed houses in the New Indigenous Quarter from the 1940s onwards borrowed several elements from the villa. The buildings they created generally had two floors and benefited from large openings with a preference, like in the villa, for high and narrow glassed windows and wooden doors. In contrast to the tube-house, the main buildings gathered all the living activities and segregated them into specific functional spaces. Some new roles, unheard of in the old merchant city, also made their appearance: entry hall, office, dining room, maid's room, and pantry. In this exclusively residential area, buildings did not need to open directly on the street, as was the case in the merchant city. Front setbacks were therefore inserted, with small gardens enclosed by a main gate reminiscent of the colonial villa's exterior buffer and representational space. (see Figure 12.4)

Like the villa, the houses built in the New Indigenous Quarter during the 1940s adopted various shapes and styles. Neoclassicism, French regionalism, art deco, and cubist shapes of the modern movements were summoned and integrated in turn by their designers (see Figure 12.5). Interactions between French and Vietnamese architectural

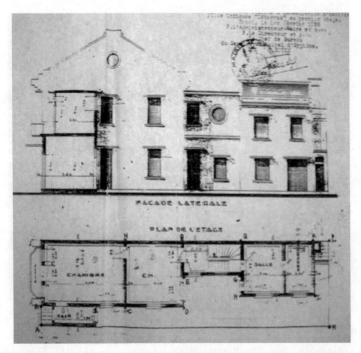

Figure 12.4

Original plan of the house located at 93 Trieu Viet Vương Street (People's Committee of Bui Thi Xuan, Hanoi)

cultures also transited through the appropriation of new materials and construction know-how. Doubtlessly influenced by the precepts taught at the EBAI and by the groundbreaking works of Ernest Hébrard, many of the houses built throughout the 1940s showcased tropical adaptations of the art deco style, combining open spaces such as balconies and flat roofs, with pergolas, canopied windows, loggias, louvers, screen-walls, and verandahs. (see Figure 12.5)

The houses built in the New Indigenous Quarter were more than the entanglement of two archetypes; rather, they were an amalgam of both models in terms of space and function. In this hybrid house, each constitutive element of the model retains some of its original quality in a final product that can hardly be seen as a simple variation of an existing housing type. This illustrates in very concrete terms the reality of a co-production of housing space in Hanoi—which, if proceeding in parallel to the French initiative—was nevertheless, in its physical reality, the result of shared and interactive cultural processes.

Figure 12.5

New Indigenous houses built in the 1940s (photographed in 2005, Quang-Vinh Dao)

Conclusion

The urban development of the New Indigenous Quarter symbolizes a fascinating moment in the architectural history of Hanoi. Tucked between the French neighborhoods and the vernacular peri-urban areas, this sector became a meeting point, revealing how professional training institutions, administrative ambitions to domesticate indigenous suburbs, exogenous and local housing cultures, and an emerging Vietnamese middle-class coalesced during a short but highly vibrant period of cultural exchange. For the first time in Hanoi, a group of local actors—consisting of developers, clients, and architects—proceeded, by themselves, to a synthesis of the vernacular models of the Vietnamese city and the more consciously structured one of the colonial villa. In this sense, what happened in Hanoi at the crepuscule of the French imperial era echoes Homi Bhabha's "in-between spaces": "the terrain for elaborating strategies of selfhood—singular or communal—that initiate new signs of identity, and innovative sites of collaboration, and contestation, in the act of defining the idea of society itself."[34]

But as demonstrated in the chapter, the forming of this urban space resulted from complex and diffuse processes controlled—if unevenly—by various social groups. Their changing roles in the production of urban space in Hanoi go beyond the mere oppositions of dominant/dominated and colonizers/colonized. Hence, the EBAI intentionally undermined the French administration by exceeding its mandate to produce technical assistants. This institutional insurgency, coming from the colonizers' own ranks, allowed the EBAI to play an important role. For several years, it oriented architectural practices and circulated models and ideas not only from Europe but also from the colonies that influenced the practice of architects in Hanoi. Most importantly, the progressive curriculum taught by the school prepared young Vietnamese architects to engage with dominant concepts from the metropole, proclaimed to be universal and liberating, and to translate them into local spatial practices. As a result, young Vietnamese professionals did not stay in the shadow of their French counterparts—as the colonial authorities had wished—but assumed an increasingly important role in the redefinition of Hanoi's built environment.

The circumstances by which these architects were able to participate in the creation of a "proper" suburb for an emerging, indigenous middle class were not without problems. These conditions resulted from a long period during which the municipal authorities put enormous pressure on pre-existing populations, acquiring communal lands by force, and pushing poor households out of the city through enforcement of restrictive regulations on housing. What appears, from one point of view, as the "emancipation" of Vietnamese architects through production of residential space for their compatriots also implicitly involved a collaboration in the colonizers' gentrification plans. This might explain why the architectural value of those houses was not acknowledged by the communist regime in the 1950s to 1960s, and why most of their designers remained unknown.

Yet a genuine attempt to create a Vietnamese architectural identity came out of the urban renewal operation led by the French authority in the New Indigenous Quarter. The Vietnamese practitioners took advantage of what we can call, following Michel De Certeau, a "generative power relation"[35] to reinvent their own tradition of inhabiting domestic space. The houses built in the New Indigenous Quarter during the 1930s and 1940s dealt inventively with the constraints posed by the regulatory requirements of the colonial administration and with the new housing aspirations of their first occupiers. In co-producing these houses, both French and Vietnamese architects went beyond plagiarizing and artificially applying local and exogenous styles. Instead, they integrated two seemingly irreconcilable architectural systems into a robust housing type that remains, to this day, highly appreciated by Vietnamese urbanites. Following Vietnam's socioeconomic reforms in the late 1980s, new foreign architectural models are, once again, penetrating Hanoi's urban landscape. In this context, we can hope that the New Indigenous house will teach Vietnamese architects of the twenty-first century a lesson on the reinvention of an architectural identity that is both contemporary, open to external influence, but still rooted in local urban space practices.

Notes

1. See for instance: Gwendolyn Wright, "Indochina: The Folly of Grandeur," in *The Politics of Design in French Colonial Urbanism* (Chicago: University of Chicago Press, 1991), 161–233; William S. Logan, *Hanoi: Biography of a City* (Sydney: UNSW Press, 2000), chap. 3; Nguyen Van Ky, "The French Model," in *Hanoi: City of the Rising Dragon*, eds. Georges Boudarel and Nguyen Van Ky (Lanham, MA: Towman and Littlefield, 2002), 47–73. Nicola Cooper, "Urban Planning and Architecture in Colonial Indochina," *French Cultural Studies*, no. 11 (2000): 75–99.
2. Benedict Anderson, *Imagined Communities: Reflections on the Origin and Spread of Nationalism* (London: Verso, 1991), 163.
3. The material and analyses presented in this chapter borrow heavily from the authors' graduate studies. See Caroline Herbelin, "La section architecture de l'Ecole des Beaux-arts de l'Indochine: Une introduction à l'architecture vietnamienne du XXe siècle" (Master's thesis, Université de Paris IV Sorbonne, 2004); and Quang-Vinh Dao, "La fabrication d'un paysage urbain à Ha-Nôi: identité architecturale et valeurs patrimoniales de l'habitat du quartier Bui Thi Xuan" (PhD diss., Université du Québec à Montréal, 2010).
4. National Archival Center No.1, Hanoi, Fonds de l'Inspection générale des travaux publics, carton 2716, *Formation des élèves architectes à l'Ecole des*

Beaux-arts de Hanoi, Lettre 5 mai 1937 à Hanoi, de l'Architecte principal, Chef du service des bâtiments civils, Godard, à Monsieur l'Ingénieur en Chef de la circonscription du Tonkin.

5. See Henri Bernier, *Atlas statistique de l'Indochine* (Hanoi, Imprimerie d'Extrême-Orient 1914), 129.

6. Centre National des Archives d'Outre-mer, Aix-en-Provence (France), Fonds du gouvernement général de l'Indochine, carton 51039, file no. 1, dossier 2, p. 8, Victor Tardieu, Sur l'enseignement des beaux arts en Indochine, et la création d'une école centrale de dessin à Hanoi (authors' translation).

7. The EFEO was created by the Governor-General Paul Doumer in December 1898 to pursue research in archeology, history, linguistics, and ethnography in Indochina. It became both a renowned scientific research center and an operational institution conducting archeological excavations and restoring monuments. A significant number of architects were part of this institution, rooting modern Indochinese architecture into scientific and historic grounds.

8. These student sketches are now valuable documents for the study of pre-colonial vernacular monuments of Vietnam. Examples can be found in Charles Batteur, *Relevés de monuments annamites anciens* (Paris: Van Oest, 1932).

9. See Gwendolyn Wright and Paul Rabinow, "Savoir et pouvoir dans l'urbanisme moderne colonial d'Ernest Hébrard," *Les Cahiers de la Recherche Architecturale*, no. 9 (1982): 26–43; Haris Yiakoumis and Christian Loddis de Pédelahore, eds, *Ernest Hébrard, vie illustrée d'un architecte planétaire. De la Grèce à l'Indochine* (Paris: Picard, 2001).

10. Other important figures from the first generations of Vietnamese architects working in Hanoi include: Ngô Huy Quỳnh, Tạ Mỹ Duật, Nguyễn Văn Ninh, Nguyen Văn Ninh, Huỳnh Tấn Phát, Nguyễn Ngọc Chân, among many others.

11. For more details on Nguyễn Cao Luyện's involvement in affordable housing productions during the colonial period, see Caroline Herbelin, "Des HBM au Viet Nam: La question du logement social en situation coloniale," *Moussons* 13–14 (2009): 123–46.

12. Published in the magazine *Phong Hóa* in 1934, quoted in Quốc học Tùng thư, *Việt Nam văn học sử giản ước tân biên*, vol. III (Saigon, 1965), 433.

13. National Archives Center n°1 (NAC1) Inspection Générale des Travaux Publics (IGTP), C.2716, « Formation des élèves architectes à l'Ecole des Beaux-arts de Hanoi, Lettre de l'Architecte Principal, chef de l'arrondissement des Bâtiments Civils Léo Craste, à M. L'ingénieur en Chef de la circonscription de Cochinchine », Note 12 juillet 1937, de l'architecte de la sûreté des Bâtiments civils, Jacques Lagisquet sur la valeur des architectes indochinois.

14. Like many streets and neighborhoods of Hanoi, the New Indigenous Quarter was renamed after Independence in an effort to reinforce national identity through the celebration of pre-colonial Vietnamese heroes. Since 1981, the area has therefore been known as the "Bùi Thị Xuân neighborhood" after the name of a famous female general who fought the Chinese invaders in the late sixteenth century.

15. ANV, HD, M.7, 3311, *Demande de cession d'un terrain sis au huyen de Kim Lien et huyen de Tho Xuong pour la construction d'une fabrique d'allumettes formulée par la Société française des allumettes 1890–1893*, f. 14 and s.

16. ANV, Mairie de Hanoi, 3258: *recensement des habitants et maisons de Hanoi, 1890*.

17. Jules Boissière, *L'Indochine avec les Français* (Paris: Louis Michaud, 1913), 191 (authors' translation).

18. The French called the Vietnamese "Annamites" in reference to the Chinese appellation of the Northern Vietnamese region.

19. ANV, RST, series H.3, no. 6379, *Au sujet de la création d'un quartier au sud de la Ville de Hà-Noi*, f. 2–6, « Extrait du procès-verbal de la séance extraordinaire du 3 mai 1901 » (authors' translation).

20. Ibid.

21. Under the 1883 Treaty of the Protectorate, all land in Northern Vietnam was under the ownership of the *Résidence Supérieure du Tonkin*. The city of Hanoi only existed as a French municipality due to its status as a concession and, up to the end of the nineteenth century; it owned almost no public land except for a small area in the old merchant city.

22. Phillippe Papin, "Des villages dans la ville aux villages urbains: L'espace et les formes du pouvoir à Ha-Noi de 1805 à 1945" (PhD diss., Université de Paris 7, 1997), 294.

23. ANV, SCDH, series D.651, no. 415, *Démolition des paillotes construites dans le quadrilatère défini par l'arrêté du Maire de la ville de Hanoi du 7 juillet 1922 (1922–1929)*.

24. This estimation is based on ANV, MH, Série 88, no. 3272, *Recensement de la population indigène de la ville de Hanoi 1920–1921*. We should nevertheless consider these data cautiously: the colonial administration assessed its own census as "unsatisfactory" because of the difficulty to enumerate *"the floating population of day laborers, coolies, and petty traders who regularly change house as to follow the work opportunities on which they depend."* Ibid. (authors' translation).

25. Nguyen Văn Tuyen, "La question des logements insalubres à Hanoi" (PhD diss., École de Médecine de Hanoi, 1938).

26. ANV, SCDH, series D.651, no. 415, Arrêté no 120 du 26 novembre 1928 (authors' translation).

27. Reflecting this group's arrival in the area, the New Indigenous Quarter is to this day still referred to by the inhabitants of Hanoi as the "Vietnamese civil servants' and traders' neighborhood."

28. ANV, RST, Série H.3, no. 79013, *Règlement sanitaire pour la protection de la santé publique à la ville de Hanoi (1920–1930)*, f. 2 « Procès verbal de la séance 4 décembre 1920, Service des Travaux et de la Voirie ».

29. «Logements à bon marché et vente de terrain à long terme», Conseil Municipal du 30/11/1936 and 16/12/1936, *Bulletin Municipal de Hanoi*, 1936, 1315 and 1493 (authors' translation).

30. ANV MHN 4228, « Extraits des délibérations du conseil municipal de la ville de Hanoi », 30/11/1936 (authors' translation).

31. ANV, MHN 4228, Procès verbal du conseil municipal, séance ordinaire du 25/02/1937, 2.

32. François Decoster, et al., *Hanoi: Fragments de mutation* (Hanoi: Urban Planning Institute, 1995).

33. Records of land and housing transactions dated from the period 1920–40 exist at the National Archive No. 1 in Hanoi, but remain inaccessible due to ongoing litigious affairs about property. Yet according to interviews conducted in 1999 and 2000 with owners of houses in the New Indigenous Quarter, their residences had been designed by Vietnamese professionals in the period preceding the first Indochinese War (1945). We also know that graduates from the Architecture Section were employed by the *Service Municipal d'Architecture de Hanoi* and that others were commissioned by the *Office Public d'Habitations Économiques de Hà-Noi* to design affordable housing in this area.

34. Homi Jehangir Bhabha, *The Location of Culture* (London: Routledge, 1994), 45.

35. Michel de Certeau, *L'invention du quotidien* (Paris: Gallimard, 1990).

27. Reflecting this group's arrival in the [illegible] Cholon [illegible] to [illegible] still referred to by [illegible] civil servants and [illegible].
28. ANV, [illegible] nov. 1913, [illegible] pour la protection de la [illegible] publique [illegible] de Hanoi [illegible]; Procès-verbal de la [illegible] 4 [illegible] 1930, [illegible].
29. [illegible] et [illegible]; Conseil [illegible] du 20.11.1930 and [illegible] Bulletin Municipal de Hanoi, 1930, [illegible] (author's translation).
30. ANV, [illegible] 4228, « Extrait des délibérations du [illegible] municipal [illegible] » [illegible] (author's translation).
31. ANV, [illegible] 4228, [illegible] séance ordinaire du [illegible] 1923.
32. [illegible], Dictionnaire [illegible] (Hanoi: [illegible] 1995).
33. Records of land and housing transactions dated from the period [illegible] exist at the National Archives No. 1 in Hanoi, but it was too [illegible] due to [illegible]. Yet according to interviews conducted in [illegible] and 2000 with owners of homes in the New Quarter, [illegible] Quarter residence had been designed by Vietnamese [illegible] in the period preceding the [illegible] independence [illegible] employed by the [illegible] and [illegible] were commissions [illegible] de [illegible] from the [illegible].
34. [illegible] The [illegible] (London: Routledge, [illegible]) [illegible] (Paris: [illegible]).

13
Afterword

The European built form in Asia was a colonial enterprise from the very beginning—an expression of imperial aspirations in challenging environments. Once the gun smoke cleared, the diplomats, traders, and sovereign agents used the built form to send a clear message of new order: a court representing European justice, the government house on a hill representing power, the banks representing financial might, and hospitals representing progress, along with schools, parks, and churches.

The cities explored in this volume involved different forms of foreign authority—formal colonies, treaty ports, leased territories, concessions, and settlements, yet they were all based on unequal treaties. "Colonial" dominance was both real and symbolic. Real, because it carried social, legal, military, and economic privilege. Symbolic, because it visually expressed "superior" European presence, and the urban forms and architectural styles that came with it. It was also idealistic—some urban spaces were seen as a *tabula rasa*, upon which modern plans could be imposed in order to avoid the problems plaguing European cities. Yet the reality was more complicated and the foundations of these colonial enterprises were shaky, as they were dependent on the acquiescence of the local populations. Risk and insecurity were integral parts of these colonial projects. The threat of revolt from local populations was real too, making it necessary to keep gunboats and a regular police force. Moreover, the process of building and maintaining these colonial forms was complicated because each location presented different sets of obstacles: geographic, climatic, and logistic.

The large span of time covered in this volume was necessary to present the constantly shifting face of colonialism. The early entrance of France and Britain gave them enormous, but not exclusive, influence.

The colonial experience on the China coast cannot be measured solely by the standards of French and British experience or models. As the articles in this volume demonstrate, Russia and Germany, despite being latecomers to this region, were able to create their own enclaves and cultures in a short period of time. Japan was later able to build on various European experiences to pave the way for its own empire in this region. Railroads were crucial built forms used by these powers to expand their influence into the interior, becoming the foundation for the growth of new towns, industry, and trade.

China and Vietnam also underwent changes. In 1911, the Qing dynasty collapsed in China, and the new republic was left fragmented due to rivalries among the northern and southern governments and the warlords. Local developments forced European powers to renegotiate previous terms with emerging new forces. Wealth was increasingly shared, making it possible for Chinese and Vietnamese elites and merchants to move closer to the places once reserved for Europeans and renegotiate the terms of trading, banking, and sharing of labor and resources. There were also a growing number of Western-educated professionals who understood how to operate in this particular environment. Between the two world wars, these treaty ports were becoming increasingly cosmopolitan, and conflict ceded ground to dialogue and interdependence. This was reflected in more diverse architecture, best expressed in the emergence of eclectic styles. New alliances, unthinkable in the past, were formed: for example, when a wealthy Chinese merchant hired a Western architect, or when a hybrid building designed by a French-trained Vietnamese architect was erected. New buildings reflected the changing tastes of emerging international bourgeoisie and new wealth. Yet, these changes were not uniform—colonial attitudes remained strong in Hong Kong, French Indochina, and the treaty ports.

All of this changed during World War II. When the Japanese invaded the continent, their hegemonic plans included reshaping the European urban enclaves to their own preference. They presented the notion of pan-Asian brotherhood to the Asian populations; yet, their actions were nothing more than the replacement of one form of colonialism with another. Japan's reliance on military force and violence triggered anti-imperial sentiments among the indigenous peoples, contributing to growing nationalism, which shook the foundation of colonial rule across Asia after World War II. These different, competing colonialisms left their permanent marks in the cities discussed in this volume; their material layers have to be uncovered and further explained.

The fate of the colonial built environment in the twentieth century has its own controversies. While losing its original significance a long time ago, it had practical and aesthetic qualities that appealed to local governments, banks, and corporations. Despite sporadic outbursts of nationalism and anger over a colonial past, the local governments and elites still prefer to house their offices in such surroundings. Moreover, in places like Dalian and Harbin, the commercial value of these built forms have created demand for new apartments, boutique hotels, shopping malls, villas, and even historical theme parks built in pseudo-colonial styles.

The advocates of preservation of colonial architectural heritage argue that the future generations should remember colonial history and at the same time appreciate the architectural value of the remaining colonial built forms. In the old districts of Harbin, Qingdao, Shanghai, and Tianjin, major colonial buildings were given a face-lift, serving both as administrative and office spaces as well as tourist attractions. In Changchun, the former palace of the supreme ruler of Manchukuo, Henry Puyi, was lavishly renovated to become an important museum of Japanese colonialism in China. Yet, other colonial buildings did not survive the test of time; many have been destroyed to clear land for new urban development, while others were left to their own fate. The conflict between the rapidly rising price of land and the value of heritage buildings is easily found in Hong Kong Island, where the government is struggling to determine the fate of the British colonial police head-quarters. Another example can be found in Shanghai, which during the last decade became a battleground between real estate companies and landowners, resulting in the disappearance of many colonial villas. At the same time, the Bund with its former banks and the famous Peace Hotel still remained a postcard view of Shanghai.

For historians of European and Japanese imperialism in Asia, the battle for the meaning of the colonial built environment is not over yet. Nationalistic narratives of imperialism tend to simplify the accounts of everyday experience and of individual activities. Colonial built forms cannot be understood on their own terms: they need to be placed in concrete historical circumstances, and any human activity surrounding them thus scrutinized. Otherwise, they remain silent symbols of a colonial past, mere skeletons without flesh and soul, devoid of the stories of human drama behind them. People who planned, built, and lived in these settings provide a more powerful testimony to the uneasy relationship between imperial powers and Asian societies.

Index